The Economy, Media and Public Knowledge

Studies in Communication and Society

Series editors: **Ralph Negrine and Anders Hansen**
University of Leicester

Also published in this series:

The Mass Media and Environmental Issues
Edited by Anders Hansen
TV News, Urban Conflict and the Inner City
Simon Cottle

The Economy, Media and Public Knowledge

edited by

Neil T. Gavin

Leicester University Press
London and New York

Leicester University Press
A Cassell imprint
Wellington House, 125 Strand, London WC2R 0BB, England
370 Lexington Avenue, New York NY 10017-6550

First published 1998

British Library Cataloguing in Publication Data
A catalogue record for this book is available from the British Library.
ISBN 0-7185-0095-4

Library of Congress Cataloging-in-Publication Data
The economy, media and public knowledge / edited by Neil T. Gavin.
    p.   cm.—(Studies in communication and society)
Includes bibliographical references and index.
ISBN 0-7185-0095-4
    1. Journalism, Commercial.   2. Mass media—Economic aspects.
I. Gavin. Neil T.   II. Series: Studies in communication and society
(Leicester, England)
PN4784.C7E36   1998
070.4'4933—dc21   97-47698
                                                            CIP

Typeset by BookEns Ltd, Royston, Herts.
Bound and printed in Great Britain by Bookcraft (Bath) Ltd, Midsomer Norton

Contents

List of figures and tables

Figures

Tables

List of contributors

John Corner is Professor in the School of Politics and Communication Studies at the University of Liverpool. His recent books include *Television Form and Public Address* (1995), *The Art of Record: Critical Studies in Documentary* (1996) and the co-edited collection *International Media Research: A Critical Survey* (1997). He is an editor of the journal, *Media, Culture and Society* and Visiting Professor of Media Research at the University of Stockholm.

Evan Davis is a BBC Economics Correspondent and is formerly of the Institute for Fiscal Studies.

Erik Fichtelius has been head of the news department of Swedish Radio. He is Senior Political Correspondent in the news department of Swedish television's TV1 and is, at present, Visiting Professor of Journalism in the Department of Journalism, Media and Communication (JMK) at the University of Stockholm.

Neil T. Gavin has research interests in the field of media, economy and public opinion. He has published in *Parliamentary Affairs, Representation, Media, Culture and Society, The British Elections and Parties Yearbook, 1996* and *British Elections and Parties, 7.* He is co-editor of *Britain Votes, 1997.*

Peter Goddard teaches and researches in Communication Studies at the University of Liverpool. His published work includes contributions to *Popular Television in Britain*, edited by John Corner, and to *Media, Culture and Society.*

Håkan Lindhoff is a lecturer in Media and Communications Studies at Stockholm University. Originally an economist, he has published in Sweden on consumer perspectives of advertising. With Professor Kjell Nowak and Bo Mårtenson he is at present carrying out a project on Swedish journalism and the economy, covering the years 1970-98. Results from this project have been published, in Swedish, in *Medierummet* (*Media Space*).

Peter Malmqvist is an economist, and has worked as an accountant and financial analyst. From 1989 to 1996 he was an economic reporter and commentator with the Swedish newspaper *Svenska Dagbladet* and with the news programme *Aktuellt* on TV1. He is now chief analyst with a Swedish stockbroker.

Bo Mårtenson is a Lecturer at the Department of Journalism, Media and Communication (JMK), Stockholm University. He is co-author, with Stig Hadenius, of *Press och ekonomisk politik*, case studies of the Swedish press coverage of economic policy in the early 1990s. Along with Håkan Lindhoff and Kjell Nowak he is currently undertaking a research project within the JMK ('Journalism on the Economy, 1970-98') concentrating on the construction and reception of economic news on Swedish popular television.

Kay Richardson is co-author, with John Corner and Natalie Fenton, of *Nuclear Reactions*, and co-editor, with Ulrike Meinhof, of *Text, Discourse and Context: Representations of Poverty in Britain*. She has contributed articles to the journals *Media, Culture and Society, Text, Social Semiotics* and *Language and Communication*.

David Sanders researches in the fields of electoral studies, European elite attitudes and political forecasting, and is editor of the *British Journal of Political Science*. He is author of *Losing an Empire, Finding a Role: British Foreign Policy since 1945*, and has published extensively in *Electoral Studies*, the *American Political Science Review*, and the *British Journal of Political Science*.

John Williams is a political columnist for the *Mirror* newspaper.

Acknowledgements

I wish to thank the Economic and Social Research Council, the British Council, the British Academy and the Bank of Sweden Tercentenary Foundation. Their generous financial support for the different aspects of the UK and Swedish projects that lie at the core of this book has made the endeavour possible. There are many (on both sides of the North Sea) who also deserve grateful thanks. These include Kjell Nowak and Peter Dahlgren as well as Paul Whiteley and Sonia Livingstone. I also wish to thank Yvonne Janvier, Marian Hoffman and Alison Ross, as well as support staff at JMK. Last, but by no means least, I need to thank our focus group respondents in Liverpool for their generous help and patience.

For
Jean and Charlie

1
Introduction

Neil T. Gavin

Political issues come and go. There is an ebb and flow in media (and public) interest in the political concerns of the day. Interest in a humanitarian tragedy abroad can easily give way to concern for a domestic issue like the environment, school standards or food safety. Many issues are, by their very nature, transient – commanding the public stage for a period, before retiring to the wings. This is less obviously the case with regard to the economy and economics. The economy is always with us – both as an issue of public concern and as a regular object of news coverage. Different economic events and sub-issues (such as international agreements, interest rate fluctuations, stock market crashes, unemployment, inflation, and so on) are more or less prominent at any given time, but economics, the economy and economic discourse are common and recurrent themes in news and current affairs coverage across a wide range of mass media. The interest in economics shown by the media is, perhaps, hardly surprising given that the economy and economic events have a profound effect on the shared fortunes of any community and, on a more personal level, are an integral and important part of the lived experiences of the public – through a wide array of everyday transactions (from buying, selling and employment to every sort of mortgage or credit arrangement). The economy touches us all.

Given the centrality of this issue in civic and private affairs, politicians have become acutely aware that their own reputations often hinge on the public's direct experience of the economy and on popular perceptions of the government's handling of economic affairs. Party-political controversy often revolves around precisely these sorts of issues, and the media form the arena where the battles are fought out. Harold Wilson once said, 'All political history shows that the standing of the government and its ability to hold the confidence of the electorate at the General Election depend on the success of its economic policy.' But it is frequently the case that what constitutes 'success' (or, indeed, failure) is not at all obvious, and press and television coverage often centres on precisely this sort of issue – as well as communicating to the audience more specific signals about the health or otherwise of the economy. Several decades after Harold Wilson uttered these words, an *aide-mémoire* in President Clinton's office at the 1992 election read 'It's the economy, stupid' – a reminder of the centrality of the issue to the public and, therefore, to the campaign. Politicians are increasingly aware that television and the press play a crucial role in explaining this complex and often abstract domain to the public. In this context, the ways in which the media handle the topic and inform civic consciousness are therefore important aspects of contemporary politics – with implications for the effective functioning of the democratic process.

Given this set of circumstances, it is somewhat surprising that scholars in communication studies (and, indeed, in political science) have taken less of an interest in economic news and economic discourse than it deserves. Some of the earliest and perhaps most controversial work on economic news focused on the perceived lack of impartiality in television coverage. The Glasgow University Media Group (1976, 1980) focused on the structure and language of economic reporting as well as the news agenda, and looked at the political and ideological implications of what they saw as the distorted and partial portrayal of the economy regularly conveyed to the public. Though not without its critics (Harrison, 1985; Anderson and Sharrock, 1979), this research involved an in-depth assessment of the way in which news output reflected economic realities – concluding that it gave a distorted picture of the economic crisis prevailing at the time and that this reflected badly on organized labour and the Left in general.

Since this early work there has not been a great deal of sustained scholarly attention given to press or television reporting of economic matters (and even less to issues of audience reception of such coverage). There have been only a few studies in the UK, the USA and elsewhere that deal with the issue. Some of these do so in a rather indirect fashion. Herman (1982), for instance, looks at what he perceives to be the ideological role of the economists and business professionals who figure regularly in economic news. Dreier (1982) looks at the relationship between the business community and the media, and at attempts by the former to have its affairs and interests reported in a more favourable light. Both of these studies touch on economic coverage, but it is not their central theme. On the other hand, work by Jensen (1987), Gavin (1992), Emmison (1993), and Rae and Drury (1993) has had a firmer focus on the form and substance of economic news. Jensen's (1987) study deals with economic news on US television, suggesting that the coverage under-emphasizes explanations for economic events and processes. Coverage, it is suggested, is abstract where, 'agents are typically missing in accounts of economic processes' and 'economic variables tend to lead lives of their own' (Jensen, 1987, pp. 16-17). More recently, Gavin (1992) looked at the nature of political coverage in the run-up to the 1992 General Election in the UK, finding that the agenda (and the coverage of some key economic issues) seemed to favour the Conservative Party over its main rivals. Emmison (1993), on the other hand, has used discourse analysis to evaluate portrayals of the economy over the course of the present century and, on the whole, finds that it is commonly reified as an object or entity beyond human control – a portrayal that has important political implications. This is a theme which is amplified in Rae and Drury's work (Rae and Drury, 1993) on press coverage of the 1990 recession.

These pieces of research are firmly within the communication studies frame of reference. However, some have attracted critical attention, not least on the grounds that their empirical focus is too narrow – confining their analysis to a short time-frame, or skating too thinly over coverage that straddles decades (Gavin and Goddard, 1998). More importantly, none of these cited studies has a sustained processual dimension. They explore content alone rather than probing the issues of journalist practice, agenda-setting (or 'agenda-building') and public knowledge that are explored more fully in the work of, for instance, Schlesinger et al. (1983), Gamson (1992), Neuman et al. (1992), Deacon and Golding (1994) or Schlesinger and Tumber (1994) – mostly in relation to non-economic topics. It could also be suggested, with some justification, that by its very nature content-orientated research is also unable to deal with the issues surrounding public engagement with coverage. Attention to this dimension of the communicative process is much more clearly discerned in the work of Morley (1980), Lewis (1985), Jensen (1990), Corner et al. (1990) and Schlesinger et al. (1992).

If we turn to the political science community, we find that it has always taken a keen interest in the relationship between the economy and the popularity of governments (Nannestad and Paldam, 1994). Yet it has been slow to extend analysis to the role of press and television in the equation. Only recently have scholars involved in opinion research begun to take an interest in what might be loosely termed the 'effect' of economic news. In the UK, the earliest work by Mosley (1984) looked at the relationship between one newspaper's reports on the economy and trends in government popularity. However, this theme was not developed until Sanders et al. (1993) explored in a much broader way the connection between national press coverage and public perceptions of the economy. This sort of relationship has also been explored in the USA, although the focus is often on one particular medium (the press in Mutz, 1992), or indeed, on the impact of one particular newspaper (Goidel and Langley, 1995; Blood and

Phillips, 1995). And if we turn our attention from the press to television, we find that, to date, there has been only one study in the UK that focuses on its role (Gavin and Sanders, 1996). It suggests that television economic news has a modest (but stable and significant) relationship with public views on the government's competence in economic management. These perceptions are, in turn, reflected in government popularity.

The limited nature of the literature that broadly touches on 'news-and-the-economy' (within both the media studies and political science traditions) leaves a number of questions outstanding. These include issues of journalistic practice, news structure and content, as well as audience engagement with economic news output. The economic agenda can change quite markedly in a short space of time (and a great deal in the medium to long term). And, in like manner, the preoccupations of the journalists covering the economic beat change and evolve over time (Parsons, 1987). But why do particular economic themes come into focus at different times; what prompts change over time; and how do journalistic practices influence the nature and pace of economic reporting? How, and under what political and journalistic pressures, does the economic agenda evolve? If our focus turns to the form and content of economic coverage, what, we might ask, are the characteristic structures of economic news reporting (in the press and on television) and how do these compare to the way in which other news topics are reported? Do different countries deal with issues surrounding the economy in distinctive ways? Finally, if we turn to the audience, how does the language of news discourse differ from the language of everyday public talk about the economy? How does the public understand, appreciate and use the news that reaches it, particularly through television? How is economic news evaluated by the audience and how far does economic coverage contribute to the formation and development of public opinion? Does economic news make a difference to government popularity (and, if so, how)? These are among the key issues addressed by the contributors to this book.

From a range of theoretical and sub-disciplinary perspectives, the issues are addressed in relation to two countries – the UK and Sweden. On the one hand, Sweden is chosen as a useful comparison because the two countries have a shared membership of the European Union (EU) and have undergone comparable economic restructuring in recent times. Moreover, as we began our research at Liverpool, we became aware that a team at the University of Stockholm was developing a similar project on economic news and we quickly saw the value of exchanging ideas and data. On the other hand, Sweden offers some useful contrasts. It has sustained a greater degree of social democratic consensus for longer than the UK and has traditionally boasted one of the most well-developed welfare state structures in Europe. Although this has begun to change (along with the economic structure),

Sweden has come late to the sort of market restructuring that the UK has undergone since the early 1980s. Sweden is also a late entrant to the EU, with a distinctive economic and geographical position in relation to other Nordic countries.

Over the last 10–15 years the UK has undergone a series of sustained periods of economic crisis, recovery and restructuring. The UK government's extensive deregulation, privatization and marketization programmes have greatly altered the social and economic terrain, and the overall balance of state and private provision of goods and services. This has been the backdrop to an economy that has lurched from the boom of the late 1980s to the slump of the early 1990s, and has seen upheavals brought about by currency speculation and the ignominious withdrawal from the Exchange Rate Mechanism in 1992. Since the mid-1990s, an economic recovery has taken place which appears to be strong (at least by European standards). The depth and sustainability of this recovery has, however, been a topic of dispute between politicians and among economists. Some observers, indeed, have suggested that the recovery is more imaginary than real – largely a rhetorical fiction rather than a fact. This is a theme regularly reflected in the media coverage.

The economy of Sweden has experienced similar trials and changes. Starting somewhat later than in the UK, the Swedish economy has experimented with the deregulation of foreign exchange markets (beginning in 1984) and the loosening of credit restrictions. As in the UK, tax reforms (particularly reducing the burden on those in the top tax brackets) have been a feature of the Swedish approach to economic restructuring. And again as in the UK, the debate over the balance between interventionist and *laissez-faire* economics has been played out on television and in the press. This has been the backdrop to a Swedish economy that has experienced a series of traumatic crises. The banking crisis brought on by the burgeoning and unregulated extension of credit has led to a restructuring of the banking system and the introduction of a stricter regulatory regime. The large-scale unemployment in the banking sector that accompanied these changes has placed a heavy burden on state finances, precipitating cuts in public expenditure and state employment. These economic problems and challenges facing the UK and Sweden have, of course, been mirrored in the experiences of many other countries.

The book essentially is split into three parts. The first, and by far the longest, deals with the different elements of the Liverpool University Economy Study, 1993–95. The second looks at some of the work done in Stockholm on Swedish television and press reporting. The latter part includes comments by working economic journalists as well as the methodological reflections of a number of the authors. The opening chapter in this book focuses on a year-long study undertaken by the Liverpool Public Communication Group. It deals, in part, with the structure and form of economic news reporting on television – with its distinctive style and characteristic formats. However, the main focus is on audience comprehension and evaluation of television coverage. Here, focus groups were used to gauge audience engagement with selective screened material. The results tend to suggest a complex and contingent web of influence, under-standing and, indeed, alienation. The information that emerges from television is generally credited by viewers with factual integrity, even where the audience disputes its relevance or interprets it in line with partisan predispositions. Under a number of sub-headings, the Liverpool team analyses the specific terms of economic news viewing, paying particular attention to levels of partial understanding and the way in which this causes dissatis-faction or, more often, resigned acceptance.

From the various materials collected for the Liverpool study discussed in the opening chapter, Kay Richardson in Chapter 2 explores the linguistic character of mediated economic discourse, and the terms upon which that discourse enters into the respondents' own constructions of the economic. The chapter focuses upon how respondents speak, as well as upon what they say; and particular attention is paid to the vocabulary of economic affairs and their reportage. Respondents show some resistance to economic vocabulary, sometimes dismissing it as jargon and waffle; nevertheless, elements of that jargon certainly have, at points, become part of their own linguistic/conceptual resources. The chapter also considers the significant syntactic constructions which belong to the idiom of mediated economics, focusing especially upon the use of narrative syntax alongside (and in interaction with) the syntax of comparison.

In Chapter 3 John Corner looks at the communicative organiza-tion of economic news, developing some of the themes which emerge in Chapter 1. What questions of journalistic *performance* are raised by reporting in this area? What shifts from 'the national' to 'the local', from the abstract to the concrete, from 'today' to more long-range perspectives does the news involve, and how are language and image used to accomplish them? By taking a small number of items and working at the level of the complete report rather than the selected extract, Corner is able to raise questions about the particular difficulties of reporting change in this area and assessing whether it is 'good' or 'bad'. He is also able to explore the extent to which the economy is seen as a sphere of political management, in which 'tonics' can be found, and the extent to which it is regarded as the product of forces beyond direct political control.

The following chapter, by Peter Goddard, examines coverage of the economy through a focus on one specific case study of *press* reporting of economic news. Newspaper accounts of the economy tend to draw upon a narrow range of credible, professional sources and are characterized by heavy dependence on signifiers of precision such as numbers. They tend to concentrate on the insertion of new information into pre-existing explanatory frameworks and to focus in varying ways on strategies which relate economic events to the immediate concerns of readers. Drawing upon press coverage of a single economic event (a cut in interest rates announced in March 1996), this chapter looks at its treatment in five UK newspapers. It investigates the range of coverage and the explanatory frameworks in which the event is situated. Enlarging upon the work of van Dijk (1988), it suggests that the stylistic and rhetorical strategies employed are involved not only in reporting and explaining the change, but in persuading readers of the authority and facticity of newspaper stories about it.

From within the political science tradition, the authors of Chapter 5 (Neil T. Gavin and David Sanders) deploy time-series techniques to look at the relationship between television economic news and public opinion. Content analysis of economic coverage is used to assess the impact of television news on public perceptions of the government's competence in handling the economy. The formal models deployed take into consideration what political scientists often term 'the real economy' (ostensibly, government-derived statistics), as well as poll measures of the direct economic experiences of the public. The results suggest that television economic news has a stable, consistent and statistically (as well as politically) significant impact on public opinion – over and above that of personal financial circumstances and the 'real economy'. This prompts the authors to question the rational choice assumptions underlying much of the contemporary work in this area, and to consider a reconceptualization of what precisely is being measured by the statistics that constitute the 'real economy'. The authors also critically reflect on the practice of modelling the relationship between the 'real economy' and economic news output.

Two chapters then look at the Swedish context and at the style and substance of Swedish television and press coverage. With special reference to budget coverage, Bo Mårtenson, in Chapter 7, deals with the dominant ways in which Swedish television approaches economic affairs. The chapter also explores the way in which television reporting has adapted to changing economic circumstances. Mårtenson shows how television's economic coverage has developed more of a future orientation – with predictions, portents and possibilities featuring more prominently than they used to. More importantly, he points to the increasing relevance and centrality of the voice of 'the market' (especially the judgements of the share and currency markets) in structuring television news reports. Mårtenson also focuses on the pivotal role of economic journalists as 'experts'. He explores the way in which this can often translate into a journalistic dialogue in which the roles both of 'citizen' and 'informed authority' are assumed.

In contrast, Håkan Lindhoff (in Chapter 8) focuses on the press and, in particular, two prominent newspapers – *Dagens Nyheter* and *Expressen*. After briefly outlining the contours of the economic crises endured by Sweden in the 1990s, the author uses a full-text database to perform a quantitative analysis of the terminology that forms the basis of what he terms the 'crisis discourse'. This suggests that of the multiple crises that Sweden faced, the economic one was by far the most prominent in press reporting. However, particular dimensions of this crisis (notably banking and financial turbulence) were given more sustained attention than others (notably, unemployment). There then follows a more intensive analysis of isolated articles. The author comments on the rather narrow range of voices heard in this sort of context. He uses a typology developed by Ekecrantz and Olsson (1994) to explore the types of journalistic strategies and temporal perspectives deployed in the construction of press copy on the economic crisis. The results suggest that reports have both a synchronic and a diachronic dimension, but that the latter are dominated by journalistic constructions with little narrative depth. Finally, Lindhoff looks more closely at some of the discursive features of economic news. He notes that stories are often dominated by considerations of the future. The 'symbolic' dimension (encompassing expectations, evaluations and specula-tions) is also seen as a recurrent feature of economic news – as was the emphasis on the macro-level (as opposed to micro-level). The author also notes that notions of the operation of market processes are rarely articulated to those of 'crisis', and that, where they are, 'the market' is seen as part of the solution rather than as part of the problems facing Sweden.

Finally, the book turns to issues of journalistic practice and research method. The way in which economic journalists approach their craft is the subject of Chapter 8. A range of press and television journalists from the UK and Sweden were invited to discuss and comment upon the sorts of issues that were raised in Chapters 1, 6 and 7. They also comment more broadly on the sorts of pressures they experience in their work and on the sorts of problems faced when reporting the economy, and on the way in which decisions about coverage are made. The last chapter deals with method. Here some of the authors reflect on the theoretical and methodological questions raised by the research and on their implications for media studies generally. They also flag the direction that might be taken in any future research on this topic. Certainly, it is part of the general project of this book to stimulate further enquiry, as well as to offer a range of substantial analyses for debate.

1

Economic news and the dynamics of understanding: the Liverpool project

Peter Goddard, John Corner, Neil T. Gavin and Kay Richardson[1]

Introduction

Coverage of the economy is a routine aspect of UK television news for most viewers. For many it provides the principal source for information about economic issues and for evaluating economic policy and the competence of its execution. The way in which UK television news reports economic issues is therefore an important factor in the formation of popular economic understanding and the development of an informed citizenry. Its importance, however, is no guarantee that viewers currently respond to it with appreciation, since its subject matter is often thought to be hard to understand and of limited viewing interest.

In this chapter we present some of the findings from a Liverpool University research project exploring how economic news is reported on television and the extent to which television audiences are able to make sense of this reporting. Although this is a study of UK television news, the issues raised have a wider resonance and connect with several strands of international media research. The first is that of news analysis, with its concern for the news as political and social knowledge and, increasingly, for the communicative organization of its images and speech as it bears on this. Leading studies in this field include Brunsdon and Morley (1978), Cottle (1993), Ericson *et al.* (1987) and Glasgow University Media Group (1980). Equally prominent within our perspective is the field of reception studies, with its broad interest in modes of interpretation and the use of which media items are put. In this area, of which Morley (1992) provides a valuable recent overview, Morley (1980) made an early and influential intervention which included some discussion of budget coverage, whilst Lewis (1985) and Jensen (1990) have made further important contributions. Our study also relates to recent enquiries into the way in which media accounts contribute to the development, and at times the emergence, of 'public issues' (e.g. Corner *et al.*, 1990; Deacon and Golding, 1994; Schlesinger *et al.*, 1983) and to questions about knowledge and citizenship (addressed, for instance, by Gamson, 1992 and Neuman *et al.*, 1992).

Our choice of economic news as the focus for this study was motivated not by a wish to enquire into economic issues themselves but out of an interest in the range of questions about public communication which the topic raises, given the importance of the 'economic' to the modern political process. Economic news discourse has a distinctive character as a result of the statistical and 'systemic' nature of most of the events which are reported, the sourcing and regularity of those events and the directness of their relationship 'upwards' – to questions of political management – and 'downwards' – to the ordinary life of the nation. Economic exposition and analysis increasingly poses problems for journalists as the economy becomes a more complex and contentious area of public debate, with public perceptions of it now established as a factor of paramount importance in the formation of popular political opinion (see Gavin and Sanders, 1996; Newton, 1993; Philo, 1993; Sanders, 1991). Indeed, this being the case, work on economic news is surprisingly underdeveloped, with few studies of any kind and no major research in the UK.

Our approach both to television reporting and to viewer interpretation is informed by a recognition of 'the economy' as essentially a systemic notion.[2] That is to say, as an entity, 'the economy' is dispersed across a range of interrelated processes, states and indicators (including interest rates, unemployment levels, exchange rates, balance of payments, public sector borrowing and inflation). But the configuration of this dispersal is subject to change in various ways. Different factors can be included or excluded as parts of the system, the relationship assumed to be desirable between parts (the economy in balance) can vary, and the priority accorded to given parts can also alter.

As the introduction to this book outlined, over the course of the economic restructuring undertaken by many countries in Western Europe during the 1980s there has been a tendency for political debate about economic management to become more 'technical', with macro-theories and predictive models playing a more prominent role in public debate than before. This has been part of a general shift in which key factors of national economic performance have become as much a function of the international economy as they are of national policy, with governments adopting varying, and often strategic, stances towards this, thereby opening up questions of responsibility and controllability which have often been adopted as themes in economic journalism. In the UK, the move into a period of 'recession' in 1990/91, a designation initially resisted by the Conservative government, had the effect of making not only the management of the economy, but also national economic *direction*, an area of open contention and, finally, of crisis. Nightly, the economy was foregrounded on television news – the symptoms, causes and possible cures providing the premier domestic running story as well as becoming the principal battleground of the 1992 General Election. Only in spring 1993 did a run of figures across the whole economic system herald the beginning of a transition from 'recession' to 'recovery'. As a slow consensus formed about the 'fact' of the transition, news values shifted on to whether or not the recovery was 'sustainable', thus carrying the narrative forwards to a new phase of conflicting predictions and statistical implications around which stories could be told. A further criterion, the degree to which people actually experienced improvement (the 'feelgood factor'), became a marker for coverage from late 1994 onwards, accompanied, by late 1995, by speculation about the relationship between the Conservative government's economic management and its pros-pects for re-election. As the recovery became established, fears of 'overheating' and the role of interest rates in controlling UK economic growth also began to emerge as common topics in news coverage.

In what follows, we base our findings on research covering the period from March 1995 to February 1996, during which we examined the form and content of television economic news. In order to investigate questions of comprehension and evaluation by viewers, we set up a range of focus groups to which we showed selected extracts from economic news coverage collected at three notable points in the course of the year.[3] This chapter is organized into two broad sections. First, we discuss the difficulties raised for economic news reportage by the nature and complexity of its subject matter and examine the forms which it commonly takes. Then, in what is the main section of this chapter, we look at some of the findings of our respondent study and at how it suggests economic news coverage is received by viewers and put to use in their construction of understanding and formulation of judge-ments. It is here that we get closest to some of the factors determining the role of television news in the dynamics of public knowledge.

The economy as image and speech

The ways in which viewers understand the economy are dependent, as we shall illustrate later, on quite fundamental questions of comprehension. Economics, it is widely thought, is 'difficult' technically and also a subject notorious for the wide range of views which can be held about the same data. The modes of reporting the economy, then, present distinctive problems for broadcast journalism. The nature of the economy as a systemic entity, in which shifting relations between the parts provide the main focus of news, means that the 'news event' for most coverage is abstract and cannot be visualized directly. As in diplomatic coverage, images may sometimes be available of the secondary events associated with the news focus (e.g. airport arrivals, cars drawing up at government buildings, the inside of conference chambers) but a good deal of economic news uses visuals not to precise illustrative ends, but to provide broad *thematic support*. So, for instance, shots of busy trading rooms may be found *under* commentary on City reactions, shots of job centres under details of unemployment figures, shots of various industrial processes under accounts of the state of manufacturing and shots of high street counters under reporting of consumer spending.

This means that the core depictive material for many economic reports is *voice-over across diverse images* in which the speech is strongly dominant. In many of the accounts in our survey, this is interspersed with sections of *voice-over across graphics*. Here, the communicative profile changes and the visual depiction becomes primary, as the reports attempt by various devices to render abstraction and (statistically based) complexity in terms of visual symbols. A third use of reportorial speech is the *piece-to-camera*, in which the reporter offers exposition, mostly from a location having significance for the news theme. Location reporting of the kind found elsewhere in television journalism is less common in economic items for the reasons noted above, but thematically supportive settings are often used. These have a more direct role to play in the account, and are thus given more emphasis, when the report is cast in the narrative form of a visit – e.g. to a region, to a factory, to a shop or to a particular household. Visit formats, invariably involving a degree of typification in which the visited site represents more general conditions, form an important part of economic reporting and we shall say more about them both in this chapter and later in the book.

Transitions between speech over supportive image, speech over graphics and speech to camera often produce an interwoven account rather than sequenced, discrete blocks, although the convention of closing the report with a piece-to-camera is widespread across the channels, and, not surprisingly, we have found that the discursive summarizing that this involves weighs quite heavily in viewer response.

We have noted the different modes of reporter speech but one of the most important elements of economic reporting, as in most television news, is the *interview*. Interviews are mostly 'location' sequences, although on big stories (Budget Day would be an obvious example) there may be studio interviewing after the location report has concluded. Interview speech feeds into the report the accounts of political actors, experts, and a range of citizens variously related to economic events. In economic reporting, it is most often 'evaluation' (rather than 'information' or 'experience') which is sought. Interviews reflect the economy as both multi-aspectual and as the object of a (potentially chronic) number of 'professional' as well as 'lay' interpretations.

These various uses of image and speech in the economic report almost always follow an introduction by the news 'anchor' and may follow a main headline too if the item is high enough in the bulletin's running order. *Headlines and anchor speech*, with their special density and framing role, are key aspects of any journalistic discourse, signalling the essence of a story and often situating it within the broader classifications and topography of the newsworthy. Along with the reportorial usages we have outlined, they are an important constituent of those dynamics of understanding which the latter half of this chapter explores.

The reported economy

In this section, we want to examine three different dimensions of the economy as reported on UK television, each of which is to be found across the range of our taped and transcribed material as well as featuring with varying degrees of directness in respondent comment. These dimensions are the economy as figures, the political economy and the sectored economy. By using the term 'reported economy' we wish to draw attention to the uncontestable point that of all the various activities and circumstances that constitute 'the economy', only a selection receive television treatment. This is the inevitable result of preselection within the political sphere and the sphere of economic debate combined with further selection within the terms of broadcast journalistic practice, a field with its own institutional constraints (including those on time) as well as its commitments to specific audience groups. However, observed discrepancies between the nature of 'the economy' and that of the 'reported economy' have often been used in criticism of broadcasters by politicians and academics, and they are also to be found in the accounts of our own respondents, discussed later.

The economy as figures

We have noted earlier how the abstract, systemic, contingent nature of economic events and conditions often poses a challenge for journalistic story-telling. The reporting of significant statistical change in the context of expectations provides the core of most economic news items. New figures are significant longitudinally, against a background of recent history and prediction, and laterally, in relation to other economic indicators. The longitudinal setting may be one of high volatility in economic affairs, or one in which relative stability has been maintained. The significance of figures consequently varies with immediate context – a 0.5 per cent rise in retail sales figures might be dramatic in one period and unremarkable in another. The lateral setting is affected by those indicators which have become highlighted for particular attention, as a result most often of government targets or, for instance, strongly expressed concern within industry.

As we have already indicated, the broad movement during the period of our study was out of recession and towards recovery. At the beginning of our study, strong news values still surrounded the question of whether recovery had 'really' started; at the end of our study the question of its 'pace' and its 'sustainability' provided the strongest news framing, with the 'feelgood factor' having become a dominant marker against which demand-side statistics were read. During such a period of uncertain transition, readings can generate news interest from confirmatory or contradictory indications almost equally, and we have found reversals of evaluation occurring within one week on the same channel.

'New figures' may not only have news value as indicators, of course. They often also have value as the grounds of *dispute*, not just of their significance but of their reliability and provenance. The disputing of significance is sometimes carried out by journalists themselves but in recent years economic broadcasting has used 'experts' from the banking and finance sector more extensively. This has provided a way of opening up the reporting of economic shifts to variable interpretation whilst obviating the need for reporters either to initiate a strong critical framing themselves or to pass the story over to the more predictable differences of party politics (although the political colouring of comment drawn extensively from City employees has not gone without comment; referred to in Gavin (1992). However, opposition political parties are available to provide regular and news-credible challenges to more fundamental questions of statistical probity.

The political economy

The reported economy is political not only because it is the subject of parliamentary concern but because it is the object of government measures and a primary indicator of government competence. The extent to which the government itself claims responsibility for the problems and the successes of economic performance varies but, despite the recognition both of domestic and international market factors outside of direct or even indirect regulatory action, the Chancellor of the Exchequer is understood to be the main 'actor' in the UK economy. His appearance in economic reporting is routine, from brief references to sustained interview. As well as his being main 'actor', news coverage often casts him as the nation's official 'interpreter' of economic conditions, his pronouncements here acting as a major source of news comment (Budget Day being a special case). During the period of our study, his regular, minuted meetings with the Governor of the Bank of England to discuss economic planning provided an element of personalized 'theatre' in economic reporting, strengthened by differences between the two on the interest rate – inflation relationship.

The extent to which economic reporting develops its political dimension (sometimes thereby requiring further commentary from parliamentary correspondents) varies not only with the extent of government involvement in the immediate news event, and the journalists' attribution of political causes even where these are not self-proclaimed, but also with the wider political climate. During the period prior to an election, for example, the party-political aspects of economic affairs become most obvious.

An economy of sectors

Reporting of the economy takes place largely within a national narrative, the reported shifts attaining significance in respect of their implications for UK interests. At the level of the 'political economy' (see above), it is a view of the UK economy as a relatively discrete entity in political stewardship which informs economic dispute. This dispute is a main source of news material and news comment. However, the economy is also reported as a sectored one, in which there exist not only separate sectoral interests (e.g. the building industry – much featured in our data – being differently related to economic controls when compared to high street stores) but also potential conflicts (e.g. between the overall beneficiaries and overall sufferers from a given cut in interest rates). Reporting sectoral interest within a framework of national interest (overlaid by the perspectives of parliamentary commentary) further complicates both the formats and the discourse of economic news. Sector spokespersons are accessed by news accounts to speak for their area and they vary in the extent to which they align this with national interest or place it in explicit conflict with the interest of other sectors. The variation here provides journalists with different tasks in the illustration of conflict and commonality around their new theme.

There is a further aspect to sectoralism too. This is the location of the UK economy as a 'sector' within the European and then the global economy. This has both market and political dimensions. The multinational ownership of corporate giants means that an element of internationalism feeds into what might otherwise be domestic aspects of performance (e.g. the car industry, telecommunications), whilst competition between nation states (with an element of protectionism) remains a dominant framework, alongside co-operation, in the conduct and the reporting of international developments. Economic news makes regular reference to conditions elsewhere among 'Britain's trading partners' and occasionally to the broader league tables and predictions drafted by international bodies, the news value of which is often to provide a 'shock' indication of the UK's declining status. The UK economy within the EU was essentially a contentious background story, and essentially a 'political' rather than 'economic' item, during the period of our study. With the moves towards a single European currency, however, it is certain to impact upon economic performance and planning much more directly, further modifying the national framing of reports.

Analysis of the classifications and themings of the reported economy would benefit from a more ambitious typology than has been provided here, but these broad strands provide a good basis for looking more closely at coverage and interpretation.

Themes and responses

The 'managed economy' – statistics, politics and scepticism

A question you often ask yourself when you see these figures is where do they come from?

(Garage workers)

The news reports on an economic realm which is 'official' in at least two important ways. News items are often grounded in the release of statistics from governmental or government-related institutions, although throughout our study period news bulletins frequently indicated the contested character of these statistics. News items also routinely report the condition of the economy in terms either of the consequences of past political action or of likely future political action. Moreover, they reflect on economic competence as a feature of the broader parliamentary contest.

In our respondent groups, as we shall indicate, we found that these features of the reported economy connect with different strands of scepticism. First of all, there is a scepticism about the 'truth' of economic conditions reported so extensively through the use of government statements. This may impugn the integrity of the broadcasters themselves as 'carriers' of such statements, despite their attributions and the accessing of counter-claims. Related to this, but more specific, is a scepticism about the integrity of statistical information as an indicator of economic conditions. This may derive from a belief in the 'fiddling' of economic statistics by governments or it may be a more general scepticism about statistical representation *per se*. Then there is a strand of scepticism about the degree of actual control over the economy which government can really exert. Again, this is different from, though often related to, specific criticisms of policy and policy statements. Not surprisingly, we also found a degree of partisan scepticism, in which interpretation of the news items was strongly framed in terms of political affiliation. Since most of the news items involved the direct actions of members of the Conservative government, this kind of scepticism showed up most clearly in the comments of Labour-supporting viewers. In what follows, we look first of all at the specific issues posed by statistics, and then at the broader question of how 'political management' of the economy (and of economic news) is perceived.

Statistics

As we have noted, the value of statistics can be doubted for a variety of reasons, including specific concern about the calculations upon which particular figures are based and a more general scepticism about the employment of detailed figures in public discourse. This latter position may regard incomprehensibility as a general failing as serious as unreliability. For instance:

But do these figures mean anything for ... like? I mean, they throw these fig ... But there's so many different figures at you and, like you said before, they're putting in percentages and that ... These sort of figures that get thrown at you – different figures all the time – they don't mean anything really. (Sixth-form students)

Even more directly, there may be the implied idea that not just miscomprehension but deception is at stake:

I think figures are things that blind people, more than anything. (Hotel workers)

Around unemployment, scepticism often became more focused on particular limitations of statistical indicators, drawing on alternative knowledge of this problem in the UK and the government's record over many years:

It suggests that for months and months, and going on years, that all that ... how much it's rising ... how much it's been going down – and they've been claiming it's good that it's been going down ... they've been doctoring the figures so much that ... people on training schemes don't count and everybody else doesn't count towards the figures and then they're seasonally adjusted and after everything else ... (Sixth-form students)

Or, similarly:

Well, I'd like to know, the graphs that they're quoting, they haven't got 16 to 17-year-olds on ... Right, because they can't sign on the dole. They've got to go on YOP [Youth Opportunity Programme] schemes or whatever, whatever else. Now, how can they come up with an accurate picture of what the economy's like if their own graphs are ridiculous? (Garage workers)

Both of these examples display a political reading of the statistics as unduly 'managed' in the government's favour in the light of specific exclusions, a dominant trend in our respondent groups. However, when we showed material critical of the government's record in the context of a slight rise in unemployment, a reading of bias *against* the government was forthcoming in one group. This item, in the context of a very small rise in national unemployment figures and a fall in retail sales, featured a report by Peter Jay, the BBC's chief economic correspondent, on location in Bristol. Jay was shown standing at the docks in front of the classic early steamship SS *Great Britain*, once a model of efficiency and power, later an abandoned hulk and now a tourist attraction.[4] The metaphoric implications were given full weight, illegitimately so in the view of this speaker:

Well they only gave one side as well, didn't they? I mean, I think the unemployment's been falling for the last ... ooh, several months at least. It's gone up by 200 and I think they've really overemphasized the fact the economy is perhaps worse than it is. By using the SS *Great Britain* and, you know, saying ... I mean, I thought that was really over the top to use that. I mean, had it been going up and up and up for the last 12 months, I'd say, yes, fair enough. But they only put one side of the story. They didn't speak to any government ministers or even speak to a firm who might have taken on three or four workers. (Library workers)

Other respondents were better able, if sometimes only partially, to relate to statistical information as both comprehensible and of use, but the *apparent volatility* of the economy itself – evident in some of the quotations already given – sometimes comes through as a reason for doubt about the validity of the indicators. Here, the reference is to the 'positive' and 'negative' implications carried by news items on successive days:

Again, I can't see how two things could come out like that 24 hours apart. It doesn't gel to me. (Rotary Club members)

We explore below the way in which partisan considerations affect interpretation, but we can note here how, compounding the problem of rapidly shifting indicators and statistical obscurity, there is for some respondents the problem of the starkly contra-

dictory political interpretations which the news rhetoric employs
on a routine basis:

To be honest, I find it very difficult to decide how it is going because
you've got one set of politicians saying we're doing marvellously well
and everything's fine and on the other hand they're saying no, it's not,
it's the worst position we've been in for nine, ten years. So you really
don't know. (Library workers)

This general uncertainty is returned by one respondent to the
question of the 'figures' and their high level of dependence upon
party-political perspective:

Are they a Labour figure or are they a Conservative figure, if you like?
… I'm sure if the Conservatives had come up with a figure, Labour
would come up with another figure and totally contradict it. (Garage
workers)

The possibility that statistics are part of a news concern with
description which displaces *explanation* is also raised. Thus, for
example, the garage worker's comments below refer to the value
of the pound sterling against other currencies. The value of the
pound is one of the indicators used in discussing the health of the
economy, but it is not the focus of this report. So this respondent's
questions – 'why is the pound at an all-time low?' and 'whose fault
is it?' – could be seen as tangential to the 'point' of the story, were it
not for the fact that he perceives the omission of information to fit
in with an underlying logic (whether of the government or of the
broadcasters is not altogether clear): 'they always seem to be
preparing you for tales of gloom and doom':

To be honest, I start asking myself questions, you know, about the
pound and … why is the pound at an all-time low? And they're showing
you all these people with computer screens in front of them and I go:
well is it their fault that fell then? Whose fault is it? But they always
seem to be preparing you for tales of gloom and doom all the time. Do
you know what I mean? Oh well, inflation is at such-and-such a per cent
but the pound is at an all-time low and … You know, the pound is the
basic thing that sets everything in perspective, isn't it? And yet they
never really go into why the pound's at an all-time low, and why it can't
compete in Europe, and why we're well below Italy and Spain, you
know, in the European group. (Garage workers)

Political management

Just how far people feel that politicians *are* 'responsible' for the
economy is clearly a factor in their ascription of cause and their
discrimination amongst different political 'solutions'. Viewers'
attribution of responsibility is likely to differ with the aspect of
the economy under scrutiny. For example, when in our pilot study

we asked respondents about inflation, a number of them saw the government's responsibility in the most direct of terms:

I just feel like they sit and make a decision. That's what it is going to be, end of story, no argument, you know. The Chancellor of the Exchequer, simple as that, you know.

or:

The government, yes. Yes, you'd have to blame the government. That's what I'd say …It's up to them isn't it? They're the ones managing the country.[5]

There are indications that this belief in the 'controllability' of the economy is stronger during the budget period than at other times – this is not surprising, considering the focus on economic management of budgets and budget news. Indications of 'control' are, of course, a routine dimension of economic news coverage. The question of *how much* control in relation to *what non-controllable* factors a particular policy measure can expect to exercise forms a regular object of journalistic scrutiny and a key part of the interface between economic and political reporting.

As we noted earlier, however, questions of controllability are often linked to the issue of partisanship. Partisanship was expressed in a variety of ways.[6] One of its most common manifestations was in respondents' willingness to read the overall tone of television commentary in accordance with their own partisan perceptions. In some groups, Labour-supporting respondents found it possible to find negative implications in stories which were actually substantially positive, as in the following case, where a fall in the inflation figures was reported:

R1:   If the government's strategy on the economy is so good and they've got inflation down, why is the pound its second-worst it's ever been? It's just a small thing.

R2:   At an all-time low.

R1:   At an all-time low. Well, just above it all now but … And why can't it … it can't even come a decent third to the American dollar and the German Deutschmark.

(Garage workers)

Conservative partisans sometimes manage this kind of interpretative move in reverse. One report illustrates the poor state of the economy with a case study in which a small trader (a baker) has been obliged to make a member of his staff redundant:

… he made the point that, *despite what the economic condition was* [our italics], people still have birthdays, weddings and christenings and he was doing OK making his cakes. I mean, that's the … what he started off by saying. (Rotary Club members)

Sometimes this results in disagreements within groups as to the overall 'positive' or 'negative' tone of reports, underpinned by political divergences. Below, responding to a story on unemployment, R1 is a Labour partisan, R2 is neutral and R3 is a Conservative partisan:

Q: So you think the report was saying … overall everything was all right?

R1:   It's painting a rosy picture of the economy whereas there isn't.

Q: Yeah. Did any of you feel differently about that?

R2:   I didn't think it was painting a rosy picture.

R3:   I thought it was doom and gloom really. To make things look like they were bad.

(Garage workers)

Partisanship could also be expressed in the respondent's reactions to those commentators or experts who were perceived as coming from the wrong side of the political divide. This is epitomized in the following extracts, where the BBC's economics editor, Peter Jay, is castigated for possible bias – right-wing bias for the garage workers, and left-wing bias for the Rotarians:

R: I'd say no [the report did not have an appropriate selection of speakers] because from what I know of that Jay – his name's Jay, isn't it? – he's a Tory … he's a Tory … affluent Tory, isn't he? From what I've heard of him.

Q: Yeah? I don't know.

R: And if that's the case, he's only reporting on government politics which makes him biased.

(Garage workers)

R1:   No, I'm sorry, I don't [have faith in Peter Jay] because Peter Jay, as you know, is …

R2:   The son-in-law of …

Q: Callaghan.

R1:   Callaghan.

R3:   Been in Parliament.

R1:   And he's been in Parliament. He's been here, there and everywhere. I'm sorry, I've no time for Peter Jay.

(Rotary Club members)

In this section we have attempted to illustrate aspects of the relationship to the 'managed economy' which news viewers bring to their interpretative action. Around the statistical core of economic news, a number of questions of use and validity are generated, often related to matters of comprehension, but rarely manifested as *merely* matters of comprehension. Some of the scepticism has a directly political character. When the focus shifts to political control over the economy (the actions behind the figures), the political dimension frequently displays a partisan character, which can be used to evaluate not only politicians, but accessed experts and the broadcasters themselves.

Broadly, the playoff between the terms of management of the 'official economy' and scepticism is a key dynamic in our respondent data. However, informing this is the further dynamic between perceptions of national interest and perceptions of personal interest.

Comprehension and involvement: national news and personal perspectives

As soon as they put something like that on the telly, I know I don't understand it all. Generally lose interest in it. It's way over my head. (Garage workers)

It was looking at the individual really rather than the economy as a whole, which is what I tend to find most people are interested in. (Geography postgraduates)

A common characteristic of television economic news resides in its abstracted nature. Consequently, stories discussing aspects of national economic management, often accompanied by statistics and specialized terminology, may present viewers with difficulties in identifying their own interests with what is presented as the national interest, and with impediments to comprehension.

We have found that television news, with this presumably in mind, adopts a variety of formal strategies to 'personalize' national economic shifts or to relate them more closely to the everyday lives of viewers. Amongst these are the use of 'typical families' to gauge the likely effects of economic measures, the foregrounding of the principal actors involved in national economic management as 'personalities', the use of sectoral 'case studies' to illustrate the impact of measures across the wider economy, the employment of non-economic metaphors in economic reporting and the imaginative use of graphics to portray economic measures in straightforward terms. Whilst such devices may be desirable to increase viewers' identification with and comprehension of economic stories which might otherwise appear remote or obscure, they may also risk distracting viewers from the national perspective and oversimplifying complex phenomena, sometimes to the detriment of comprehension.

We were interested in the extent to which viewers showed themselves to be able to comprehend and identify with the national, as opposed to their personal, economy, as presented in news accounts, and in the effect on this of devices of personalization which news stories employed. For our viewing material, we selected both strongly abstracted and strongly personalized texts to investigate respondent engagement and to assess how helpful such devices were. In what follows, the 'national' frame of reference will be our starting point, and we will then attempt to discuss how respondents respond to material which either refracts national issues through more 'localized' reportage, or concentrates upon the personal and sectoral effects of economic policies and events.

Certainly, viewers are aware that there is a national story which they themselves are more or less implicated in:

The main thing I think of when people mention the economy is how the pound's doing abroad and stuff like that, mainly the stock exchange and the *Financial Times* share index and all that. I mean, I don't fully understand it but that's what I think of when people mention the economy. (Garage workers)

They also appreciate as citizens the duty that television news journalism has to report that story. But this appreciation has its limits. The details of the most abstracted accounts are almost impenetrably difficult to follow, even for the most educated groups which acknowledge the greatest degree of interest in economic news; and there is a marked preference for more 'personalizing' strategies because these are not about the national story but depict 'effects' at the level of individual families. The problem is partly that the personal is immediately interesting, whilst the interest of the national has to be worked at by the broadcasters and by the viewers themselves, but also that the national ought to be about effects at the experiential level, so that the more abstracted accounts represent a kind of mystification.

This difference can be seen by comparing responses of different groups to the same extract: an item from *Sky News* on Budget Day 1995 which employed the 'typical families' strategy and opened thus:

Well, so far we've heard the view from Westminster and the world of business. What did people up and down the country make of the budget? We've been talking to three families on very different incomes.

The response to this item was a favourable one across every group that we talked to, and their approval was registered as something to do with comprehensibility:

Well, that showed you exactly who the budget affected. Who it benefited and who it didn't. You couldn't get more clear than that as far as I'm concerned. I mean, people at the lower end of the ladder are being hit again. The guy there with the high-income family, if you like, smiling from one ear to the other. That's a ... good piece of news, if you like. I mean, it's the ... You can't get more clear than that as far as I'm concerned. (Garage workers)

I liked that because I like the way they, you know, went to the actual people, showed the effects, rather than having these discussions and the terms I didn't understand. It makes it more lively. (Sixth-form students)

I thought it was very ... it was entertaining – I mean, most people would be able to follow that ... (Library workers)

It was looking at the individual really rather than the economy as a whole, which is what I tend to find most people are interested in. So I think people would get more out of that than the previous thing. (Geography postgraduates)

Can I say that I found that much more easy to understand? It was far simpler and maybe that's why it appealed to me, because it was ... I quite liked the idea of them going to the three separate families and getting the views of it. (Rotary Club members)

Are there any differences between these responses to this item? We may notice that more than one account carries some recognition that the Sky item complements a preceding more general account of the budget. As it happens, all groups had watched and discussed just such a general account (a BBC item) before watching the Sky extract, and this experience is partly responsible for the comparative terms of reference which they all employ. However, it is not obvious that the garage worker is thinking in terms of complementarity. The speaker here is the garage worker whose Labour partisanship, and its influence on his interpretative approach, is discussed in the previous section of this chapter. His comments connect his experience of the item's clarity to the delivery of the message that the rich are going to benefit from the budget and the poor are going to suffer from it. He is better able to approve the item because it is about these relativities. But if that is the case, Sky's item is being taken as an alternative rather than as a complement to a general, nationally focused account.

However, it is impossible to discriminate in any firm way between the 'complementary' reading and the 'alternative' reading of the Sky item. Viewers' formulations indicate a real uncertainty concerning how, in these terms, the broadcast material should be judged. So, for example, the idea that viewers are 'more interested in' (geography students) the budget's effects on families (including their own) than upon the national profile allows for a fudging of the issue as to whether they should, as citizens, allow themselves such a preference.

It is perhaps unsurprising that this extract, the most personalized of all those which we showed to our groups, should unanimously have been greeted as the easiest to follow and the most readily comprehensible. None of our groups seemed unduly worried even about the representativeness of the 'typical families' chosen. Material which was more intrinsically 'difficult' was less likely to generate wholly favourable responses even where formal strategies had been employed to encourage viewer involvement or identification. A noteworthy example of this came in the report by Peter Jay, referred to earlier in this chapter, marking the first rise in unemployment figures for two years and a fall in retail sales. Jay's report set the release of the unemployment figures in a general context of economic slowdown in the UK and employed a number of devices which might be expected to encourage viewer identification despite the 'difficult' subject matter. It was located in a troubled suburban shopping street in Bristol with an independent bakery as its focus – familiar territory for many viewers. The problems affecting the baker (who has laid off an employee and 'can't remember a tougher time') and the street are made to stand as a case study illustrating the impact of economic slowdown more generally ('Out in the high street, in Bristol as elsewhere, there are few signs of confidence').

Outwardly, this encouragement of viewer identification through the use of personalized and sectoral coverage to give significance to economic statistics was quite successful. Overall, the report was taken to be clear, and complaints about comprehensibility were focused on the economic terms within it. One group actually commented that the setting made identification easier:

I think it showed an everyday scene of a high street, everyday shop that everybody's been in at some time in their life. You could identify with the ordinariness of it all. (Rotary Club members)

But within our groups there was some disagreement about whether the form of coverage made the report easier to understand. One garage worker thought that the report was 'filled with irrelevance':

Q: Did you think that sort of … 'game' made it harder to understand …?

R: Yeah, yeah.

Q: … Than just presenting the raw figures?

R: I mean, the figures – they showed you a graph and then surrounded it by *irrelevant stories* [our italics], if you like.

(Garage workers)

Moreover, the wealth of supplemental personal and sectoral information given to viewers by this form of coverage sometimes caused its own problems of interpretation. Group members were inclined to read more into the choice of the bakery or the location of the report than was perhaps intended, and in some cases this undermined their ability to generalize from it or to take it as representative. Groups tended to discuss the particular problems of the bakery trade:

Well, to be honest I was surprised to see a baker like that that had survived for a hundred years. That's what I thought when I seen it. Perhaps ... you know, I'm surprised he's still going because the supermarkets have swallowed people in places like that up, you know. That's the first thing that hit me when I seen it. (Garage workers)

Another group went so far as to count the local bakeries which their own local high street had recently lost. Others read it as suggesting a distinction to be made between the effects of economic slowdown on small and large businesses, or as commenting on the decline of traditional trades:

Q: Apart from the central point about unemployment figures, do you think they made any other points in this?

R: A lot of small businesses, how the economy's affecting them. Like it showed you that baker's. That's been in use for years. Now they've all of a sudden had to make someone redundant. When was the last time they had to do that? It's, like, shows you, like, small businesses seem to be suffering.

(Sixth-form students)

Q: Can you think of any other issues that you didn't think were so prominent but that also came across in that extract or were raised in it?

R: The decline in traditional trades. The baker's finding it very hard to run his business the way he has done for hundreds of years probably.

(Library workers)

There was also considerable confusion about the significance of Bristol:

Q: Do you think Bristol's likely to be representative?

R: No.

Q: ... Or not too representative? No? Why not?

R: It hasn't got, like ... I always think of Bristol like they're all fairly well off ... It doesn't show, like, a wide representative of the different classes, Bristol. It's like ... one particular ... I don't know.

(Sixth-form students)

To close this report, Jay employs an entirely different device – the non-economic metaphor – with a piece-to-camera before the preserved steamship SS *Great Britain*:

The steamship *Great Britain*, once the biggest in the world, mirrors Britain's economic decline. For half a century she dominated the world's sea lanes, before being beset by great storms, abandoned as a wreck in the Falkland Islands and now displayed as a relic to tourists in Bristol. If John Major's Great Britain is to avoid a similar fate, the Chancellor will soon have to get the economy moving again. Right now, he's got two weeks before the budget to find the right tonic.

Reaction to this device was mixed. All of our groups understood it and were able to explain its intention, although the Rotary Club members were dismissive about others' ability to grasp it:

Q: So you feel that it tied in nicely?

All: Yes.

R: Half the country will have missed it, mind, anyway.

However, there was some disagreement amongst the garage workers about its relevance and, as the following comments show, the library workers questioned its appropriateness and fairness:

R1:   Well, I felt that it was cliché. Yes, I ...

Q: Did the rest of you?

R2:   No.

R3:   Yeah, I didn't think that it sort of went with the article at all. I mean, I think they probably just used that because maybe they passed by it as they were filming and thought, well, maybe we'll try and get that in somewhere. I thought it was a bit of a nasty comment at the end. You know, to say ... to compare it to John Major's government. I mean, I'm not saying they're perfect but I don't think it was fair to say that at the end.

Q: No. R4, did you?

R4:   I thought it was quite a good comparison. A bit melodramatic but ... you know, a bit different.

In this news extract, then, formal strategies which might increase viewer involvement in nationally focused and otherwise abstracted and densely statistical economic stories embodied a trade-off between increased viewer identification and problems introduced by the formal devices themselves. However, reactions to other extracts confirmed that such an approach has a positive part to play in sustaining viewer interest in nationally focused economic news.

The importance of viewer interest was another factor to emerge from our discussion with viewing groups. Across our groups, denial of interest was a common response to much of our screened material. Respondents frequently admitted to 'switching off' either literally or metaphorically when confronted with such news in the normal context of everyday life. Some respondents told us they had mentally 'switched off' even during the research screenings: one Channel 4 item used in the research produced a fairly uniform response of this kind. Denial of interest is a significant response in this context, of course, because it does indicate the possibility of detachment from the national picture. Very few groups listened to national economic news with no sense of membership in the nation whose fortunes were at issue. All groups spoke of the recession as something happening to 'us', for example. And yet there certainly were respondents for whom the national 'we' was a rather long way away from the immediate 'I' about to pay more for cigarettes – or less for whisky.

Q: Do you think it's unclear because what it needs to get across is a difficult thing to get across, or is it just that ... they've organized it badly?

R: That might be part of it, I think, with people who aren't particularly interested in the economics anyway. And myself I'm not.

(Rotary Club members)

R1: I don't think we're stupid because I can think of a lot of people who wouldn't be able to understand that. I think my mum and dad could sit down and watch that and have the same sort of reaction as we've got.

R2: You have to be interested in it really to understand it.

(Sixth-form students)

One particular respondent group went much further than this. Educated and articulate, but living – by their own description – below the poverty line, as part of 'the underclass', 'in a totally separate reality', our arts workers were alive to news visuals and formal strategies (which they often read as ritualistic, self-referential or self-parodying), but commonly described themselves as 'alienated' by the discourse of the news itself:

R1: It's the idea of democratic society, like, really, isn't it? It's like, here we are, information for all you people who are part of UK Limited, and it's for you to read, like. And unfortunately we're not part of UK Limited, I don't think.

R2: We've no shares, have we?

(Arts workers)

In part at least, it is the discourse of economics which viewers find themselves rejecting. Some groups said as much, as comments cited elsewhere in this chapter demonstrate. The vocabulary and reasoning characteristic of this discourse produces even greater confusion when it is used, less characteristically, not to explicate national economic fortunes but tax cuts as a matter of direct personal relevance. This was made evident to us in the responses of our groups to an item presented on Channel 4 by Steve Levinson. In mid-November 1995, Levinson set himself the task of explaining the reasoning which would make income tax cuts more likely or less likely in the forthcoming budget. A 'traffic light' graphic was used as a visual metaphor: green meant 'more likely', while red meant 'less likely'. But this visual symbolism was not enough to deliver a clear message about tax cuts. Through its assumption that personal benefit via tax cuts is self-evidently desirable, the item was in tension with the more customary news emphasis on a 'national' perspective, with the result that indicators which are normally 'bad' for the national economy were depicted as 'good' for their effect in increasing the likelihood of tax cuts. We were told, for example, that 'the economy's stagnating' rather than 'overheating', but stagnation, although normally 'bad', of course, was here presented as 'good' in the sense that a stagnating economy is more likely to result in tax cuts. The strategy of the programme thus demanded a *green* light at this point in the delivery. Furthermore, Levinson's dependence upon economic discourse (usually associated with the 'national' frame of reference) is in tension with an approach essentially based upon relevance to the individual, and the result for many respondents is confusion and rejection:

R1: And what was the point of having the traffic lights on the screen when you just didn't understand what it said anyway?

R2: I know. I spent more time thinking about what the hell that meant.

R3: The reporter did say that the pound's weak, the pound's at an all-time low. I mean that was helpful enough, rather than having to work with all the things with traffic lights and spinning numbers. It's ... seems to defeat the point.

(Sixth-form students)

R1: Giving you a negative view one minute and then mentioning inflation going down, the lights change to green ...

R2: In that order.

R1: ... And then back on to red again – something negative – so ... it's difficult to make out what they're trying to say to you really.

(Garage workers)

The economy as public knowledge

In the previous section we examined the interplay between news discourse and viewer interpretation as it operated across two recurring themes within our selection of news material. The issue of comprehension arose frequently and in this section we explore its implications more directly. We look first at the extent to which the coverage was perceived to be fair and the consequences of this for comprehension, and then at viewers' comprehension of the material more generally, identifying the causes of some comprehension difficulties and reflecting on viewers' ability to make partial sense of economic news nevertheless.

For television to be successful in informing the public about the economy (or any other topic, for that matter) it is obviously important that it be perceived to be free from manifest unfairness in its presentation. That most of our respondents did consider BBC and ITN coverage 'fair' in this way is less revealing than the criteria which they employed in judging 'fairness'. One important criterion seemed to be television's perceived ability to deploy 'the facts' about the economy:

I suppose you have to say it was fair. They presented *the facts* [our italics] and ... yes ... (Rotary Club members)

Interestingly, where accounts were read as less fact-based, they were often criticized as being 'speculation' and consequently of scant relevance:

I'd rather it was factual than ... speculation, the way it is in certain items, I mean ... Rather than if it speculates over something, say ... If it's something that you've got no control of anyway, so ... you know, why speculate? (Garage workers)

Of course, the adequacy of any selective presentation of 'the facts' embodied in the news coverage might be open to challenge (and, indeed, many of our respondents did challenge the unemployment statistics in particular). However, it is clear that *information* conveyed in news is taken seriously – not least in judging the fairness of the overall package.

Audiences are also sensitive to perceived attempts to give a story a particular inflection or spin. The following comments suggest that audiences are capable of judging television coverage to be unfair if it is seen to 'guide' a story:

Q: Did you feel that the item struck you as being fair reporting?

R: I didn't feel it was, no ... I mean they gave one side and they gave it quite well. I would have liked to have seen another viewpoint for it to be fair.

Q: Right. Was there anything in particular that was unfair about it? It was one-sided, but did you feel that they selected things or ...?

R: Well, I'd say that they selected it ... selected the item to make the point that they wanted to make.

(Library workers)

Finally, it appears that a viewer's *comprehension* of a particular item has a bearing on their own perceived ability to judge the fairness of a story:

Q: When we were talking about the other item we asked whether you thought it was fair, the way it was reported. If it was a fair report. What about this one? Is this fair?

R: It would be fair if you understood it properly and you had time to sit and think about it, but you don't get the chance to with that one no matter how hard you try and follow it. You can't ...

Q: It's too complicated?

R: You know, you've got to take their word for it, haven't you? You've got to believe what they're telling you is the truth. But you can go into it hundreds of different ways.

(Garage workers)

R: I have got no opinion about fairness and that, cos I just didn't understand it.

(Arts workers)

Judgements of fairness or otherwise are dependent, of course, on the sense which people are themselves able to make of the news material. Some of our respondents were prepared to speculate on the fairness of particular items despite admitting to having only partially understood them. We reflect further on the consequences of partial comprehension below.

On the question of their general ability to comprehend the news material, our respondents' own assessments suggested varying degrees of success, with a marked variation between and within groups and in relation to different types of text. Few people, for example, expressed difficulty with the 'typical families' extract referred to above. Of all of our groups, the Rotary club members expressed the least difficulty overall. This may perhaps be explained by the fact that they were experienced, professional people, having some interest in the subject matter, who were able, consequently, to bring more prior knowledge (see Höijer, 1993) to bear than most.

Broadly speaking, those who responded to general questions of comprehensibility ranged from those who professed little difficulty with the material, except in relation to the more arcane terms or concepts touched upon, to those who, initially at least, claimed almost total incomprehension:

Q: What kind of issues do you think this piece was trying to raise?

A: I haven't got a clue.

(Sixth-form students)

I got very little information from that at all. (Arts workers)

No idea at all. Sorry. (Garage workers)

I just feel terrible because, like, that just washed over me, and I tried my hardest to concentrate then. (Geography postgraduates)

These were among the most extreme comments, amounting almost to a rejection of comprehension (and, in two cases, an apologetic one).

In general, however, our respondents did their best to engage with what they acknowledged at times was difficult material for them and claimed, if not total comprehension, then some at least:

Q: Can anyone remember any of the details of the arguments in that?

A: Can't say that I can, no, the *details* [our italics] of it.

(Garage workers)

Q: Did you find it clear apart from the graphs?

A: I knew what it was talking about, yeah, but …

(Sixth-form students)

I can go along with the *gist* [our italics] of it but obviously I couldn't go along with the finer details of it. (Garage workers)

A variety of explanations were put forward for poor comprehension, including mode of address, specialized terminology, lack of contextualizing information, over-reliance on comment perceived as speculative rather than fact-based, speed or lack of clarity in verbal delivery, mismatches between verbal and visual cues, and either too many or too few graphics.

Furthermore, even most of those who initially claimed almost total incomprehension were able, when questioned further, to recall some information from the screened material and to piece together a general sense of its meaning. So it would appear that in most cases our respondents, like the garage worker quoted above, were able at least to pick up what might be termed the 'gist' of the news reports even where the finer details remained elusive. These 'gist readings', if we may so term them, appeared to be available despite a failure to engage fully either with the terms in which the story or its significance were expressed, or with the propositional structure and coherence of a story, or despite difficulties of engagement arising from particular elements within a story.

However, the idea of these 'gist readings' must be treated with caution. It depends upon the explanations of our respondents and arises out of their own conception of and explanations for comprehension. It is in the nature of 'gist' to render comprehension difficulties less problematic for respondents; to have got the gist is to have understood (or to feel that one has understood) a story *despite* difficulties in comprehending it. Hence there is a sense in which it may be used, consciously or unconsciously, in self-appeasement. The significance of and attraction for our respondents of 'gist' may arise in part from a desire to resolve the cognitive dissonance involved in partial comprehension, where the alternative is to admit a failure to comprehend. Respondents may be keen to impose some sort of closure on the screened material even where they do not feel that this is satisfactorily provided by or can be adequately comprehended from such material. Hence, 'gist readings' partially remove the need for confessions of failure or apologetic rejections of comprehension.

In a few cases, however, respondents' difficulties in comprehension did not resolve themselves in this way and instead an outright rejection of the terms in which economic news is presented was proposed, as in the following response to a sequence reporting figures for economic growth:

I think sometimes as well when it's reported like that it puts a lot of people off. I'm not saying, like, a lot of people are stupid but a lot of people are put off watching the news because either they won't understand it or they lose interest because it's not in their language. (Hotel workers)

The issue of viewers' ability to comprehend economic news is an important one. In a democracy where the economic realm is highly complex and abstract but yet of paramount importance to the evaluation of political performance, television news is, for many, the principal source for civic information and knowledge about the workings of the economy and its management. Where people distrust, are baffled by or despair at the complexity of news accounts of the economy, it is likely that they will be hampered in making the informed appraisal of politicians and government actions upon which the democratic process depends.

Our findings show that many of our respondents found considerable difficulty in making sense fully of the extracts which they were shown, and the likelihood is that the circumstances in which they were asked to watch them (including the foreknowledge that they would be asked questions about them) would encourage closer concentration than would be normal in a domestic environment. Nevertheless, most of our respondents were able to make partial sense even of that material which they found most difficult. This was sometimes partial in terms of specific, understood detail but it was also often partial in terms of general understanding and the according of significance. This latter kind of partiality we have called 'gist'. In most cases the level of achieved 'gist' made it less likely that a sense of alienation from the entire report would occur and made it probable that a capacity to evaluate economic policy and management and to be engaged as a citizen was an active dimension of news viewing. However, the adequacy of 'gist' is primarily a function of viewers' own sense of cognitive satisfaction – a device for staying above a threshold of understanding below which retained bits and pieces simply don't 'add up' at all. With difficult material, 'gist' may be a reactive strategy used to achieve 'closure' in the face of disconcerting openness or to resolve potential points of cognitive dissonance. Where a 'gist' reading is developed early, it is likely to determine (either through selective attention, selective meaning or both) subsequent understandings (see Lewis, 1983, on the incremental character of interpretation). Although it carries us beyond the bounds of this specific study, we might note here that research on news and public knowledge may benefit from more attention being paid to the schemas and practices of 'gist' and the moves, some of them documented earlier, by which viewers 'figure out' what essentially is at issue in a news story. As an established way of coping with extensive, diverse or difficult information and of being content with quite high levels of communicative slippage, 'gist' might indicate some problems and even dangers for emerging forms of mediated citizenship.

Conclusion

It is our hope that we have been able to open up for enquiry some of the themes and issues which bear upon, first, the exposition of economics in television news, and second, the reception (comprehension and evaluation) of that material by the viewing public. The analysis undertaken here has been conducted as a snapshot within the particular context of a mature democracy at a particular time and its generalizability must be limited. Yet it is worth remembering that in the UK most of the agencies of national news distribution have long publicized economic policy and economic change of the kinds we have been concerned with, constructing their audiences as co-members of a community whose interests and fortunes are shared.

Whilst it can be assumed that any felt sense of co-membership is itself a sign of media influence upon consciousness – albeit an influence which must work over the long term – there are more specific patterns of 'effectiveness' or influence which are worth commenting upon. Amongst these are the inclination to credit the truthfulness of basic factual information even while disputing relevance, or significance, in a broader context, or whilst reinterpreting factual information in accordance with partisan themes. However, we have noted signs, too, of *in*effectiveness – at least if the intended goal is to produce viewers who are themselves capable of entering into, and reproducing, the logic of economic reasoning on the basis of the short reports which constitute 'economic news' within the framework of daily news programming. Fragments of economic argumentation are very frequently offered to viewers, along with the visual aids, metaphoric allusions, and location and sectoral reports we have discussed above. But any expectation that viewers will produce correspondingly coherent articulations as a result of exposure to such reports is not confirmed by the present research. Viewers do not understand, or they do not remember, the details well enough to organize them into accounts that reproduce (or challenge) those offered by the broadcasters. Generally, they remember 'the gist' and are satisfied that this is adequate. If this is a 'danger sign' for the public communication process, as suggested above, it is at the point where the strategies of the broadcasters and those of the viewers conspire to excuse the latter from attending to the details; where the unspoken convention of the exchange is that the details are unimportant. Clearly, this problem is more than a matter of communicative 'good faith' – it relates to the whole funding and regulation of broadcast journalism as well as to its changing conventions of practice in a situation of multi-channel competition.

We might note, finally, the specific lines of research which our project has not followed but whose value it has certainly underlined. More work on the practices of economic news collection and processing would be valuable, following the broad lines taken by other 'newsbeat' ethnographies and touching upon concerns expressed by journalists. Although it can sometimes obscure as much as illuminate, comparative study would be of great use in this area too – since the media themselves are becoming more international in character, while there is a degree of convergence, at least in Europe, in economic systems, their 'ailments' and proposed 'cures'. The whole area of reception analysis is fraught with difficulties (see the discussion of research problems in Chapter 9) but we have found our emphasis on comprehension *and* evaluation a productive one here and we believe that selective, deeper study of the interpretative resources upon which viewers draw in forming knowledge from television (in a sense, the construction of 'viewing biographies') would contribute to further progress on our main theme – the relating of media signification to public understanding.

Acknowledgement

This research was funded through the generous support of the Economic and Social Research Council (Ref: R000235976).

Notes

1   These individuals are members of the Public Communications Group, Liverpool University, based in the School of Politics and Communication Studies.

2   See Emmison (1983) for a historical account of the term as indicating a sphere of national polity.

3   The two principal UK weekday television news programmes, BBC's *Nine O'Clock News* and ITN's *News At Ten*, were videotaped throughout the research period as a baseline archive of television news coverage. For our principal audit periods (18 September to 30 November 1995; 15 January to 26 January 1996), from which all of the material used in our audience study phase was taken, we supplemented these news programmes with ITN's *Channel 4 News*. For Budget Day itself (28 November), we collected live and news coverage from all BBC, ITN and *Sky News* bulletins.

From this material, three screening tapes, each containing three recent stories, were prepared and shown to focus groups; the first about six weeks before the November 1995 budget, the second immediately after the budget, and the third at the end of January 1996. In selecting material for the first and third screening tapes, we sought stories which were drawn from more than one news organization, embodied a variety of presentational forms and covered the reporting of a range of economic and associated political variables. For our second screening tape, material was drawn exclusively from Budget Day news coverage, differentiated by channel and presentational form. The full transcripts of all screened material can be accessed through Liverpool University Politics Department web site. The address is:
http://www.liv.ac.uk/~polcomm/polhome.htm.

We aimed to recruit groups to reflect as wide a range as possible of occupational, social and economic circumstances as well as offering a balance of age and gender. Although full sociological representativeness was not sought in the range of respondents consulted, we tried to guard against obtaining a misleading picture by being too narrowly selective. We recruited four 'core' groups from which we gathered responses to each of our three screening tapes within a week or two of their original transmission. These were groups of garage workers, Rotary club members from an affluent suburb, public library workers and sixth-form students. To broaden our range of respondents and to control for the possibility of these groups becoming sensitized by repeated exposure to economic news, we interviewed further groups on a once-only basis, showing our second set of screenings also to groups of unskilled cleaners and geography postgraduates, and our third set to Church of England workers, hospital nursing staff, Liverpool and Everton football supporters, Townswomen's Guild members, hotel reception staff, arts sector workers, fire-fighters and first-year veterinary science undergraduates. Twenty-two group sessions were conducted in total. The average group size was four members. In all, 58 group members were involved.

Following each screening, group members were asked a set of questions from a prepared inventory about their responses to the material and the issues it raised for them. Such a method ensured intra- and inter-group comparability, while allowing the flexibility to ask follow-up questions and probe more fully where appropriate. In addition, each group member completed a short questionnaire, giving background details including age, political orientation and media use and exposure.

4   We return to this example in more detail in the following section of this chapter, where we discuss reactions to various formal strategies used by broadcasters to increase viewer interest in stories about the national economy.

5   As indicated, these quotations belong to the pilot study phase of our research. In the pilot study we interviewed individuals after screenings rather than conducting discussions with respondent groups. These participants were asked directly about the power of the government to control the national economy.

6   It is necessary to register here some reservations regarding the attribution of partisanship to the speakers in these respondent groups. A written questionnaire, using the standard political science measure of partisanship, was administered to respondents before the first session with each group, and one of the questions asked them to indicate their political preferences, if any. We have drawn upon this evidence in writing the current chapter. However, such self-attributed partisanship should not be taken as indicating firm knowledge of, or consistent commitment to, the policies of the supported parties. It is, rather, a general indicator of political sympathies in a very broad sense.

2
The economy and public language

Kay Richardson

The textualization of economics

Like Chapters 3, 4 and 5, this chapter is an attempt to extend the
scope of the primary research of the Liverpool group (see Chapter
1) by undertaking an 'aspectual' study. Accordingly, my concern
here is with the language of economic news reporting, and
specifically with the way in which language is used in television
news broadcasting to mediate accounts of national economic
circumstances.[1] It is also very much concerned with the language
used by respondents ('the viewers') in their own constructions of
the national economic situation and their place within it. In
Chapter 1 we raised some important questions concerning the
influence and effects of televised economic news upon its
audience. In the present chapter these questions are indirectly
pursued by concentrating upon the ways in which viewers
appropriate the *idiom of mediated economics* into their own talk
and thus into their understanding of economic affairs. The
argument will be that, because respondents are not under the
same expositional obligations as the broadcasters, the discourse of
the former lacks the complex inter-articulation of comparative and
narrative syntax which is characteristic in the discourse of
mediated economics. Instead, respondents invoke their memories
of the national economic past, more or less concretely, using these
recollections to construct a sense of the present as different from/
the same as the past.

Mediated economic discourse

The national economy, as understood in professional macro-economics and by the would-be managers of the economy in political life, has a systemic character such that it is deemed to consist of various components, related in complex ways to each other and, in their interactions, capable of generating effects of different kinds and at different levels. The profession of economics is dedicated to the attempt to understand this complexity, and thus to predict the consequences of actions and events of an economic character.

In economics the preferred mode of reasoning is abstract, formal and mathematical. The systemic nature of economic reality is to be captured by formal models, which will crunch numbers according to the properties and formulae with which they have been provided. This mathematical discourse provides the 'public' discourse of economics with one layer of its meaning, although, for the most part, both in Parliament and in the mass media, economic argument is conducted not in the formulae of macro-economic models but in ordinary language, and with any amount of reference 'out' from the economic realm to those of politics, industry, finance, international relations and even 'ordinary life'. In television this results in the kind of audiovisual discourse discussed in Chapter 3. The present chapter is directly concerned with the linguistic component of that discourse.

To begin with, it is worthwhile to be reminded of the lexical and thus semantic density[2] which can be found in even quite short reports:

In his budget just over two-and-a-half years ago, Norman Lamont planned a deficit soaring to £50 billion in 1993 in order to fight the recession, then falling back to £30 billion over the next four years. Kenneth Clarke aimed to cut the deficit from £50 billion to almost nil over five years. Last year, he trimmed that back to reach balance by 1998 and a surplus the following year. Today, he has gone back to the position after his first budget, postponing balance and surplus by a year. (*Peter Jay*, BBC, 28 November 1996)

This is not the most 'difficult' exposition in our material: it is at least cast in narrative mode, so that each sentence takes the chronology one stage further, and the verbal discourse has supporting illustration in the form of a graph. The graph's lines 'grow' in synchrony with the words, with appropriate legends; each stage in the story produces a new line, whilst the superseded lines 'fade' progressively. But it is difficult enough. Four previous budgets are referred to (Lamont's in spring 1993, and Clarke's in autumn 1993, autumn 1994 and autumn 1995). Each budget plans the future, but it is a different future in each case. The future planned by Clarke today is more like the future he planned in spring 1994 than the one he planned in autumn 1994. In 1993 he expected to balance the books in 1999; in 1994 he expected to balance them in 1998, and in 1995 the balance was planned for 1999 again.

Kenneth Clarke in 1995 was the UK Chancellor of the Exchequer, which is the most important government post from the point of view of economic affairs. As such he takes advice from economic experts (the six so-called 'Wise Men' have themselves become newsworthy in recent years), whilst his role requires him to operate at the intersection of professional and lay versions of economic understanding. He belongs to a small group of actors who are in such a position. This group includes the politicians (especially the ministers and shadow ministers) and civil servants with Treasury-related posts. It also includes the specialist economic correspondents and editors within the mass media. The personnel within these groups have complex tasks of mediation to undertake, whilst the politicians in particular are understood to be participants within the economic realm as well as mediators of it to a wider audience.

The point of this mediation is, of course, to disseminate some degree of understanding to the widest possible audience – the mass electorate. And it is beyond question that economic propositions are indeed distributed on a national scale, to every household, every family, every individual, ultimately via the news component of national broadcasting and press organs. Economic news is a ubiquitous component of a ubiquitous media genre.

As far as news form is concerned, the ubiquity of this content calls for a certain formulaic character to the coverage. Formulaic repetitions of style, format and expression can be seen as providing for a degree of familiarity with such coverage that will allow the print reporters and broadcasters to introduce the newsworthy changes, deviations or 'events'. Yet at the same time this formulaic character mediates ritualism: repetition for its own sake as part of the mystique of national life. In this perspective, our participation as readers and viewers requires us to respond to the familiarity of the formulae, not the novelty of the latest development. We even had some respondents who themselves made this point:

It's become so ... it's such a genre, the delivery of the news, that something like *The Day Today* [a popular comedy show which parodies the news] can exist. And so really the information content and what it's actually imparting is a sideline ... from it being like a ritual for the people that watch it. (Arts workers)

In this piece I want to discuss the textualization of economics not only in the broadcast news itself but also in the discourse of our respondents. The focus will be upon the linguistic forms, including the stylistic and rhetorical tropes that are used, with a particular emphasis upon the importance of *time* and time relations within these contexts.

Time and process in the discourse of economics

Time is of the essence in understanding 'the economic': economics is concerned, above all, with the passing of time and what this means for national wellbeing. Measurements are taken at regular intervals, and the significance of those measures is judged in the context of the national story: depression, recession, recovery, etc. However, in reporting the economy, different time-frames are relevant to different stories and parts of stories. 'The present' is constituted not only through its similarities with and differences from 'the past' but also through expectations with regard to the future. So broadcast news can carry economic stories about falls and rises in official statistics (a timeline ending 'today' but beginning at some earlier point) or stories about the establishment of expectations (a timeline starting today and ending some time in the future) or some combination of these. Linguistically speaking, this reportorial necessity calls for complex interplay between the syntax of *comparison* and the syntax of *narrative*. The nature of this interplay will become clearer if we look at some examples.

In one short BBC item on 22 January 1996 the news lead is the national growth rate figure for October, November and December 1995 – a rise of 0.5 per cent. This kind of figure is intrinsically one of change through time. A quantum of economic productivity at one point in time is compared with that same measure at a later period of time. The news is not the size of the measure (productivity) but the degree of change within the audit period. The trope of 'growth' lexically foregrounds the movement from the earlier to the later figure, whilst doing so in terms of a quantification, a percentage, which can be compared with other percentages. A comparison is duly made. We are told at the outset of the story that this is 'the slowest rate of growth for nearly three years'. The actual rate of growth, then, must also be compared with an 'ideal' (healthy) growth rate. All growth is good, but the Chancellor is looking for growth as good as or better than the 'healthy' rate. We can see from the way this report ends that the Chancellor's efforts to achieve this are seen to take place not strictly month by month, but over a longer time-frame: the 'gap' to which the report refers is envisaged as closeable (with difficulty) within the decade.

Today's figures for the output of the whole economy show that the gap between the normal healthy level of output and the present depressed post-recession level is getting wider and has been doing so for three quarters running. To reverse that trend and close that gap would require output to rise for the rest of the decade at the brisk 3.5 per cent rate forecast by the Chancellor for the next year. At the moment, that looks optimistic. (*Peter Jay*, BBC news, 22 January 1996)

Thus, not only does the economy need to grow by 3.5 per cent for

1996; it needs to continue at that rate for 1997 and 1998 as well to stay on target.[3]

It is in this fashion, within mediated economic discourse, that the tension between synchronic and diachronic perspectives is managed. Change is at the heart of that discourse: change is constantly monitored and presented as present reality. The linguistic consequences of this in the 'textualization' of economics include an interesting set of intra-textual relations between forms expressing *states* and forms expressing *processes*. For example, economic exposition permits and requires that comparative formulations in which 'then' is compared with 'now' coexist with formulations which represent these two distinct times within the framework of a present which consists of the transition itself. Relations of this kind can become quite complex, as in the following example:

The national unemployment picture now also reflects the sharp economic slowdown this year. At the end of the late 1980s boom, it fell to a low point of 1.6 million and then rose for two and a half years to a peak of almost 3 million. Since then, it's fallen for three years. Today's rise has come when unemployment is still 600,000 above the 1990s low point. (*Peter Jay*, BBC news, 15 November 1995)

In this short paragraph (from a story reporting a small rise in the numbers of people out of work and claiming benefit – an item also discussed in Chapter 1), the final sentence is clearly a comparative formulation. 1990 is compared with 1995. The 1995 picture is worse. This comparative perspective, coming at the end of the paragraph, is presented as a kind of corrective to unwarranted optimism in the face of recent positive trends, and as reinforcement for the negative view of the economy's fortunes with which the paragraph begins. Between these two utterances focused upon the present time, we are given a short narrative to take us from the past (the late 1980s boom) to the present.

At one level (as in the Budget Day example cited earlier concerning Clarke's continuing revisions of the budget deficit), story mode is needed for the representation of process and comparative mode for the representation of state. But at another level, the distinction breaks down: 1990 and 1995 are more than simply different states. They are also part of a single state, though not a static one: and the questions concerning this state have to do with the direction in which it is moving. Unemployment was (relatively speaking) low in 1990. It was higher in 1995 and rising again. This is a perspective in which the falling trend of recent years (the smaller time-frame) can be treated as less significant than the rising trend of the larger time-frame. It is an interpretative perspective: the broadcaster's informal judgement has played a part in applying time-frames and in reading particular moments within the smaller or the larger frame. The negative tone of the introductory sentence is not within the same time-frame as that of the closing sentence. The terms of the introductory sentence have narrow time horizons, focused on the trend this year; those of the closing sentence relate to wide time horizons, the narrative from the 1980s boom to the present.

Needless to say, there is much about all of this which is controversial. No real case has been made that this year's economic trends are indeed downwards. Such a case would have to invoke other evidence besides the unemployment figures, and in doing so would be moving beyond the immediate 'news' remit of the broadcast. Neither is it self-evident that the benign downward trend of the unemployment figures in recent years belongs only to a narrow and self-contained time-frame, as the broadcaster's interpretation tends to suggest. In short, the bare facts allow scope for interpretation and argument as to significance, and different interpretations give different weightings to different periods in the national narrative. 'Unemployment still rising' (from the sixth-form student group) is a possible interpretation if the falling figures of the recent years are played down. But, as we have noted elsewhere, an alternative view is possible which gives greater weighting to the more recent trend:

Well they only gave one side as well, didn't they? I mean, I think the unemployment's been falling for the last ... ooh, several months at least. It's gone up by 200 and I think they've really over-emphasized the fact the economy is perhaps worse than it is. (Library workers)

Economic understanding in respondent discourse

The first thing to say about the ways in which respondents 'talk economics' is that they are not required, as the broadcasters are, to produce sustained coherent exposition. Whatever economic understanding they possess can only, in the context, emerge in fragmentary form – sometimes with greater and sometimes with lesser generality according not only to their own interests and concerns but also to the context of the talk. Questioned by interviewers about the state of the national economy, respondents gave appropriately general answers; questioned more specifically about the use of a particular statistic in a news report, they made more focused points, at least those respondents who felt they had understood and had something to say:

It seems to me there's a shift going on. I don't get the impression things are improving. It seems that certain aspects of society are, you know, getting ... doing better for themselves. Others are getting worse off. You know, there seems to be a greater divide happening and a shift of wealth more, but I don't get the sense that there's an overall huge improvement for everybody. (Arts workers)

Lack of optimism, again, in what the government's trying to put across, and, that he's really trying to force the pace. But unrealistically, 'cos they're obviously not up for it at all, the Bank of England guy or whoever. And they're only tiny little ... well, I know it's a lot in monetary terms, but it's very small, isn't it, the amounts they were talking. Quarter of a percent or whatever. And they're worried and don't want to have any truck with it. (Arts workers)

In the second case the speaker has been asked what the main points of the broadcast item were. The item in question is one reporting a cut in the base rate from 6.5 per cent to 6.25 per cent. The context within which this is reported makes it clear that the cut has been made by the Chancellor against the advice of the Governor of the Bank of England. Our respondent's reply here mixes description with evaluation: the cut of 0.25 per cent is registered as 'very small', whilst the interpretation she offers of the 'lack of optimism ... in what the government's trying to put across' is implicitly attributed to the journalistic framing of the event.

The research context gives limited opportunities for respondents to make explicit the extent of the economic knowledge which they possess prior to the screenings, and make use of in making sense of those screenings. It is therefore of interest, as noted in Chapter 1, that more than one of the four core groups question the official statistics on unemployment and do so in terms which do draw upon such independent knowledge:

People on training schemes don't count and everybody else doesn't count towards the figures and then they're seasonally adjusted and after everything else. (Sixth-form students)

An expression like 'seasonally adjusted', as used by this sixth-form student, can be seen as part of the idiom of mediated economics. This idiom is partly a matter of vocabulary, and partly a matter of the ability to construct the kind of exposition examined in the previous section, with its characteristic mixtures of narrative sequences and comparative ones. Both of these matters, vocabulary and expositional style, deserve further comment.

Economic vocabulary in respondent talk

First, a comment about the vocabulary of the screened 'source extracts' used in this research, compared with the vocabulary used by respondents.[4] In the nine extracts used with respondent groups, the commonest 25 words included seven whose meaning clearly belongs to the discourse of mediated economics: the words *cut*, *tax*, *economy*, *chancellor*, *budget*, *rate* and *government*. Significantly, a number of these reflect a concern with the political management of the economy. In addition, the top 25 words include five which directly express a concern with time and the passing of time: the words *year, now, next, last* and *month*. Four other terms are worth mentioning: *all* and *more*, two very common quantifying terms, as well as *up* and *down*, two very common expressions of movement. This patterning should be seen in the context of a point made earlier – that news broadcasts on this subject are semantically extremely dense.

The patterning looks rather different when the vocabulary of the respondent discourse is examined. The top 25 words of this corpus do overlap with those of the source material, but very few of the terms mentioned above are concerned in this overlap. The common words in both sets of texts are *is, have, will, we, all, get, go* and *say*. 'All' is a common word in both sets: the rest are verbs and the pronoun 'we' (which should probably have been included in the stoplist). I want to make two further points: first, that the top 25 words in the source corpus all feature in the top 155 in the respondent corpus, which has a total of 5241 words; and second, that the top 25 words in the respondent corpus have a lot to do with the interactional context in which the data were elicited – not just in terms of pronouns, many of which were eliminated through the stoplist, but also in terms of interaction markers like 'well', assent terms like 'yes', hedges like 'just', and forms indicating an epistemological position, like 'say', 'think' and 'know'. One other term that was common in the respondent material and much less so in the source data was the term *people* – perhaps reflecting the greater interest that respondents had in the effects of economic management, compared with that of the broadcasters. If we broaden the context to consider the first 300 words in the respondent corpus, we notice another set of terms not found in the other material: words referring to television itself and to the broadcast extracts in particular. This list would include such words as *television, bias*, and *channel*, and the names of some of the reporters, especially *Peter Jay*.

But it is not just the presence/absence of economic terminology which needs to be explored in investigating this material. What is of more interest is the kind of stance which respondents adopt in using these terms, and this cannot be identified mechanically. It will be necessary to examine some examples:

They explained but I don't think they went into enough detail. Because it got people's attention to find out more, whereas some people just sort of might just watch it and think well, oh yeah I would like to find out more about this, but it didn't sort of ... I mean, obviously time is a factor where you've got a short news bulletin, but it didn't really go far enough to make you actually see, you know, what they were trying to do, why the government should make tax cuts. Because the average person just thinks, yeah, tax cuts – great, we pay less tax and we get more money. We get more spending power. But they were saying no. I thought, well, hang on a minute, why isn't this as good as people say. (Librarians)

This is a comment following the screening of a Channel 4 report in November 1996. The report took place two weeks before Budget Day, and it set itself the task of reviewing the likelihood of a 'tax-cutting' budget, which required it to mention a wide range of economic factors which would enter into the calculation: inflation rates, interest rates, growth, taxation revenues in the previous year, the size of the budget deficit, etc. It is a comment which recognizes the reporter's serious attempt to explain the economic reasoning for and against tax cuts, but which sets that perception alongside a perception of 'deeper' explanation failure. The thought behind this comment is that there ought to be a national economic rationale for tax cuts, as well as an ideological, individualistic one, and there is in fact such a rationale within the political sphere, but this is the one element which is missing from the account of the 'practicalities' presented in the report under discussion. The rhetorically interesting feature of this paragraph that I wish to draw attention to is the shift from 'more money' to 'more spending power'. The respondent paraphrases herself and in doing so shifts from one kind of idiom, that of personal interest, to the idiom of mediated economics and an (implicit) national perspective. Her problem is that, through no fault of her own, she cannot take that perspective further in her attempt to understand why tax cuts might be desirable (or undesirable) as well as possible, at this particular point in time.

This is a relatively unselfconscious use of economic idiom, though a use which, as the respondent presents it, has 'nowhere to go' within her own discourse. It can be contrasted with various examples where the use of economic vocabulary is decidedly self-conscious – beginning with cases where lexical items from that idiom are registered as unfamiliar/incomprehensible.

Sometimes the deployment of economic language is used by a respondent as grounds for non-engagement with what the report is trying to say about the economy. The Channel 4 report referred to above certainly generated such a reaction at times:

It seemed to waffle on. It wasn't to the point. It was like: uh, we'll use all these economic terms and blah blah, then we'll move on somewhere else and waffle on about them for a bit, then we'll fly over to Ford's, then we'll go back to the stock market, then we'll go and stand by the Thames with all the buildings in the background and waffle on a bit more just for the change of scenery. (Sixth-form students)

There is no reference here to any of the particular terms/concepts used which provoked this reaction. This is also the case in the following cases, from different groups responding to different items:

I lost it on a couple of sentences where they used some of the financial in-words. (Library workers)

I think it could have been clear if we hadn't had that big, jargonistic thing at the beginning and it just made me go: right, oh, I don't know what they're talking about ... (Arts workers)

The rejection of economic idiom is not absolute. Many respondents show that they are familiar with the sound of economic expressions but disavow knowledge of the concepts to which those terms refer:

I mean, public expenditure and all that, it's just, like, phrases I don't really understand. (Garage workers)

The budget and inflation and interest rates. It's all terms I've heard of, but I don't really understand them. (Sixth-form students)

FTSE share index. I've never known what that meant. (Sixth-form students)

I find it particularly confusing and difficult when they start talking in terms of the money markets and the FT index. (Librarians)

In examples such as these, our respondents reproduce bits of economic discourse, like 'FTSE share index', but do so in a quotative way. The discourse itself is not their own, merely something that they have been exposed to and remember parts of – if only the sound. This inter-textual or inter-discoursal mixture is characteristic of the discussions; we may note too how respondents attach marks of distance/suspicion to particular expressions drawn from mediated economics:

So-called market forces, I mean what are they? They're not [the] real ... turn-round economy that people can make a living from. (Garage workers)

When I try and equate it all, I think back to a few years ago when there was a so-called boom and everyone was going out and spending money they didn't have, you know, on credit cards and that. And I thought, well, what's wrong with that, you know? The high street shops are doing well and everything, and then they want to sort of raise interest rates and stop you spending. And to me it doesn't compute. I think, you know, if people have got money to spend and they want to spend it, keep them spending. (Garage workers)

Time and process in respondent talk

I have already discussed the task of economic news reportage as one which, among other things, involves the discursive management of time-frames to convey the state of the economy and the rate and type of economic change. In the discourse of respondents there is much less elaboration of temporal frameworks than there is in the broadcast extracts. There is no lack of reference to the past in what the viewers have to say, but here there is much less attempt to inter-articulate the comparative and the narrative modes than there is in the television material. Some respondents did try to produce their own stories of the national economy in this fashion, but examples of the kind illustrated below were the exception rather than the rule:

I don't think we're on an upturn, I think we're on a downturn. I don't think we've ever been on an upturn. I think it's increased slightly a couple of years ago, and then they increased taxes and other things, and that's sort of had a downward spiral on the economy. (Garage workers)

Elsewhere, however, the tendency was to produce either comparative observations about the economy (this year versus last year) or narrative sequences (this happened, then this, then this), with little or no attempt to relate the two. Narrativization occurs principally when respondents are attempting to recapitulate the 'message' of the broadcast:

Q: What was the point?

R: Basically, that the economy ... unemployment had risen for a time, and then fell and then sort of steadied off.

(Garage workers)

This is the most straightforward kind of narrative, with one phase of national economic life following another phase, in temporal sequence. It does involve one compound tense, establishing the earliest moment in the sequence; the subsequent tense forms are both simple past tense. But it is much less troubled by the problem of assessing the significance of the shifts than Jay was when presenting them in the original broadcast, and thus some information (e.g. on the duration of different phases) is omitted here.

It is when we look at the comparative formulations in respondent talk that the interesting differences between the discourse of respondents and that of the broadcasters begin to appear. In respondent talk, comparative formulations are very prevalent. One of the constraints on broadcast news – its orientation to the present moment – is experienced much less by respondents. In consequence, respondents are able to reason by analogy much more overtly than the news broadcasters can – and, in doing so, to invoke collective memories of the national past with an economic aspect, and to draw lessons from those recollections:

Well, I mean, from what they were saying there, and they were predicting, I mean, you've only got to look back a couple of years to the ERM fiasco.[5] So what makes you think that they're going to do any better now than with that? (Garage workers)

Some respondents would construct a stable 'past', significantly different from the present. Businessmen in their fifties as well as school kids in their teens both conveyed to us a sense that things used to be different, albeit from different levels of engagement with the conditions of national economic life:

Governments have used the construction industry as a means of controlling the economy. When things have been going well, they've in fact turned off the tap to say no more investment in the construction industry. When things are going badly, it used to happen that the government would put money into local authorities to say: spend more on schools, build more council houses. That doesn't happen because money does not now flow directly to local authorities for housing, for schools and the like. (Rotary Club members)

But the economy is still in a really bad state 'cos look at the way they're fighting for business. You walk down the high street now and there's constant sales on. It used to be like there's a sale in January and a sale, like, summertime. Now everywhere you go there's always sales on somewhere. (Sixth-form students)

The past is constructed by respondents as better than the present, sometimes because the present is characterized by a permanent changefulness which potentially renders all attempts at prediction and control futile:

And I think we saw employment's in the balance. Employment goes up and then it's down and then it's up and then it's down, and people aren't buying any more. Don't know next week whether you're going to have a job or not. There's all this uncertainty. (Garage workers)

Thus, the reporting of economic movement is subject to (re)framing by viewers in terms of chronic volatility, where movement does not equal change (the movements are too small; the direction is not constant; the intervals are too frequent). Furthermore, so long as viewers engage with economic reportage from a starting point in which 'lost prosperity' (personal or national) is an important axiom, they are not satisfied with economic news which indicates positive direction, but falls short of restoring that lost prosperity:

R: But, say, it doesn't seem to be going anywhere in any great steps. Just seems to be steady plodding along.

Q: So it's getting better, but too gradually?

R: It's very slowly, and there doesn't seem to be any light behind ... you know, round the corner. Coming out the dark tunnel or anything like that.

Q: In terms of what?

R: Er, jobs. Prospects or any financial commitments or anything like that. You'd be very wary of making any financial commitment at the moment.

(Garage workers)

Several groups made explicit their own personal point of reference, claiming to be and to feel worse off in 1995/96 than they did five or so years earlier.

I feel I'm worse off than five years ago. Definitely. I find that, say, things are just ... I mean, just for sort of items that you can't really see. I mean, things like service charges on the utilities like electricity, British Telecom, the biggest rip-off on this planet, you know. But unfortunately these are what people need and it's because it's a captive audience, isn't it, that you have no choice. I don't feel particularly well off at all. (Librarians)

The notion of lost *national* prosperity is less determinate: respondents cannot easily call up relevant statistical comparisons, and there is scope for elision of the national with the personal here, so that positive national statistics are less likely to carry conviction to the extent that they conflict with personal experience. Or conversely, as here:

... and they say there's no confidence in the public to go and spend money. You know, walk down the streets of Liverpool on a Saturday and you can't move so I don't know what to make of the pictures I've seen on the television where they say people won't go out and spend money. I didn't look at it the way A [another respondent] did. When he was talking about industries and that, I only see, you know, likes of high street shops and they start mentioning on the television how they didn't make as much as they did last year, but the street seems to be full of people spending money so ... That's why I put down sometimes I don't understand what to make of television programmes where they say people aren't spending. The shops are full. (Garage workers)

At the outer limits of propositional specificity (triggered, for example, by the Peter Jay item featuring the SS *Great Britain* in Bristol – seen in Chapters 1 and 3), there is a background image of lost national prosperity in terms of 'the story of Britain' as a country in decline since the loss of Empire and the (re)growth of other national economies at the UK's expense. Where this epic narrative is allowed to set the parameters of success and failure, it would be difficult for any rhetoric of achievement to obtain purchase upon the national imagination, and certainly there is little evidence that our respondents were susceptible to such rhetoric. I would not wish to argue that our respondents are *consciously* comparing the UK economy of the 1990s with that of the nineteenth century, or that such a comparison, in non-mythological terms, would obviously favour the earlier period (if the question concerned general living standards). I am only suggesting that: (1) the epic historical narrative provides some of the contours for 'reading' present-day economic news; (2) this narrative operates at an imaginative level which escapes easy propositional 'grounding' (the story of the rise and fall of the British Empire is a matter of national mythology); (3) if the economic realities of the late twentieth century are read within the epic, they must be read as bad realities or indifferent ones; and (4) this may be a factor in our respondents' lack of enthusiasm for the economic 'good news' reported in the extracts they viewed.

It must be admitted that the last point is hard to assess. There is little or no explicit 'epic' discourse in respondent talk. It is true that respondents are, generally speaking, unimpressed by vaunted 'signs of change'. But this lack of enthusiasm may have multiple causes. It may indeed spring from an appreciation that such changes are too small and too local to constitute any kind of meaningful episode within the grand national narrative of which they are a part. But it may as well (or also) be that within their pragmatic and/or self-interested frameworks the national epic is simply irrelevant; more proximate points of comparison (in space or time) should provide the economic managers with their yardsticks of success or failure, and citizens with their criteria for judging the managers.

Conclusions

I have attempted to compare the discourse of mediated economics with the language of respondent groups – mediations of mediations. The difficulty of economic representations, coupled with a professed 'lack of interest' amongst a large proportion of the viewers, encourages an expectation that the respondents would have much 'simpler' things to say about the national economy than the broadcasters. In one sense, this is true. But, as I have suggested, it is not appropriate to assess what the respondents say purely in terms of how faithful they are in reproducing broadcast accounts, since respondent talk goes beyond the frameworks adopted by the broadcasters, and respondents can orient to points of reference which broadcasters cannot address within their constraints of immediacy, relevance and time restrictions. What remains to be explored is the more global 'conditioning' of respondent frameworks by the media – a process which takes place not item by item, but over much more extended time periods and in interaction with other sources and agencies of representation.

Acknowledgement

This research was funded through the generous support of the Economic and Social Research Council (Ref: R000235976).

Notes

1   For a more linguistically focused account of related matters, deriving from a pilot study for this project, see Richardson (1997).
2   For an interesting discussion of lexical density in different text types, see Stubbs (1996), Chapter 3.
3   Within the discourse of economics, mediated or otherwise, it is a matter of consensus that growth is good. Halliday (1992) is a linguist who has commented upon the extent of the 'conspiracy' within English to promote this view and its consequences for the possibility of thinking alternatives.
4   These comments are the result of employing lexical analysis software (Wordsmith Tools) on the source data and on the respondent data (Scott, 1996). For the purpose of the analysis, the top 100 words in both data sources were lemmatized, and a stoplist of 20 function words excluded from the count.
5   The ERM fiasco is a reference to events in 1992 when the Conservative government was forced, in crisis conditions, to withdraw sterling from the European Exchange Rate Mechanism.

3
Television news and economic exposition

John Corner

Introduction

In this chapter, I want to look in some detail at how UK television news communicates economic events through its news formats and its specific usages of language and image. In order to achieve a complementary relationship with other chapters in this volume (particularly Chapters 1 and 2), I shall draw on examples which were used for the screening sessions conducted with respondents during the period of the 1995/96 Liverpool project. Thus at several points I shall be looking closely at the organization of items which are referred to elsewhere in this book in terms of viewers' understandings and judgements.

The analysis of television news discourse

There is a strong and rapidly developing international literature on the communicative character of television news. This literature has to be distinguished from studies whose concern has exclusively been with news 'content', taking matters of visual and verbal signification, the nature of the news discourse itself, as broadly for granted. Studies which have put news discourse under scrutiny have varied in the extent to which they have also wanted to develop arguments about specific news themes or 'content'. Some of them have worked with an emphasis on general questions of form and styling which, although meant to be relevant to substantive inquiries, has not been carried through in relation to specific news themes, except by brief illustration (e.g. Brunsdon and Morley, 1978; Corner, 1995; Graddol, 1995; Hartley, 1982;

Lewis, 1985). Other studies have attempted to use closer formal analysis as a means to develop their understanding of particular areas of news coverage (e.g. Cottle, 1993; Glasgow University Media Group, 1976; Jensen, 1986; Schlesinger *et al.*, 1983). The Liverpool project took this latter approach, necessarily so since one of its primary objectives was to investigate the terms of viewer understanding – a significatory as well as a thematic issue.

As a way of providing routine public surveillance of events selected as 'newsworthy', the conventions of television journalism have a distinct communicative character. With many variations, there has emerged an international model of how to 'do' television news. Passage through a sequence of items is managed 'live' by a newsroom anchor, who introduces the larger items before handing over to reporters who typically provide a pre-recorded mix of in-shot presentation, voiced-over film report and interview. Increasingly, 'live' updates and studio/location links may be used at the end of the item if the immediacy values of the story appear to warrant it. It is the reporter's job to organize what are judged to be the relevant elements of an event into a 'story' which possesses adequate levels of coherence and comprehensibility across its diverse parts. This is a very different discursive requirement from that made on print journalists, since television is a time-based, visual medium and television reporters have to manage a temporal relationship between what they say and what the viewer sees. Television journalism is also a genre of performance – journalists offer their accounts from significant locations, providing a *mise-en-scène* for stories (which in the case of war reporting can, of course, be extremely engaging simply to view). Other people's acts are recruited to the performative dimension of news, as observed behaviour and/or as interview speech. Given these factors, the narrative dimension of television news is thus often of a prominent kind, shaping the elements into a story form which meets the needs both of time constraints, popular accessibility and good levels of viewer engagement. In a fascinating historical study, Brian Winston (Winston, 1993) looked at the early formation of these features in CBS, as the technology of location reporting and the conventions of studio address were combined into something that differed both from the established practices of the radio bulletins and those of the cinema newsreel.

However, despite this, news items are not able to be narratives in the way that television fictions are, since their primary task is expositional. They have to explain things as well as to organize them as stories, even though explanation itself sometimes involves the use of another level of narrativization. Elsewhere (Corner, 1995) I have commented on the nature of the expositional/ narrative tension in television news, noting a tendency among many cultural studies researchers to over-emphasize narrative creativity and understate the requirements of expositional adequacy. To use another set of terms, this is often to let the 'poetic'

dimension of news obscure the extent of its 'referential' obligations. In the detailed examples presented below, I think this
tension or playoff manifests itself in a number of interesting ways.

The character of economic news

In Chapter 1 a brief account was given of some of the features
which mark economic news as an area of coverage. Three such
features deserve mention here. First of all, news about the
economy is often highly statistical, putting a very special kind of
pressure on spoken exposition and often requiring the use of
supporting graphics. Moreover, it is not merely statistical in
development, but is routinely statistical in its core 'news event',
whether this is the release of new figures or the actions of a key
economic 'player' (e.g. the Chancellor of the Exchequer, a multinational company or major European finance houses). Second,
economic news does not normally allow for any direct visualization (for example, one cannot see the pound 'sliding' or
unemployment going up) and the result of this is a certain reliance
on generally illustrative stock shots (job centres, city dealing floors,
car factories, etc.) and a strategy of indirect - metonymic and
sometimes metaphoric - depiction which will be well exemplified
below. Abstractions are routinely being condensed into concrete
illustration, although a certain irreducible level of abstraction
usually provides a direct challenge to reportorial exposition, here
often accompanied by graphics. Given these difficulties in
visualizing economic news, it can be seen that what is perhaps
the most frequently made general criticism of television news
services - that their selection and treatment is too heavily dictated
by pictures - hardly fits the case here.
   Third, economic news is highly relational, in that the significance
of 'what has happened' is closely (and indeed often densely)
related to other factors, some of which may be long term, and
some of which may be undergoing simultaneous change with the
event which provides the story's main focus. Of course, most if not
all news stories are to some extent relational, relying on contexts
external to the news account (see Lewis (1985) on this point). It
has, indeed, been another frequent charge against broadcast
journalism that it pays too little attention to developing story
contexts and too much to presenting its items as almost free-
standing, thus strengthening their narrative intensity and 'view-
ability' (and commercial competitiveness). However, as the
introduction to this book noted, economic events have an
inescapably systemic character which is both diachronic (in terms
of a history) and synchronic (in terms of ongoing developments
across the various indicators and sectors of economic activity). A
given reported economic shift may be simply 'unreadable' in terms
of its significance unless its relation to other factors is brought into

the report. It is not surprising, then, to find in economic news reports the kind of relational headline where one economic event (change) is read in terms of another factor (change or no change) or even more than one other factor. Nor is it surprising that economic news accounts have frequent recourse to a syntax of qualification ('yet', 'but', 'whilst', 'nevertheless'). It is the relational character of economic events which provides economic journalism with its high level of speculative commentary – given so many variables, what *is* happening, let alone what *might* happen, provides generous scope for different judgements and for different anticipatory ('what if … ?') frameworks.

As I shall illustrate below, this kind of 'openness' has implications for the economic judgements that reports can make, about what is 'good' news and what is 'bad'. One might note here, finally, how the possibilities for narrativization in economic news items are often constrained by the fact that the 'core events' around which such items are constructed often have no duration in themselves (compare, for instance, reporting of accidents, crimes and political scandals) even though they can be placed within different types of time-frame. In what follows, I want to use selected reports from our corpus to develop an account of three routine dimensions of television reporting of the economy – the reading of statistical change, the linking of economic conditions to the state of the nation and the reporting of present and possible future actions by the Chancellor (often involving an assessment of his 'options'). Rather than selecting brief extracts from a wide range of instances, my analytical purpose within the overall terms of this book is best served by giving a full transcript of each report before considering its communicative design and delivery. In these considerations, I shall draw on a five-fold scheme of basic analysis (developed from Hartley (1982) to close in more tightly on the news discourse. The scheme highlights key phases as follows:

- *Heading* (how the news item is headlined, 'framed' in relation to other events and moved to the level of detail).
- *Naming* (how key parts of the story are identified and classified).
- *Showing* (how the story is illustrated by still and moving images).
- *Accessing* (who gets to be interviewed in the story, on what terms and in what relation to its development).
- *Closing* (how the story is concluded, how the strands are brought together and an overall significance given to what has happened).

This is a simple scheme, but it is an aid in the development of a more complex account.

Reading change

My first example comes from the BBC's *Nine O'Clock News*. It is a report by its chief economic correspondent, Peter Jay, on 15 November 1995 (visuals in italics):

Newsreader (*to camera; caption: JOBLESS*):
> The number of people out of work and claiming benefit rose last month for the first time in two years. Retail sales also fell slightly. (*v/o (voice-over) graphic; caption UNEMPLOYMENT FIGURES*) Seasonally adjusted unemployment figures for October rose to 2,265,500, a rise of just 200.

Peter Jay, economics editor (*v/o Wilton's Bakery*):
> Wilton's Bakery has served the Fishponds road area of Bristol on this spot for over 100 years. (*ovens*) The oven, which bakes the loaves and cakes, is almost as old, and the skills of the staff are even more traditional. (*cake decoration*) Weddings, birthdays and Christmas still come in the toughest economic times, but the baker can't remember a tougher time.

Laurence Levitt, manager, Wilton's Bakery (*to camera*):
> I'm afraid it's particularly difficult at this point in time, and as a direct result of that, economics have dictated that unfortunately I've had to make a person redundant, very much against my will.

Peter Jay (*v/o graphic; caption: UNEMPLOYMENT (table showing rise/decline 1990–95)*):
> The national unemployment picture now also reflects the sharp economic slowdown this year. At the end of the late '80s boom, it fell to a low point of 1.6 million and then rose for two and a half years to a peak of almost 3 million. Since then, it's fallen for three years. Today's rise has come when unemployment is still 600,000 above the 1990 low point.
> (*v/o suburban shopping street, establishing shot*) Out in the high street, in Bristol as elsewhere, (*facia: Mortgage Advice Co.*) there are few signs of confidence. (*shop chalkboard: 'Any 5 bars for £1'*) New national figures today for sales contradict the brief hints of improvement in the early summer, and almost all indicators now confirm that the recovery of the economy from recession is at a halt.
> (*v/o SS Great Britain; various shots of hull, bows and mast*) The steamship *Great Britain*, once the biggest in the world, mirrors Britain's economic decline. For half a century she dominated the world's sea lanes, before being beset by great storms, abandoned as a wreck in the Falkland Islands and now displayed as a relic to tourists in Bristol.
> (*to camera, before SS Great Britain*) If John Major's Great Britain is to avoid a similar fate, the Chancellor will soon have to get the economy moving again. Right now, he's got two weeks before the budget to find the right tonic. Peter Jay, BBC news, Bristol.

This item has a strongly statistical heading given by the

newsreader, framed in terms of previous economic circumstances. (The 'studio still' behind the newsreader shows a man outside a job centre and has the story caption 'jobless', although the item ranges much more widely than this.) It is a story about two slight movements – an increase in unemployment and a fall in retail sales. 'For the first time in two years' seems evaluatively ambiguous as a way of contextualizing the former movement – it could indicate either that on the whole the government's record is good in this area or that the rise should be interpreted as part of a new, potentially bad, long-term trend.

Peter Jay's job is to 'take this down' to local level, using Bristol to sample and to show a little of the real experience which lies beneath the figures. This format is a routine device in Jay's reporting but his visit to Bristol develops a more marked 'heritage' character than usual. The bakery's age and even the age of the ovens become significant in an account of traditional and enduring community life and family routine against which the unprece-dented economic difficulties are set. Within this account, the baker's personal experience, connecting with the new general statistics, is that of having had reluctantly to lose a member of staff.

Here, the story on the ground is interrupted by a return to the abstract level of statistical trends. Again, the ambiguous complex-ities of economic 'rises' and 'falls' are apparent as Jay offers a potted, two-sentence synopsis of unemployment-level phases since the late 1980s. There *is* now a rise, but its significance has to be read relatively against a wider context of 'highs' and 'lows'.

Back at ground level again, Jay turns to the second part of the story – retail sales. The visual indicators of Bristol shop fronts serve, representatively, to contradict the 'brief hints' of improve-ment which appeared earlier in the year and to support the idea of a recovery which is at a halt.

Jay's story is closed with a strong visual and figurative flourish in his final voice-over, and then piece-to-camera, in front of the SS *Great Britain*. Rather than remaining indirect in its implications, the ship is brought into the closing comments as an explicit simile, mirroring economic decline. The mode of this sequence retains a degree of journalistic naturalism (the ship *is* in Bristol, so why not pick up on its symbolic resonance?) which (just) provides it with a legitimacy which would certainly be denied to any more contrived use of such an image (as could be got from using archive or stock-shot material, for instance). Finally, the long-term, historical view is exchanged for a tightly personal and short-term finish. It is the Chancellor who has to get the economy moving again and he has only two weeks in which to do it. Staying in the figurative vein, Jay sees this, not in terms of any specific policy measures, but in terms of finding the 'right tonic'.

This item 'reads change' by adopting a two-level approach, the general and abstract against the specific and concrete. The two levels are interrelated by having general and abstract exposition take place *within* the setting, in relation to concrete indicators. Discursively, this gives a good level of coherence and continuity, especially with the figurative finish, although the 'fit' between the news lead itself and what is reported about Bristol is necessarily a loose one. The snapshot of Bristolian affairs relates to a broader set of economic circumstances than 'today's figures'. But Jay, and the viewer, can nevertheless contemplate this snapshot in terms of the latest news. More importantly, by placing himself within the composition of the snapshot, Jay is able to connect his abstract reading to tradition, community, ordinary people and an ironic allegory of national history.

My second extract is taken from *Channel 4 News* a day later, 16 November 1995. *Channel 4 News*, provided by ITN and going out at 7 p.m., reaches a minority audience with a high percentage of professional-class viewers. It thus is able both to give more time to individual items and to address them in ways which might prove inaccessible to audiences for BBC and ITV network bulletins. This said, the differentiation in economic reporting is perhaps less marked than for other areas of coverage, for the reasons noted above (notably, the limitations of real options):

Newsreader (*to camera*):
    The chances of a tax-cutting budget have been increased by the government borrowing figures, which were much better than expected. The inflation rate also dropped sharply, down from 3.9 to 3.2 per cent. That increased speculation that the Chancellor may cut interest rates at the start of next year.
    (*v/o graphic: FTSE 100 3,610.8 up 39.4*) As a result, the index of 100 leading shares rose nearly 40 points to an all-time high. (*graphic: Pound vs. Dm, dm2.1920 up 0.8pfg*) But the pound remained weak, rising 8/10ths of a Pfennig against the German Mark and by (*graphic: pound v dollar $1.5587 up 0.1*) 1/10th of a cent against the dollar.
    (*v/o moving 'title-page' graphic: Budget boost*) Our economics correspondent, Steve Levinson, assesses how the latest figures have given the Chancellor a pre-budget boost.

Steve Levinson, reporter (*v/o City of London skyline*):
    The City's convinced tax cuts and interest rate cuts are (*City dealing room*) on the way. That's a shot in the arm for share prices, which climbed to record levels today, but unnerving for the pound, which is only just above its all-time low. One way or another, the volatility means the markets now expect tax cuts of 5 or 6 billion pounds in the budget.

David Owen, UK economist, Kleinwort Benson (*v/o City dealing room*):
    We are looking for approximately 5 billion of net tax cuts all targeted at the floating voter, namely the consumer. (*to camera*) I think the clever move would be to get the basic rate down to 20 per cent, get the rate down to the long-term target in the life of this parliament, and then they can go into an election campaign,

potentially next year, stating that they have got their 20 per cent long-term objective.

Steve Levinson (*v/o City dealing room*):
And on interest rates, the debate is no longer if they're coming down but when, with the consensus going for early next year. (*petrol station, with prices displayed*) This latest bout of market euphoria came on the back of much better than expected inflation figures. The petrol price war which knocked 4p off a gallon last month was partly responsible for a sharp drop in the inflation rate. Lower mortgages and food prices also helped. (*Inland Revenue, tax return form-feeder*) The icing on the cake for budget optimists, however, was a surge in government tax receipts. That was due mainly to higher corporation tax revenues (*tax file boxes*) which helped to bring down government borrowing and increased the scope for budget tax cuts.

Angela Knight MP, Economic Secretary, Treasury (*to camera*):
What we have always said that we were aiming to do was carry on growing the economy, sustainable growth. We have an inflation target which we are all set to meet, and bring down the public sector borrowing. Now what these figures show is, that is precisely what has happened.

Steve Levinson (*v/o graphic (traffic lights on red); caption: INFLA-TION*):
That means the Chancellor may now feel able to override the warning signals which threatened his tax cuts. There were worries about inflation but (*traffic lights: green*) recent news has been reassuring, with (*graphic adds: raw materials fell 0.3%, House prices fell 0.3%, Retail prices fell 0.5%*) raw material costs, house prices and now retail prices all falling in the last month. (*graphic: (traffic lights on red); caption: ECONOMY*) Tax cuts might also have been halted by an overheating economy. (*traffic lights: green*) But in fact the economy's stagnating, (*graphic adds: Manufacturing fell 0.6%, Retail sales fell 0.1%, Unemployment up 200*) with manufacturing output falling, retail sales in decline, and unemployment starting to rise. (*graphic: (traffic lights on red); caption: BORROWING*) The third hazard was an overshoot on government borrowing. (*traffic lights: green*) But today again, tax hopes were boosted (*graphic adds: PSBR surplus, 1.3bn, Corporation tax receipts up 33%*) with the government finances in the black last month, and corporation tax receipts up by a third. But despite the temptation to go for big tax cuts, some warn the Chancellor it would be folly to do so.

Richard Brown, British Chambers of Commerce (*to camera*):
The temptation for the Chancellor is to stimulate a rather short-term boost in consumer confidence and demand. If we suddenly see everybody rushing out to the shops spending, of course it will make our retailers quite happy, but the demands it places – the pressures it will exert on the rest of the economy – will be highly dangerous.

Steve Levinson (*v/o Ford Dagenham factory, workers on assembly line*):

One new danger could be wage demands. Production of Ford
cars at Dagenham was disrupted today by an unofficial walkout
over pay. This after an offer of $4\frac{3}{4}$ per cent this year and $4\frac{1}{2}$ per
cent next which was rejected by unions.

(*to camera before Thames and City skyline*) Whatever the
uncertainties, expectations of large-scale tax cuts seem to be
growing almost daily, and the danger for the Chancellor is that
with the pound so weak, the financial markets could take fright
even before he stands up on Budget Day. Steve Levinson,
Channel 4 news, the City.

In contrast to the BBC news on the previous day, this is
predominantly a 'good news' lead, generating the theme of
possible tax cuts, although in fact the story contains elements
which might, independently and within a different news perspective, be read as 'bad'. The newsreader's framing highlights a
movement in borrowing figures which is positive even when
measured against positive expectation. This is combined with
positive news about inflation.

Steve Levinson situates his account from within the City, for it is
the City (in its complex dual role as both reflector of, and influence
upon, economic trends) which believes that cuts in tax rates and
interest rates are on the way. Already, however, a note of
ambivalence appears – this news, 'good' as it seems, is 'unnerving'
for the pound. Over images of a City dealing room, the site of the
significant 'belief', Levinson continues to emphasize 'goodness' –
increased tax receipts are the 'icing on the cake' for optimists. The
statement of the accessed government minister fits well into this
context of reported success.

Levinson then resorts to the traffic light model in order to bring
out the situation more clearly. However, the play-off between
'good' and 'bad' elements now emerges more awkwardly within
the schematic exposition (see our discussion of viewer problems
with this item in Chapter 1). By setting up the traffic lights idea
around 'tax cuts' (green) and indications against tax cuts (red), the
account manages to include a stagnating economy with a slide in
manufacturing, declining retail sales and rising unemployment as
'good news'!

The hazardous interrelationality of the economy is further
underlined in the closing stages of the report. Notwithstanding
the calculations which contrive to project tax cuts as the primary
economic 'good' at the present time, the 'dangers' and 'pressures'
of subsequent *overstimulation* are already being anticipated.
Indeed here, right at the end, 'wage demands' are suddenly
introduced as a new 'bad' element lurking on the economic
horizon. In front of the City skyline, Levinson finishes his account
within the terms of a system which finally resists uniform
readability, despite the direction taken in the middle of the report.
Expectations of cuts are growing daily but the weak pound could
cause markets to 'take fright'. What looked like (cautious) good

news at the start and a reassuring sequence of 'green lights' in the middle, now seems both less positive and, indeed, less clear.

Budget: locality and nation

In my first two examples, I have looked at the kind of discursive moves, and indeed tensions, produced when the reporting of 'change' comes up against certain characteristics of 'the economy' and economic affairs. I want now to look more closely at the extensive treatment of something which was there, in concise form, within the BBC report discussed above. This is the relation of the economy to the national dimension at the level of places and people. But I also want to look at another form of relation regularly appearing in the news, that between economic factors and political factors, notably the fortunes of the government (including, often, its electoral appeal). Here is a report carried by *Channel 4 News* at 7 p.m. on Budget Day, 28 November 1995:

Newsreader (*to camera; caption: BUDGET*):
So Mr Clarke said he wanted to meet the needs and address the concerns of Middle England, Middle Scotland, Middle Wales and Middle Ulster. He indicated his aim was to attract back to the Conservative fold the middle-class voters needed to win a fifth term.
(*v/o title-page graphic; caption: HEARTS & MINDS*) Alex Thomson has been getting reaction in the Tory-held constituency of Meriden in the Midlands to assess how far Mr Clarke's measures have succeeded in winning back the hearts and minds of the electorate there.

Alex Thomson, reporter (*v/o views of Meriden – river, church, street*):
If the Chancellor's deal really does boil down to something as crude as tax cuts now in return for votes come the election, then the government will have to sell it in constituencies like Meriden, (*v/o entrance to Heart of England School*) where even the names of the schools remind you that this area between Birmingham and Coventry is at the heart of England (*v/o man leaving home*) and, in theory, a safe Tory seat. But on the eve of the budget our cameras found (*v/o man arriving at Balsall Common Primary School*) Conservative voters are in anxious mood. Retired teacher John Denness was off to a meeting to protest against government plans to introduce vouchers for nursery education.

John Denness, retired teacher (*v/o Denness listening to speech at Balsall Common Primary School protest meeting*):
The people that I meet and discuss things with do not have much confidence, not only in this government, but governments generally.

Alex Thomson (*v/o audience at protest meeting*):
And income tax cuts were not top of his list.

John Denness.
It needs activity like cutting VAT for small businesses so they can live and resolve their dreams and ideas and enlist more staff.

Alex Thomson (*v/o Lady Byron Lane – (street name, houses, joggers)*):
Lady Byron Lane in the Meriden constituency is, say some, the richest road in the West Midlands. There is no doubt that many have done well even though the government has increased taxation. But there was no evidence of the fabled feelgood factor. Instead, warnings to the Chancellor (*v/o Dr Peter Lea standing at protest meeting*) about tax cuts from at least one Conservative councillor.

Dr Peter Lea, Conservative councillor, Solihull:
It's a little late in the day for this Conservative government to try and give money back to the people, 'cos they have long memories and they will show it in the ballot-box at the next election.

Alex Thomson (*v/o; delicatessen – goods being carried in, ham being sliced*):
Even in the comfortable heart of Middle England, Dr Lea's prognosis could hardly be grimmer. Tax cuts or no, the Chancellor and his party will be butchered at the next election.
(*to camera, shopping street*) Three years into what passes for an economic recovery you're seeing the kinds of concerns and anxieties among middle-class Conservative voters which you'd probably find anywhere in Britain. But what we are also seeing here is a very strong feeling that tax cuts are not the answer – nobody here is putting them at the top of their list. Some people are saying it would simply be bribery or too little too late.
(*v/o Adam French in office*) Like Adam French, beginning his career as an environmental analyst, who would still vote Conservative come the next election. What sort of things are you concerned about?

Adam French, environmental analyst:
Well definitely not tax cuts. I think that they should only come if and when the country can afford them. I think there are very many more things that ought to be done first: investment in industry and especially in the workforce.

Chris Wills, advertising sales executive (*talking on telephone in office*):
The cost of your quarter-page, black-and-white is three-forty.

Alex Thomson (*v/o*):
Chris Wills is at the mid-point of his career in publishing. (*v/o Lin Wills in kitchen*) His wife works in retailing and the family are somewhat (*v/o Wills family in kitchen*) trapped by the stagnant housing market. For two months they've been trying to move but nothing's happening. So we brought Adam French and (*v/o Adam French, John Denness, Chris and Lin Wills watching budget speech on television in Wills' sitting room*) John Denness to the Wills' household this afternoon to gauge the Chancellor's performance.

Adam French:
    Oh, here we go.

Television Screen (*Kenneth Clarke giving budget speech*):
    'I've had to consider carefully where tax cuts might fall …'

Alex Thomson (*v/o*):
    John Denness was unimpressed by changes to the inheritance
    tax.

Television Screen (*Kenneth Clarke giving budget speech, with John
    Denness watching television*):
    ' … therefore propose to increase the tax-free allowance
    substantially to 200,000.'

John Denness:
    I am sorry. That is not going to help a vast number of people in
    this country, to get the country on the move. I'm sorry.

Alex Thomson (*v/o Adam French, John Denness, Chris and Lin Wills
    watching budget speech on television*):
    And it all added up to despair for Chris Wills.

Chris Wills:
    That was not a job-creating budget. I am disappointed. And
    furthermore, as a house-owner, with all the millions of others, he's
    cut us loose. He's just letting it float and it's up to market forces, re
    our houses. So are they going to carry on falling with value? I
    don't know. I despair.

Adam French:
    He's directed it towards middle-income people totally. Nothing
    for unemployed, nothing for training, nothing for people on
    lower incomes to have any feelgood factor at all.

Lin Wills (*to camera*):
    I shan't be voting for the Conservative Party next time for the
    simple reason (*caption: LIN WILLS, Cashier, Partco*) I voted for
    them the last time because they promised all sorts and they failed.

Alex Thomson (*v/o Centre of England monument, artist sketching*):
    Outside some avoided it all, sketching the monument which
    marks the heart of England, a heart which appears to have
    rejected the electoral advances of the Chancellor. Alex Thomson,
    Channel 4 news, Meriden.

This report is a much more expansive piece of journalism than
the two previous examples. It is a feature item, developing a
documentary-like degree of 'colour' as it moves across different
aspects of Meriden life. Self-consciously, it is an exercise in
symbolic typicality, as the newsreader framing suggests. Meriden
is 'Middle England' geographically and demographically. The
establishing shots of its river, church and streets substantiate a
strong sense of the national-in-the-local which is the basis for the
'test' upon which the report is premised – how does this local
electorate regard the budget in the light of the government's

record? Will a promise of tax cuts win them over? As the item explores selected spaces in Meriden political life, canvassing opinion, it 'finds out' and repeatedly reports that the government is failing the test. This playoff between what one might assume about a place like Meriden, and what actually is the current of feeling there, provides the piece with its entire narrative design. In order for the contrast to work, an intensive visual rhetoric of 'Middle England', exemplifying its 'comfortable heart', has to be constructed from images of leafy lanes and large detached houses. But there is a mystery in these green expanses, gravel drives and well-stocked shops. It is that the 'fabled feelgood factor' cannot be found.

As well as constructing Meriden as essential Middle England with a surprising political character, the item uses another reportorial device – the small group of representative citizens. This group 'meets' to look at the budget in one member's home, giving the item a degree of immediacy value and tighter narrative linkage as viewers watch them watching the budget announcements and then hear, in turn, their negative judgements upon it. The mode is a tight mix between exposition and observation. We are told, for instance, that John Denness was 'unimpressed' on inheritance tax change, just before hearing the Chancellor's announcement and Denness's response (apparently to the Chancellor!) that it is 'not going to get the country on the move'.

Outside, someone is sketching the monument which marks the heart of England, physical indicator of Meriden's position and centrepiece of the report's own rhetorical design. Their activity is seen as 'avoidance' and appropriated for the conclusion which the item had mooted quite early on but which has now been substantiated to the report's own satisfaction by interviews with four people watching the budget. Meriden has 'rejected' the government's economic policy.

This report is much more a political report than an economic one, of course, and Budget Day coverage is particularly strong in hybrids of this kind. But by working so single-mindedly, and to some extent self-awarely, both with national 'myths' and ideas about grassroots feeling, the item connects with elements found in diluted and dispersed form in more routine reporting.

Economy and political action: the Chancellor as manager

Earlier in the book, some of the different ways in which political factors are implicated in reports about the economy have been noted. The 'political' in economic reporting often turns on what the government has done or is likely to do in response to changing indicators. Attributions of failure or success in managing the economy assume certain powers of control, and we have noted how the political discourse of economic management is sometimes inconsistent in what it is prepared to regard as 'manageable' given the emphasis on the autonomy of the private sector and the growing internationalization of both commerce and finance. In this section, I want to look at two stories which place the actions of the Chancellor of the Exchequer as central, raising questions about his managerial performance and his relation to other 'players'. The first story is taken from the BBC's *Nine O' Clock News* on 15 January 1996:

Newsreader (*to camera; caption: ECONOMY*):
  An all-party committee of MPs has cast doubt on the Chancellor's economic forecasts, in particular his prediction of a 3 per cent annual growth rate for the coming year. The Treasury Select Committee says it wants more details about the calculations on which the figures are based. And the Building Employers' Confederation have issued their own report, predicting that 20,000 jobs will be lost in their industry in the next four months.

Evan Davis, economics correspondent (*v/o lorry and workers on construction site*):
  It hasn't been a great year for Britain's builders. At the end of 1995, the building industry was 3.5 per cent less busy than it had been a year earlier. Ironically, more building firms say they are fully occupied than the year before, but that simply reflects the fact that many of the firms have become smaller. And that kind of shrinkage is set to continue.

Paul Shepherd, Building Employers' Confederation (*to camera*):
  There will be further job losses. The industry's already lost some 480,000 jobs in the last four to five years and we anticipate that a further 20,000 will go before the end of May. Many of these, regrettably, will be permanently lost to the industry, which has paid, of course, for their training. And in terms of workload, the prospects continue flat throughout '96.

Evan Davis (*v/o Treasury Select Committee examining Kenneth Clarke and Treasury team*):
  This kind of news is worrying MPs of all parties. A select committee, the Treasury Committee, published the results of its recent investigations into the economy today. Its report is sceptical about the optimistic 3 per cent forecast for economic growth published in the budget. So who came up with that number?
  (*To camera, HM Treasury*) Officially, it's a government forecast. It belongs to Kenneth Clarke, the Chancellor. And although he would have received advice, it wasn't necessarily the work of any professional economists at all.
  (*v/o Kenneth Clarke arriving by car at No. 11 Downing Street*) The Chancellor's forecast was also said to be too optimistic about investment. He thinks companies will spend 9 per cent more on new equipment or buildings this year than they did last year.
  (*v/o bricklayers at house construction site*) Builders stand to gain from booming investment, but like the Treasury Committee, they doubt the Chancellor's forecast. The industry's just hoping

he may take additional action by cutting interest rates to get near to fulfilling his prediction. Evan Davis, BBC News.

Forecasting is a key component of economic management and one of the most important ingredients in economic news-making. It is against forecasts that expectations are built and it is against expectations that economic performances are judged. The build-up of expectations around the imminent release of figures gives the economic reporter a major source of news value and narrative tension. Here, the report has a strong 'doubt' framing; questions about the Chancellor's forecast for 'growth' are all the more strong coming from an all-party committee. The Treasury Committee is the primary source of 'doubt' but this is strengthened by the more substantive assessments of the Building Employers' Confederation, whose representative is accessed to give the statistics for his sector. A return to the Treasury Committee strand reprises the headline information and raises more sharply the question of how the figures were produced. At this point, the correspondent briefly develops the story himself. In front of the Treasury, he identifies the forecast as a possession of the Chancellor, not likely to be a product of 'professional' calculation. Ambiguity about whether a falling short in the non-professional prognosis might best be attributed to incompetence or political deception is left unre-solved, although it seems important to the core news value of this item that it is there. Over a shot of the Chancellor arriving in Downing Street, the story concludes by re-emphasizing 'doubt' and by reporting the expressed hope that he will take the additional action – a cut in interest rates – which might get him near to his predicted figures.

This is a thinnish item, but its sources allow it to develop an unusually tight focus around scepticism. Bigger stories about the soundness of the Chancellor's actions would be likely to open out into a wider range of accessed opinion, blurring the sharpness of the questions which, once taken into this report, become its key, reporter-led theme. My second item in this section comes from ITV *News at Ten* three days later, 18 January 1996:

Newsreader (*to camera; caption: ECONOMY*):
> Here, the Chancellor announced another surprise cut in interest rates today, but it won't immediately affect borrowers or savers. He cut the bank base rate from 6.5 per cent to 6.25 per cent, but the banks and building societies are saying they'll not be passing on the reduction for the time being. Our economics editor, Mark Webster, reports.

Mark Webster, economics editor (*v/o busy shopping street*):
> Welcome news in the high street, where, despite buoyant Christmas sales, the outlook for the rest of the year was uncertain. Shopkeepers hope by trimming interest rates now, the Chancel-lor will give the slowing economy the boost it needs.

Fiona Price, personal finance expert (*to camera*):
The high street may see some benefit because obviously, if people are getting so little from the building society, they may be more inclined to spend. And also, hopefully, credit card rates may come down a bit.

Mark Webster (*v/o workers and crane positioning sectional roofs on construction site*):
But the beleaguered construction industry, which fears a further 20,000 job losses in the coming months, said the cut was smaller than it had wanted. Nonetheless, any reduction was a welcome relief.

Joe Dwyer, Wimpey (*to camera*):
All the statistics – employment, inflation and disposable income for consumers – are going in the right direction. This is a good signal – modest, but a welcome one.

Mark Webster (*v/o Halifax branch office*):
It's too modest for mortgage lenders to announce an immediate cut in the cost of borrowing. (*v/o graphic; caption: INTEREST RATES: Mortgage rate compared to base rate*) Mortgages haven't strictly mirrored base rates over the past 14 months. (*graphic adds: November 1994, mortgage rate 7.83%, base rate 5.75%, difference 2.08%*) In November '94, with the mortgage rate at over 7.8 per cent, while base rates were at 5.75 per cent – a difference of just over 2 per cent. (*graphic adds: December 1994, difference 1.59%, February 1995 difference 1.23%*) Over the next few months, that gap narrowed until last November, (*graphic adds: November 1995, mortgage rate 7.5%, base rate 6.75%, difference 0.75%*) the mortgage lenders took the lead and cut their rates to 7.5 per cent, taking the gap to just 0.75 per cent. (*graphic adds: January 1996, mortgage rate 7.5%, base rate 6.25%*) That's why they won't follow today's cut immediately.
(*v/o Clarke, George and aides round table at monthly meeting*) But the question is whether the Chancellor had to overrule the Governor of the Bank of England to achieve even this modest interest rate cut. Today's small inflation rise would certainly confirm Mr George's fears that caution should remain the best policy.
(*to camera, outside Bank of England*) While the Bank of England was officially maintaining a dignified silence, sources within the Bank said the Governor had indeed been reluctant to see a base rate cut now. He wanted more time to assess the impact of last month's 0.25 per cent cut in rates before moving again. Instead, the Chancellor decided that the economy needed an extra boost immediately. Mark Webster, News At Ten, the Bank of England.

This is essentially a statistical change story, similar in some respects to the two discussed above, but lacking their complexity. The second element of the headline, that the 'surprise cut' will not be passed on by banks and building societies, has the effect of 'cancelling' the impact of the first. However, as demonstrated earlier, the systemic implications of the smallest change offer a 'follow-through' route for the news across the different sectors. Here, the 'boost' effect of a trimming of interest rates is what is at issue. The report opens out into 'high street' to assess the benefits in terms of increased personal spending (although the accessed finance expert seems to be working with the assumption, against the item's own account, that there *will* be a reduction in loan rates). The positive reading is then put in semi-contrast with the more cautious one from the building sector, where fears of further losses mean disappointment at the size of the cut, though a representative shows satisfaction with the direction indicated.

The report then tackles the statistical heart of the story head on, giving us a brief, graphically supported history of recent mortgage rate changes in relation to base rates which explains the reason for the new level not being passed on straight away.

Finally, it is able to connect with the running story of the Chancellor's monthly meetings with the Governor of the Bank of England and (with pictures) to pick up on the well-reported disagreements between the two with a question about 'overruling'. A small rise in inflation is brought into the picture to reinforce the central systemic playoff between interest rates and inflation which underlies their disagreements (often posed as a dialogue between boldness and caution). The report finishes with mythic overtones in front of the Bank of England, its 'dignified silence' but implied 'reluctance' placed against the Chancellor's political need to find a 'boost immediately'.

Although, again, limited in its news strength, this account of change has been taken out to representative sectors, opened up in terms of its statistical significance and then linked with the ongoing personal and institutional 'contest' currently providing the most important (and the most tellable) running story about UK economic management.

News form and the economy: concluding remarks

Looking across those five features of a news item I outlined earlier, we have noted how economic journalism has special difficulties with 'showing'. Partly as a result of this, a greater expositional/ narrative loading falls on 'naming' and on 'closing'. This is even more of a challenge if we consider the statistical and relational character of the information in most headings. The accessing of reactions and viewpoints from different economic sectors may aid in the development of news significance, but a crucial task of synoptic interpretation falls to the reporter or correspondent. One consequence of this is a tendency for relatively lengthy and complicated closings, in which both the synchronic meaning of 'today's figures' across the economic system and their diachronic import within the national story (of, say, 'troubled recovery') are given as firm a projection as can be offered. Another consequence is the need for reports quite often to insert phases of intensive exposition-over-graphics into the more conventional flow of comment and pictures. Economic coverage routinely has to carry into its stories 'subsets' of inter-statistical significance (around base rates, for instance, or around demand forecasts) which can only be referenced if they are at some point directly engaged in this way. Rather than being dispersed across the narrative line, as other information might be, these 'subsets' require of the journalist a degree of deep exposition, often developing a density, albeit temporary, which is a frequent cause of comprehension breakdown for viewers. However, it was noted in Chapter 1 what the consequences might be for the quality of public communication of simply *evading* the awkwardness of this task.

Although they have a high immediacy value, economic events are generally instantaneous (announced figures, announced decisions) so although narratives can (and have to) be constructed around them, they do not themselves possess an event structure which lends itself to strong narrative chronology – one way in which other kinds of news event are made engaging and accessible. There are of course exceptions to this (for instance, the remarkable timetable of occurrences on the autumn day in 1992 – 'Black Wednesday' – when the UK pulled out of the European Exchange Rate Mechanism).

Economic reporting can increase its appeal and accessibility by substantiating 'downwards' into typical particulars (stronger visuals, ordinary people, real life) or 'upwards' into the world of Westminster (high-profile actors, political fortune, policy conflict). Different events will permit different possibilities here, although all economic stories are likely to be framed, with various degrees of explicitness and emphasis, as stories about a 'politically managed economy' even if the precise sphere and nature of this management are shown as being open to dispute. However, being committed to the explication of abstract, systemic change, to the 'riddle of figures', economic news has far less room for manoeuvre than other news realms. At the same time, as the entire project of this book suggests, its survival with integrity is one of the most important requirements of UK television news in the next decade.

4
Press rhetoric and economic news: a case study

Peter Goddard

Introduction

The majority of the UK sections of this book focus on television economic news and on audience engagement with it. But the press is of comparable significance in constructing and sustaining models of 'the economy', in reporting developments within it and in its contribution to the development of an informed citizenry. Notwithstanding the history of debates and experiments concerning the relative importance of press and television as sources of news and public information (reported extensively, for example, in Robinson and Levy, 1986), the two media are qualitatively very different, rendering comparisons problematic and enabling different uses to be made of each. This was a point which arose spontaneously several times within groups inter-viewed by the Public Communications Group whilst researching comprehension of television economic news (see Chapter 2).

You see, with television and with radio, completely different to newsprint, that comes into your sitting rooms. If you want, you go to a shop and you buy the newspaper you want and you read the paper you want. That [television] has got to put over a general, overall, newsy item ... (Rotary Club members)

Briefly, television and the press have different delivery systems. Television news is readily available but exists for a single and time-limited viewing, whereas press news requires the active purchas-ing of a newspaper but exists in hard copy indefinitely, leaving the reader to determine the depth of reading and degree of reiteration required. The press also offers a far larger quantity of news and often a range of news treatments of the same story, whereas, as our respondent notes, television must often aim for generality. Press readers may select their newspapers to produce the type and depth of coverage which suits them, and also because of the degree to which those newspapers reflect their own partisanship. Under the UK model, however, most television news is available in broadly similar formats reflecting a duty of 'due impartiality'.

However, similarities remain between the two media over the treatment of economic news. For press as for television, 'the economy' is regarded as a technically complex and 'difficult' area, requiring a greater degree of contextualization and explanation than many other types of news, and not readily open to visualization. Although graphics and photographs are common in press coverage of the economy, their appearance is not always geared solely towards providing explanation. As with television, 'the economy' is often depicted in the press as essentially a systemic entity dispersed across a range of interrelated processes, states and indicators. News stories about the economy often centre on changes to one or more of these, necessitating a minor redrawing of the configuration of the whole, or, less frequently, on challenges to normative readings of the range of salient factors or the priority to be accorded to particular ones. As we shall see, however, the press offers scope for a greater range of different treatments to be given to changes to the systemic configuration of 'the economy'.

Context and coverage

As an illustration of the variety of treatments which are commonly applied even to the most straightforward economic news story in the press, the remainder of this chapter will concentrate on the reporting of a single economic event across a range of UK newspapers. Like many economic news stories, the event itself represents a change to a single variable in the systemic configuration of the economy, but its significance – at least as newspapers reported it – is the product also of its 'news context', making projections both backwards and forwards from the new information reported. Of equal interest, though, is a further level of newspaper-generated significance which we might call 'newspaper context', deriving in varying degrees from the form in which different newspapers reported the event and its placement within each paper. This 'newspaper context', whilst contributing to the structure of significance placed by each newspaper on the event itself, is capable also of yielding much information about each newspaper's strategies to engage readers by constructing a sense of its own identity, authority and rhetorical style.

The event chosen as the focus of this analysis is the announcement, by Kenneth Clarke, the Chancellor of the Exchequer, on

Friday 8 March 1996, of a 0.25 per cent cut in interest rates. This event was prefigured by speculation about its announcement in most of that day's papers, where it was occasionally linked to an upward change in another economic variable, retail sales, and was reported as having happened in each paper the following day. Across the five papers sampled, it was featured in a total of 24 stories over these two days (Table 4.1).

Of the five newspapers surveyed, the *Sun*, the *Daily Mirror* and the *Daily Mail* are high-circulation tabloids, although the *Daily Mail* is a 'mid-market' tabloid – significantly less populist in its approach. The *Guardian* and *The Times* are broadsheets with smaller, elite readerships and more of a hard-edged focus (for a recent history of the UK press and its division into 'downmarket', 'mid-market' and 'upmarket', see Tunstall, 1996). The most cursory glance at Table 4.1 reveals a greater extent and range of coverage in the broadsheets. Indeed, on both days the number of paragraphs of stories in which the event is featured in the two broadsheets greatly exceeds the combined total of paragraphs devoted to it in the three tabloids. This is likely to be of little surprise, reflecting no more than normative conceptions of the differences between the downmarket and upmarket press, and might be explained, in part at least, by the greater size of the broadsheets. Perhaps more surprisingly, the *Daily Mirror*'s cover-age is the most negligible, whilst the overtly populist *Sun* devotes nearly as many paragraphs to the event in both its Friday and Saturday editions as does the weightier *Daily Mail*. As we shall see, however, much more is to be gained from close attention to the variety of formal, rhetorical and discursive devices employed by these newspapers in the construction of stories around this event than is revealed by quantity of coverage alone.

Also worthy of comment, although again not of surprise, is that this event finds its way into a wide range of different types of article beyond the news pages. It prompted an editorial in *The Times* and discussion within the 'Money' (particularly prevalent in Saturday editions) and 'Business' sections of several newspapers, both in the form of sectional news stories and as the subject for commentary by regular columnists. To some extent this extended coverage, going beyond the 'fact' of the interest rate change which has been reported elsewhere as 'news', reflects the systemic nature of the economy itself, where a shift in one variable necessitates a wholesale, if minor, reassessment of the configuration of the entire system and of its accompanying narratives of competence and future prospects. Especially in the 'Money' sections, aimed largely at individual investors, this coverage often takes the form of the reissuing/updating of financial advice in the light of this new information. However, the remainder of this chapter will concern itself with the 'hard news' coverage alone (in line with the categories employed by Bell, 1991, p. 14).

Table 4.1 Coverage of interest rate cut across five newspapers

Paper	Page	Para.	Cols	Pic./Graph	Headline	Type
Friday 8 March						
Sun	2	4	1	None	New loans cut 'today'	News
Daily Mirror	–	–	–	–	(not reported)	–
Daily Mail	5	5	5	None	Eddie ready for another loan rate cut	News
Guardian	2	16	6	1p/4g	Home loan cut set to boost Clarke	News
The Times	23	8	3	1p/0g	City hopes for rate cut despite signs of recovery	Business
The Times	25	4	2	None	As simple as cutting rates	Business/ Column
Saturday 9 March						
Sun	2	15	4	3p/3g	Home loans are lowest since '66	News
Sun	29	9	3	0p/1g	Bargain & Bingley	Money
Daily Mirror	2	9	2	None	Home loans cut joy for 6 million	News
Daily Mirror	6	6	1	None	Don't be fooled	Editorial
Daily Mail	2	16	4	0p/2g	Mortgage cut puts a spring in the air	News
Daily Mail	67	20	4	None	Tumbling Wall Street spoils our rate cheer	Business/ Column
Guardian	1	16	2	1p/0g	Jitters follow cut in rates	News
Guardian	3	18	7	5p/0g	'Bumper year' spells poll gloom for Labour	News
Guardian	3	8	4	0p/1g	Big lenders cut mortgage rates	News
Guardian	25	5	4	None	Mr Clarke eyes up polling day	Editorial
Guardian	31	11	6	1p/1g	Mortgage misery goes on despite latest rates cut	Money
Guardian	31	9	2	None	Savers pay the high price of home loan war	Money
The Times	1	10	3	0p/1g	Mortgage cut boost for house sales	News
The Times	2	7	5	0p/1g	Mortgage rates lowest since 1960s	News
The Times	21	6	2	None	Never had it so good	Editorial
The Times	25	10	5	None	Wall St slump of 171 points overshadows UK rate cut	Business
The Times	29	15	7	1p/0g	Lenders act swiftly over base rate cut	Money
The Times	29	7	3	1p/0g	A bigger boost to confidence	Money/ Column
The Times	31	3	2	None	Mutual comfort	Money/ Column

Who's in charge? Who says?

There is only a small body of existing work concerning the language of press news, and its principal texts (Bell, 1991; van Dijk, 1988; Fowler, 1991) are written more for a readership versed in socio-linguistics or discourse analysis than for a mainstream media studies audience. Nevertheless, van Dijk provides an appraisal of the common stylistic and rhetorical elements within news coverage (van Dijk, 1988, pp. 71–94) which, with some reservations, might helpfully be put to use in detailing the way in which these elements operate within the particular set of economic stories selected for analysis here.[1] Van Dijk does not look specifically at economic news. Instead, his work is intentionally generalist and forms part of his wider concern with the principles of discourse analysis as applied to a wide variety of text types, of which news is only one. Whilst this chapter makes no attempt to apply an approach based on formal discourse analysis to the examination of the rhetorical organization of press economic news, and, indeed, in applying his hypotheses beyond the bounds of such an approach, goes well beyond the scope of van Dijk's original intentions, his attention to news structure does provide a valuable starting point for the scrutiny of the stylistic and rhetorical devices to be found within our set of news stories.

To begin with a general point, one of the hallmarks of news coverage is its impersonality. As van Dijk explains, 'not only is a "you" [the reader] generally absent, but also a really individual "I"' (van Dijk, 1988, p. 75). News address is normally institutional even in by-lined stories – hence the different roles of the news story and the column. Of course, this institutionalization does not entirely preclude reporters from comment or interpretation in news stories, but it does raise two questions in the case of economic news – first, that of who is conventionally allowed to speak about the economy, and, second, that of the degree to which the economy is reported as controllable or reified as having a life of its own, an issue taken up by Emmison (1983), Rae and Drury (1993) and Gavin and Goddard (1998).

Besides the institutionalized voices of reporters, the voices accessed in the first news stories which cover this event from each of our surveyed newspapers fall into four classes: those presented as decision-makers (Kenneth Clarke alone; the Governor of the Bank of England is mentioned but neither quoted nor cited); those presented as named experts (six bank economists, three representatives from the employers' organization the CBI, one representative each from the National Association of Estate Agents and the House Builders' Federation, economic spokesmen from the Labour and Liberal Democrat parties, and Lord Desai, who is presented as both economist and Labour spokesman); unnamed voices from the City, mortgage lenders and political parties; and vague unspecified attributions whose function seems to be more rhetorical than evidential (including 'the City', 'city experts', 'business leaders', 'experts', 'some analysts', etc.). The most sweeping of these unspecified attributions occurred in the *Daily Mail*:

It [the interest rate cut] was welcomed by industry, builders, estate agents and small businesses while most economists predicted that rates will fall to 5 per cent by the end of the year. (9 March 1996, p. 1)

Coverage in the *Guardian* and *The Times* differed from that in the remaining newspapers in that both published stories on inside news pages following up specific aspects of the interest rate cut. Each carried a story analysing its implications for mortgage rates and home-owners. The *Guardian* also offered detailed coverage of its political implications, covering an intervention by Lord Desai arguing that low interest rates would herald the return of the 'feelgood factor' amongst voters, which might lead to a restoration of confidence in the Conservative government. In these stories, a wider range of named economists and building society representatives appear and there are fewer unspecified attributions. Overall, however, it is apparent that those voices deemed to be qualified to pronounce on this economic event are drawn exclusively from the financial or political communities. Moreover, the only individuals presented as being in a position of control over the economy in this instance are the Chancellor and the Governor of the Bank of England.

However, there are a number of references to more abstract influences acting upon the economy in these stories, including the movements of other economic indicators (measures of inflation, consumer spending, prices, manufacturing output, etc.) but most notably panic selling on Wall Street. As the *Guardian*'s main report explained:

... the prospects of further cuts in interest rates – seen as crucial by some economists and most of industry to sustaining consumer confidence – were hit by panic selling in the City and New York last night. Share prices plunged by more than 170 points – the third biggest fall on record – on fears that US interest rates were now in a trough. (9 March 1996, p. 1)

The Times quoted Ian Amstad, economist at Bankers Trust, who made the situation sound apocalyptic:

Ken Clarke got his rate cut in with hours to spare. It could have caused a blood bath if it had happened after the US data. The US and UK economies are closely synchronised and this is an indication that UK growth may be poised to strengthen without the help of cheaper money. (9 March 1996, p. 1)

In neither case, however, is a clear explanation offered of the manner in which US share prices actually act upon the UK economy. Nor, elsewhere, are the relationships between interest rates and other economic indicators explored in detail. Taking both the exclusivity of the voices accessed for economic comment and the lack of clear explanation, it might be argued that parts of the reporting surveyed may be counterproductive - rendering comment on economic processes as complex and technical, and beyond the grasp of the reader. There are also hints in these (and other) accounts of this news event of a strand of reporting which reflects some of the conclusions drawn by Rae and Drury (1993), where 'the economy' seems to be reified as an entity largely independent of the control of individuals, even of the Chancellor, and separated (partly by the complexity and incompleteness of the explanations offered) from newspaper readers. This is not the main concern of this chapter, however. Nor is it the primary explanation for the rhetorical structure of the newspaper stories surveyed.

Persuasive content features: emphasizing facticity

Another viewpoint on the range of voices conventionally accessed in economic news stories is provided by van Dijk. He argues (Van Dijk, 1988, pp. 82-8) that much news rhetoric is involved in a process of persuasion because it depends upon encouraging readers to accept the textual accounts which it offers. He goes on to explain that:

... the bulk of our everyday news is an instance of the speech act of assertion. For such speech acts to be appropriate the writer must express propositions that are not yet known to the listener/reader and which the writer wants the listener/ reader to know. The perlocutory or persuasive dimension that sustains such intentions in practice, then, is the formulation of meanings in such a way that they are not merely understood but accepted as the truth or at least as a possible truth. (van Dijk, 1988, p. 83)

Consequently, he suggests, one purpose of news rhetoric is to organize its content and propositional structure in order to make it as believable and memorable as possible. Of course, ideas of news as a construction, and of facticity as a defining characteristic of it, are nothing new within media studies, but van Dijk expands on his point by listing a set of 'persuasive content features' which he claims news rhetoric conventionally uses to 'emphasise the factual nature of events', to 'build a strong relational structure for facts' and to 'provide information that also has attitudinal and emotional dimensions' (van Dijk, 1988, pp. 84-5). Under the first of these headings, he lists five strategies:

1. Direct descriptions of ongoing events.
2. Using evidence from close eyewitnesses.
3. Using evidence from other reliable sources (authorities, respectable people, professionals).
4. Signals that indicate precision and exactness, such as numbers for persons, time, events, etc.
5. Using direct quotes from sources, especially where opinions are involved. (van Dijk, 1988, pp. 84–5)

The application of this table of features to the reporting of this economic event illustrates a general 'difficulty' of economic news reporting and also helps to explain its particular rhetorical character. Although common in many news stories, the first two features fall largely outside the scope of economic reporting. Unlike many other types of news, economic stories are rarely about people or tangible events, but about figures or abstract decisions in which immediacy of description has scant value. Consequently, there is little to be gained by 'describing' the event of the cutting of interest rates, even if it were possible. Nor was it an event to which there were eyewitnesses in the sense normally understood. Whilst the regular (private) meeting between the Chancellor and the Governor of the Bank of England on 7 March was mentioned in most accounts published the following day predicting the interest rate cut, its mention functioned merely as a basis for conjecture rather than to provide information about the event itself.

However, the third and fifth features are of paramount importance to the reporting of this event. Since it is based upon a single hard fact (the interest rate cut), the remainder of the story is of necessity an analysis of its consequences. The more short-term of these (cuts in mortgage rates, the reaction of the financial markets) are established in time for the stories in Saturday's press, in which they can already be presented as a secondary order of 'fact', but the remainder (future prospects for various sectors of the economy, future political prospects for the government) are the subject of opinion and speculation. For such speculation to be persuasive, to be accepted as being of value, it must be presented as being the opinion of reliable, credible, professional sources. The accessing of a wide range of such voices has already been noted, with named actors having presumably the strongest rhetorical force, but with a wide range of unnamed, generalized sources added to provide an even broader rhetorical framework as a further signifier of authority. Hence the exclusivity of the voices accessed in the reporting of this particular economic event can be explained by its particular abstract nature – being inimical to direct description, but requiring for persuasive purposes a strong rhetorical underpinning of expert opinion.

Van Dijk's reference to numbers as a further persuasive feature is also of direct relevance to economic news. Numbers are the

stock-in-trade of economic reporting and not simply because
economic indicators are commonly expressed in numerical terms.
Our sample of reports of this economic event (itself a numerical
change) is awash with numbers – pertaining to interest rate levels,
mortgage rate levels, dates, monetary values, periods of time,
rankings (of mortgage lenders, in comparisons between nations),
quantities of people, share index points, inflation rates, opinion
poll ratings, etc. The reason for the presence of so many precise
numbers in these stories is likely to be more than purely evidential,
because, as van Dijk suggests, their precision serves to emphasize
the precise factual foundation upon which the stories are
constructed and to act as an implicit guarantee of reliability.
Neither is the presence of numbers confined merely to the story
text. Most stories covering this event are accompanied by graphics
– bar charts representing numerically the recent movement in
interest rates; tables of notional monthly mortgage repayments
according to different sizes of loan, types of mortgage and rates of
interest – which add still further to the proliferation of numbers
and the signification of precision. Whilst these tables occupy
prominent positions in the story layout and serve to catch the
reader's eye (the *Daily Mail*'s are even arranged within house-
shaped boxes to enhance visual appeal), in some cases their
evidential value may be open to question because the sheer
quantity and complexity of the figures involved may deter readers
from exploring them (the box marked 'How the cut affects you' in
the *Sun* (reproduced in Figure 4.1) is a case in point). Nevertheless,
it may be that only the most diligent of readers are expected
actually to read the contents of these graphics boxes. For the
general reader, their role as a signifier of authoritative reporting
may be sufficient.

A strong relational structure

Van Dijk's other categories of 'persuasive content feature' are also
worthy of investigation in relation to the reporting of this event.
The need to build 'a strong relational structure for facts' is a
commonplace feature of most reporting and often acknowledged
as such.[2] Van Dijk (1988, p. 85) breaks it down into the following
strategies:

1. Mentioning previous events as conditions or causes and
    describing or predicting next events as possible or real
    consequences.
2. Inserting facts into well-known situation models that make
    them relatively familiar even when they are new.
3. Using well-known scripts and concepts that belong to that
    script.

Figure 4.1 Coverage of the interest rate cut in the *Sun*, 9 March 1996

4.   Trying to further organize facts in well-known specific structures, e.g. narratives.

Reference has already been made to the foundation of this story, like many economic stories, in a single core news event – in this case a cut in base rates – accompanied by little more 'new' information beyond the most immediate changes in mortgage rates which it has precipitated. The 'difficult' nature of economic news demands a relational structure in which new information is 'made sense of' in the light of previous economic trends and likely future developments. The frequent accessing of expert voices to provide authoritative (and persuasive) commentary further adds to the sense that, for this sample of newspapers, the projected consequences of this single event (which depend for their significance on a reading of previous events), rather than the fact of the event itself, provide the real story.

This is illustrated by the fact that cuts in mortgage rates provide the principal focus of the main news stories reporting the interest rate cut in four of the five Saturday newspapers surveyed (as the headlines given in Figure 4.1 testify).[3] Only the *Guardian* combined this focus with that of the government's political prospects, opening as follows:

The Government was last night hoping to reap political dividends from a pick-up in the economy after its third post-Budget cut in base rates triggered a reduction in the cost of home loans to a 30-year low.
  With a homeowner with a £60,000 mortgage now £40 per week better off than in August last year, the Chancellor Kenneth Clarke, underlined yesterday that the Government sees the economy as its best hope of overturning Labour's seemingly impregnable poll lead over the next 12 months. (*Guardian*, 9 March 1996, p. 1)

Prospects for a recovery in the housing market provide a secondary focus in the other four newspapers and are the subject of a brief reference in the body of the *Guardian* story (see below). Besides the *Guardian*'s focus on it, the rate cut's consequences for government popularity and the return of the election-winning 'feelgood factor' are referred to in *The Times*, but in the body of the story and, as later in the *Guardian*'s story, are the subject of contestation by other political parties. Government popularity and 'feelgood' are mentioned only obliquely in the *Sun* and the *Daily Mail* and not at all in the *Daily Mirror*. Alone amongst the newspapers surveyed, *The Times* and the *Guardian* introduce a further focus – the reaction of UK and international financial markets. The event of the interest rate cut itself, therefore, gives little to these stories beyond their instigation. The stories themselves concentrate on interpretations of its various conse- quences – in the realm of personal economies as they intersect with the housing sector, in the political/electoral realm, and/or in the realm of financial trading. These are realms which touch upon concepts (such as 'feelgood') already well established from previous economic and political news coverage.

In common with the discursive structure of most journalism, however, these story foci are not introduced as independent elements but as co-dependent or contingent upon one another within a relational framework. The *Guardian*, for example, follows the opening paragraphs quoted above with one which begins:

However, the prospects of further cuts in interest rates – seen as crucial by some economists and most of industry to sustaining consumer confidence – were hit by panic selling in the City and New York last night. (*Guardian* 9 March 1996, p. 1)

Here, the *Guardian* introduces financial trading as a realm upon which the political/electoral dividends which may arise from the interest rate cut are contingent. Later, the story depicts the interest rate cut as 'prompting' mortgage rate cuts and, later still, describes the Halifax, a leading lender, as 'cautiously optimistic about the prospects for property prices' because it believes that rates will be cut further. In the *Daily Mail*, the means by which a range of projected consequences are presented as dependent on the core 'fact' of the interest rate cut or upon one another is even more explicit. The propositional structure of the first two paragraphs is as follows: 'Home-owners got a spring bonus' *because* the cost of borrowing fell '*triggered*' by the interest rate cut, '*firming up* a gradual recovery in the housing market' (*Daily Mail*, 9 March 1996, p. 1).

In different ways, the coverage of this event can be seen to reflect the 'persuasive content features' which van Dijk identifies as 'building a strong relational structure for facts' and, indeed, tallies with his descriptions of common news schemata both at macro- and micro-levels (van Dijk, 1988, pp. 49–71). However, the conclusions which can be drawn from this about press coverage of economic news are not clear-cut. Indeed, this raises a real problem with van Dijk's interpretation of news rhetoric as existing to serve the purpose of persuading readers of the authority and facticity of newspaper accounts. Much of his analysis seems to concentrate solely on the 'internal' relations of newspaper texts, where he interprets those elements of rhetoric which he deems 'persuasive' principally in relation to their operation on what would otherwise appear to be no more than 'assertion'. There seems little doubt that elements such as the relational structure of newspaper stories about the economy do combine to have this effect. Equally, however, whatever their structure, newspaper stories are operating in relation to the world beyond newspapers, so story structure and many other elements which he identifies do not exist in isolation from story content. It seems likely that economic news requires a strong relational structure because it consists so often of stories based on changes to single variables within the system, necessitating interpretative moves 'outwards' to other variables or processes which may be affected by such a change. Furthermore, it is implicit in the idea of 'economy-as-system' that the economy is composed of a range of co-dependent variables, and so there can be little surprise that this is reflected in news coverage. Explanations for features such as the range of sources accessed and the proliferation of numbers might also be sought within common 'external' conceptions of the economy itself rather than merely within the 'internal' rhetorical relations of texts. In other words, and in spite of the conviction with which he mounts his case, it is not clear to what extent the content features which van Dijk identifies represent something which press coverage imposes on the economy or vice versa. Further work on the presence of such features in stories where the content itself is less likely to invoke them would be required to investigate this discrepancy further.

Some qualified support for van Dijk's position may be found, however, in the existence of some notable omissions in the range of explanatory and interpretative material through which our newspapers offer to 'make sense' of this event. None of them, for example, made reference to the causes – political or economic – of the steep rise in interest rates which preceded the fall which they are reporting and which ended the late 1980s variant of the 'feelgood factor', despite the explicit link which is made in some of these accounts between the cost of borrowing and present-day government popularity. Equally, as we have noted, there is no clear explanation of any relationship between interest rates, inflation and recovery. The existence of such relationships is implicit in all but the *Daily Mirror*'s coverage of the story, but nowhere are they explained or clarified. Even the grounds upon which decisions are made to set or change interest rate levels are not given.

Such omissions would suggest that, in part at least, the reporting of this event is imposing certain explanatory formulae on 'the economy' at the expense of others. But several further inferences may be drawn from what is absent from the coverage. Perhaps journalists have an image of their target readers as having sufficient prior economic knowledge not to need reminding of information of this type. This seems unlikely both in view of the presence of information about the economy which seems to be much more elementary and in the light of the difficulty which the groups interviewed in the Public Communications Group study (see Chapter 2) experienced in making sense of material in which similar relationships between economic variables were alluded to. Equally, perhaps these details fall outside the 'well-known scripts' for reporting such events to which van Dijk refers, or they are deemed simply to be of too little interest to readers. If either of these is the explanation, the consequence is to produce a form of economic reporting which, while outwardly possessing a coherent relational and propositional structure, requires, to be fully comprehended, a grasp of complex extra-textual information which belies the straightforward approach adopted in telling the story. In other words, these accounts may unwittingly be placing a higher premium on producing persuasive and credible assertions than on being readily comprehensible. And in the economic context of newspaper production this may even be justifiable in that the impression of authoritative reporting may be more successful in attracting readers than any duty towards public knowledge as a social good.

Attitudinal or emotional dimensions

Finally, van Dijk (1988, p. 85) suggests that the provision of 'information that also has attitudinal or emotional dimensions' when reporting news stories adds to their impact and persuasiveness. His prescriptions here are as follows:

1. Facts are better represented and memorized if they involve or arouse strong emotions.
2. The truthfulness of events is enhanced when opinions of different backgrounds or ideologies are quoted about such events, but in general those who are ideologically close will be given primary attention as possible sources of opinions.

Several examples have already been mentioned where the reporting of this event has involved appeals to the attitudinal or emotional. Amongst the most obvious is the organization of stories and/or the presence of dedicated secondary news stories in which the primary focus, often supported by headlines and graphics, is on mortgage rate cuts, with the result that personal economic benefit, where the interest rate cut most directly touches upon the lives of many readers, is prioritized. A focus on individual personal gain is likely to produce a stronger response in readers than any other focus.

Particular papers use other strategies to emphasize the attitudinal or emotional. The *Sun* and the *Guardian* illustrate their main stories with smiling pictures of the Chancellor which add little to the information value of the story but have the effect of increasing the concentration on personality. The *Guardian* takes this strategy further. In its 'follow-up' news coverage on an inside page, it calls upon five economic experts to comment on the general state of the economy. Their responses appear not only in the text of the story but also in separate boxes where they each 'speak for themselves', accompanied by a flattering portrait-style photograph. In this way, they are coded not merely as authoritative voices but as interesting individuals ('stars' in a sense) open to identification or emotional response in their own right. The narrow range of voices called upon to comment upon this event, mentioned already, supports van Dijk's second point. Whilst the various stories bring in a large quantity of commentators, some of whom offer conflicting interpretations of the consequences of the interest rate cut for government popularity, as economic or political practitioners or experts they are all broadly convergent in their social position and world-view, demonstrating that a greater quantity of voices need not necessarily introduce a broader range of opinion.

Newspapers' use of language within stories provides another opportunity to introduce attitudinal or emotional elements. Different newspapers operate different language styles which construct that newspaper's 'voice', enabling populist newspapers to adopt colloquial discourses even for 'serious' economic news. The *Daily Mirror*, for example, begins its coverage of the interest rate cut: 'More than six million homeowners were quids in last night following a cut in interest rates' (*Daily Mirror*, 9 March 1996, p. 2). The use of the colloquial 'quids in' rather than 'wealthier' or 'better off' seems to be intended to produce a connection with the reader at an emotional rather than an intellectual level, although the full story reveals a rather uneasy compromise – with precise and necessary (often numerical) information about the affected economic variables spiced up with phrases from colloquial speech ('experts *reckon* the moves will …'; 'haggling' instead of 'negotiating', 'cash' instead of 'money') where possible. This sort of colloquialism is generally absent from the editorial language of the mainstream press (with the exception of 'feelgood', which has been co-opted into mainstream press and political language) but quotations occasionally enable it to appear nevertheless (an example being Ian Amstad in *The Times* likening the circumstances of the interest rate cut to a 'bloodbath', as discussed earlier).

However, the most radical approach to the introduction of an 'emotional and attitudinal dimension' is that adopted by the *Sun* (reproduced in Figure 4.1). Here a comparatively earnest report on the interest rate cut, at least by that newspaper's standards, is pepped up by the introduction of a wealth of extraneous information on the theme that mortgage rates are as low as in 1966. This technique, which seems to be an attempt to attract readers who are less than compelled by interest rate changes to the 'feelgood' connotations of the Swinging Sixties, is an imaginative one at least – much more so than the dutiful, if almost apologetic, coverage given to the event by the *Sun*'s rival, the *Daily Mirror*. But it underlines a problem with economic news coverage for the popular press. The event is too important *not* to cover, but the economy is a dry and 'difficult' area for a populist newspaper, requiring complex explanation and contextualization which would be unrewarding for these newspapers' 'ideal' readers. The *Sun* has responded by treating readers as magpies, doing its duty to the story but hoping that something in the surrounding glittering trivia catches the eye of the least interested reader. There remains a tension between the divergent parts of this split-level approach, but if the *Sun*'s intention is to render the necessary-but-dull in as lively a fashion as possible, its approach is hard to fault.

A closer look at this story from the *Sun* may serve as a demonstration of many of the points already made about press reporting of the economy as exemplified by the coverage given to this one event. The story text covers similar territory to that in the other papers surveyed and is likely to be drawn from the same briefings. The primary focus is on mortgage rate cuts and the consequences of the interest rate cut for personal wealth. Following numerically based details of specific rates and savings, it quotes Kenneth Clarke in virtually the same words as in each other paper and opens up his interpretation for evaluation from four professional sources. Adair Turner is used as a source in the *Guardian* and, in precisely the same words, in the *Mail*, as is Gordon Brown in the *Guardian* and *The Times*. Lord Desai's intervention, although absent from the main coverage in the surveyed newspapers, is the focus of a follow-up story on the inside news pages of the *Guardian*. Only one source, Ian Shepherdson from Midland Bank, is not quoted in the other stories surveyed. Nevertheless, despite the similarity of sources and approach, each newspaper has structured the information in slightly different ways – variations in story order and prioritization, for example – although little can be read into such differences within such a small corpus of data. The *Sun*'s coverage lacks any consideration of housing market recovery or the financial markets but amplifies the comparison with 1966 (mentioned by all but the *Daily Mirror*, but otherwise merely to note that rates are the lowest for 30 years).

Besides sources and approaches, the *Sun*'s coverage demonstrates other hallmarks of economic news which are common to the coverage of this event. One of these seems to be the provision of a strong, if relatively simple, relational structure (the mortgage cuts, 'sparked' by the interest rate cuts, are detailed, after which the Chancellor's evaluation is reproduced and then contested by other voices). Combined with this, however, is evidence of the poor economic explanation at a detailed level which seems to be characteristic of our sampled coverage. To make sense of a number of statements, especially those from quoted sources, a considerable degree of extra-textual information covering relationships between parts of the economy and the meaning of specific terms is required. Clarke says the cut is 'a reward for keeping inflation down', implying a relationship between interest rates and inflation which is not made explicit. Nor is it clear who is being rewarded. Is it mortgage payers? In what way have they contributed to low inflation? And there is the question of the need for more rate cuts. Ian Shepherdson cites the benefit of 'extra money in people's pockets' (probably a reference to consumer spending) and lapses into economic vernacular to call for 'cheaper money', but the relevance of these factors to interest rate levels goes without further explanation. The other quoted sources provide additional instances where explanations appear to be lacking.

In its use of pictures, graphics and layout, the *Sun*'s story also provides support for other contentions made here about economic news. The layout of this story is oddly jumbled. The headline is clear and prominent, but the eye is not drawn beyond the first bolded paragraph of the text, whose inconsistent layout and font discourages a full reading. Instead, several other elements clamour for attention – the closely cropped grinning mugshot of the Chancellor, the capitalized sub-head 'Swinging Back to 1966' and below it the picture of the Beatles. The strong suggestion is that readers are not invited to read the story – text or graphics – in full, but to connect with any part of it which they find to be of interest. In this case, then, 'news context' (telling the story coherently) is made subordinate to 'newspaper context' (promoting the newspaper's style, authority or entertainment value to readers). A large part of this latter is geared to persuading readers of the authority (and, in the case of the *Sun*, the liveliness) of its coverage. We have already noted how, besides the authoritative and comparatively earnest tone of the text itself, this authority is signified by the referencing of a limited number of professional sources for comment. We have also noted the significance of numbers and precise information. The story text has its expected preponderance of numbers. Numbers are equally prominent in the graphics. Even the 1966 information is given an air of facticity and precision through being numerical or numerically expressed. Above the story text, the two mortgage rate graphics are of particular interest. They exemplify the kind of precision in reporting which might be expected to lend weight to the authority of the coverage, yet it is hard to imagine them being read in their entirety. That a complex chart in which repayment levels are matched against different types of mortgages and a detailed bar chart showing mortgage rate trends over seven years should be illustrating the same story as a selection of 1966 pop culture seems incongruous. Of course, the explanation is that the economic graphics are not expected to be read in full. Support for this is to be found in the explanatory text below the chart of repayment levels: 'Figures based on 25-yr mortgage with Halifax with £30,000 Miras limit and 15% MITR.' Not only is this likely to be close to incomprehensible to a non-expert reader, but it is printed in a font which is almost too small to read. Like much small print, it seems that it is reproduced out of duty rather than to inform, serving largely to underline the authority of the *Sun*'s coverage. Arguably, much of the story text itself – whose layout is hardly likely to encourage the casual or disinterested reader – serves a similar purpose, being more a persuasive marker for the facticity of the *Sun* as a newspaper than as something intended to inform its readers.

Conclusion

A case study of such limited breadth can only go so far in providing conclusions about the press and its coverage of the economy which are generalizable to other cases. And no attempt has been made here to concentrate on more than a single facet of economic news coverage – its employment of persuasive stylistic and rhetorical devices. Nevertheless, one striking conclusion can be drawn, at least from the coverage surveyed here. Informing the reader about the nature and significance of economic events seems to be by no means the only goal of economic news coverage in the press. Indeed, there is enough evidence in the coverage of this one event of contextualizing information *not* supplied or economic terms and the relationships between variables going *un*explained to suggest that this may not even be the principal goal of these stories when taken in their entirety. The main information is conveyed clearly in the opening paragraphs, as is the tone of the story (good news, bad news, mixed), but it would appear that each of our newspapers, if in different ways, is as concerned with 'newspaper context' as with 'news context' in constructing the bulk of the text. Throughout our analysis we have found evidence – in the crediting of comment to authoritative voices, in the preponderance of numbers as signifiers of precision, in the use of relational structures and of familiar scripts, and in devices to enhance the attitudinal or emotional appeal of stories – that much of the style and rhetoric of newspaper reporting of the economy is geared to persuading readers that each newspaper's assertions as to the nature of events and their significance is accurate and authoritative. In drawing this conclusion, particular weight has been given to the unlikely coverage given to the event in the *Sun*. The *Sun*, as a downmarket, populist newspaper, represents an extreme example. Here, as in other newspapers, the twin imperatives of providing information to inform readers and of providing information which persuades them of the authority and facticity of its coverage are sometimes in tension. Far more than for upmarket broadsheets, however, economic news provides a further problem for populist newspapers – how to package events which are often popularly perceived as 'difficult' and dull and which require complex, technical explanations in such a way as to make them lively and attractive for casual or disinterested readers. The *Sun*'s account is a remarkable example of a news story which attempts to perform all three of these functions with some degree of success, despite being at odds with more traditional conceptions of 'good' journalism (see Dahlgren, 1992).

Ultimately, the appearance of the 'newspaper context' within stories is geared to self-promotion and the construction of a reading 'public'. No matter how attractive the idea of the press as a 'fourth estate' within theories of liberal democracy, ultimately it is also an industry whose principal imperative is to maintain financial solvency by attracting and sustaining a readership (not only for stories, but also for advertising copy). Persuading readers of the authority and facticity of news coverage is a vital part of this imperative, as, to varying degrees, is a requirement also to entertain them. Andrew Wernick (1991) has postulated the central place occupied by promotion in all media, and the relationship between media and other cultural commodities. At first glance, economic news coverage seems an unlikely site for evidence of newspapers indulging in this interchange of promotional messages. But this is precisely what the rhetoric and style of coverage employed to report the economy appears to be engaged in. The stories we have looked at are promoting not only the adjacent advertising copy and those commodified aspects of the economy (such as mortgages) to which they refer, but above all the newspapers themselves.

Notes

1   For a broadly comparable approach based on news values, see Galtung and Ruge (1965).
2   For a general overview of news values and structure, see Bell (1991).
3   For this exercise, the principal focus of a story is taken to be the explanatory framework with which it opens; a secondary focus is one which is introduced early in the story and on which considerable emphasis seems to be placed.

5
Television, economy and the public's political attitudes

Neil T. Gavin and David Sanders

Introduction

The relationship between the economy and politics has long been of interest to the international political science community. The reviews by Paldam (1981) and Nannestad and Paldam (1994) give a clear impression of the extensive and ever-growing literature on the relationship between economic turbulence and party-political support. Much of the literature on economic voting (including studies at aggregate and at individual level) is based, implicitly or explicitly, on a conception of individual decision-making processes that owes a great deal to Anthony Downs (1957). His utility-maximizing voter has often stood in the wings as an unseen, but principal, character. This is usually embodied in formal models with the inclusion of a range of economic indicators as independent variables. Unemployment and inflation have figured in many of these models, although there has been experimentation with other economic variables (Husbands, 1985). In other words, many of the models are based on 'objective' economic indicators – notionally measuring turbulence in the real economy, but, in effect, based on aggregate economic statistics (often derived from government sources). However, a number of recent studies have begun to incorporate a wider range of factors, including aggregate questionnaire measures of economic attitudes: the public's perceptions of their immediate family financial circumstances, as well as attitudes towards the national economic situation (Kinder and Kiewiet, 1981; Sanders *et al.*, 1987; Sanders, 1991). There is still some dispute about whether the relevant variables should be retrospective or prospective in nature, i.e. embody perceptions about the immediate past or considerations of the future (Fiorina, 1981; Miller and Wattenberg, 1985; Lewis-Beck, 1986; Lockerbie, 1991; Monardi, 1994). Nevertheless, it is still the case that a Downsian appreciation of underlying dynamics is integral to many of the current studies that feature economic perceptions. Yet in the formal modelling of political support (be it at aggregate or individual level), there is often more effort expended in elaborating formal models, testing new variables and deploying advanced statistical techniques, than there is in teasing out the underlying decision-making calculus of the voter. There is sometimes little more than the dutiful nod in the direction of Downs, and more than a grain of truth in the comments of MacKuen *et al.* that 'after decades of attention, we are little beyond introspection in understanding the processes by which citizens come to perceive economic movements' (MacKuen *et al.*, 1992, p. 597).

Some recent studies have begun to explore some of the *exogenous* factors that impinge on the decision-making processes of the individual voter. Some of this research has focused on the impact of the media on policy-related attitudes. Page *et al.* (1987), Jordan and Page (1992) and Jordan (1993) have looked at the relationship between coverage of political issues and public policy preferences, and suggest that the media have an important impact on perceptions. In the area of economics, there is a small but growing body of research suggesting that media coverage has an impact on perceptions of the economy, and a direct or indirect influence on political support (Mosley, 1984; Mutz, 1992; Sanders *et al.*, 1993; Goidel and Langley, 1995; Blood and Phillips, 1995). All these studies focus on the press. Indeed, the latter two US studies focus rather narrowly on a single media source (the *New York Times*). Studies of media, economy and political support have juggled a number of broad factors, which are entered separately or all at once in the formal models. These include indicators of public perceptions of the economy (measured through polls); media *exposure* indicators (Holbrook and Garand, 1996; Hetherington, 1996); media representations of the economy (generally measured and numericized through content analysis); and a range of 'objective' economic indicators (the vital statistics of the economy). One study has used the public's *perception* of media coverage as an independent variable (MacKuen *et al.*, 1992). In more than one instance, media representations are gauged against the 'real' or 'objective' economy. A disjunction here is seen as an issue of potential distortion and, therefore, highly problematic (especially where the coverage is seen to have an impact on public attitudes).

Despite the fact that, in the UK at least, television is the public's most important and trusted source of political information (Dunleavy and Husbands, 1985; Independent Television Commission, 1996; Barnett, 1989), there has, to date, been only one comparable study of the role of television in public opinion formation (Gavin and Sanders, 1996). This study suggested that there is a stable and statistically significant relationship between economic coverage, perceptions of governmental economic competence and, indirectly, government popularity. The object of this chapter is to elaborate this model of the relationship between television news about the economy and measures of government competence and popularity. In particular, we consider the impact on the public's political perceptions of both 'real' economic variables and measures of *personal* economic experience. The first part of this chapter describes the theoretical model that we seek to test. The second outlines the precise way in which we operationalize it and the third presents our empirical findings. These are based on a time-series analysis of weekly data on television news coverage, aggregate economic perceptions, party support levels and the 'objective' condition of the UK economy for the period from November 1993 to November 1994. The results show a surprisingly weak set of relationships between television coverage of economic news and 'objective' or 'real' changes in macro-economic conditions. However, they also show a stable and robust relationship between news coverage and aggregate UK electoral opinion. We conclude by exploring some of the implications of our findings for models which rely on objective economic measures – especially where these rely on Downsian explanations of the voters' individual-level decision calculus.

The theoretical model

As noted above, the relationship between patterns of party support and the condition of the domestic economy has been extensively researched in recent years. In the UK context, there is considerable evidence to suggest that voters' economic perceptions play an important role in determining the overall levels of support for the main political parties (Sanders, 1991; Clarke *et al.*, 1997; Nadeau and Niemi, 1995). Although there are clearly a variety of ways of measuring voters' 'economic perceptions', recent studies have shown that, in the period since 1991, the crucial economic perception has been the electorate's view of the relative economic management competencies of the Conservative and Labour Parties.[1] The Conservatives' loss of their long-standing reputation for competent economic management, in the wake of the UK's ignominious exit from the EU's Exchange Rate Mechanism (ERM) in September 1992, appears to have played a decisive role in weakening their subsequent electoral support (Sanders, 1995, 1996).

But if perceptions of the relative economic management capabilities of the Conservative and Labour Parties have been so decisive in determining their support levels, the question arises as to what it is – in addition to the sort of shock associated with the 1992 ERM crisis – that influences perceptions of managerial competence. One immediate difficulty encountered in trying to evaluate this question empirically is that voters' management competence perceptions may be influenced by the very political preferences that they are supposed to 'explain'. Because a voter supports the Conservatives (for other reasons), he or she may also view the Conservatives as being more competent than Labour at running the economy. Fortunately, a recent study of the 1991–96 period shows that voters' perceptions of Conservative versus Labour economic management capabilities are exogenous to the two parties' support levels (Sanders and Price, 1997). For the purposes of the current analysis, we accordingly assume that voters' political preferences do not influence their economic management perceptions and that any causal connection between perceptions and preferences runs from the former to the latter.

We hypothesize, instead, that perceptions of the Conservatives' relative economic management capabilities are influenced by three major sets of factors: the 'objective' economy; the 'experienced' economy; and mass media coverage of economic news.

The performance of the 'objective' economy, as measured by official government statistics

Work on the relationship between the economy and party-political support has traditionally focused on unemployment and inflation as indicators of overall economic performance (e.g. MacKuen *et al.*, 1992). To these two standard measures we add two additional performance indicators that previous research has shown to be important in the UK political context: interest rates and the taxation burden on the average household (Sanders, 1996). We assume that an increase in any or all of these four indicators connotes 'poor' economic performance. The simple hypothesis that we seek to test is that poor (good) performance will be associated with a decline (increase) in the governing Conservative Party's economic competence ratings.

The extent to which changes in the 'experienced economy' are viewed positively or negatively by the electorate

It is often suggested that official government statistics on the macro-economy fail adequately to capture the economic turbulence that is actually experienced by voters. In December 1994, for example, when UK unemployment had been falling for eight successive quarters, opinion surveys showed that 61 per cent of UK voters felt 'economically insecure' and that fully 93 per cent believed that 'a lot of people are feeling that their jobs, earnings or homes are not safe'.[2] In our view, voters' experience of changing economic conditions are better captured through their retrospective assessments of changes in their own personal economic circumstances. Accordingly, we use the aggregate responses (percentage thinking that things have improved minus percentage thinking that things have worsened) to Gallup's regular survey question: 'How does the financial situation of your household now compare with what it was twelve months ago?' The responses to this question correspond strongly to the sorts of ideas which are considered to motivate a Downsian utility-maximizing voter (Downs, 1957). The question focuses explicitly on the individual and his or her family; it concerns an issue that we would expect the respondent to care about; it draws on information about which the respondent has intimate, first-hand knowledge; and it is directly comparative, inviting respondents to judge *changes* in their circumstances over time. These are precisely the sorts of calculation required for the respondent to make a judgement about the relative utilities associated with voting for party A rather than party B. In short, the replies reflect voters' direct perceptions of the impact of economic turbulence at first hand. The simple hypothesis that is suggested in this context is that aggregate improvements in voters' retrospective judgements about their own personal circumstances (i.e. rising 'personal retrospections') should serve to enhance the governing party's reputation for competent economic management; falling 'personal retrospections' should serve to damage that reputation.

The information that voters receive about the economy from the mass media and, in particular, from television coverage of economic news

While television is by no means the only mass medium to which voters are exposed, it seems clear that television's economic news coverage has the *potential* to shape voters' perceptions of the economy and, in turn, their political preferences. In the UK, millions view the BBC and ITN news broadcasts each evening. The economic coverage in such news is filled with information about (and evaluations of) the health or otherwise of the UK economy. In these circumstances, it would be surprising if the overall tenor of the coverage of economic news – in terms of whether each week's coverage was either broadly positive, neutral or negative – had no effect on the way in which voters thought about economics and politics. What is much more difficult to assess, of course, is the extent to which consistently 'bad news' might damage the governing party's image and the extent to which 'good news' might enhance it. In the absence of any detailed research on the types of news frame that might maximize the impact of economic news on public perceptions, our simple hypothesis about television news is that a greater weight of positive coverage of the economy will, other things being equal, tend to lead to an improvement in the ruling party's relative management competence ratings, while more negative coverage will be associated with a ratings fall.

Our initial supposition, then, is that voters' assessments of the incumbent party's relative economic management capabilities are likely to reflect the *objective* condition of the macro-economy, voters' direct experience of the economy (reflected in their reported personal retrospections), and television coverage of economic news. Such a claim, however, immediately begs another obvious question. What determines the type of television coverage of economic news (positive, negative or neutral) that is presented during a given time period? One obvious possibility that commends itself is that coverage reflects, more or less accurately, what is actually happening in the 'objective' economy (an assumption whose adequacy we will explore more fully below). In this case, improving economic indicators should be associated with 'positive' economic news coverage, and worsening indicators with negative coverage. This expectation, moreover, should manifest itself it two ways. First, coverage in relation to any given economic category (in our case, unemployment, inflation, interest rates or taxation) should be shaped by objective changes in the corresponding official statistics. Second, the overall balance of coverage (positive, neutral or negative) should reflect the 'objective' health of the economy, again as measured in the relevant official statistics.

A second, and much more elusive, general factor that may also affect coverage is news editors' views about the issues that are of concern to the audience. In this respect, editors may be loath to offer interpretations of economic developments that they believe will be markedly at odds with voters' actual economic experiences. The assumption here is that a news programme which consistently reports economic stories that are seriously at variance with the direct experiences of its viewers will soon find itself without an audience. Given the difficulty of establishing how news editors assess the receptiveness of their audiences to different sorts of news story, one immediately available measure of such receptiveness is the sort of personal retrospective economic perceptions variable referred to above. Although news editors are unlikely to be aware of the measured values of such a variable, their beliefs about the economy as experienced by their potential audience may reflect the same sort of intangible factors that generate aggregate changes in personal retrospections. With this in mind, we wanted to assess whether news coverage was at variance with the public's perception of its own financial circumstances.

While it is obviously and necessarily a simplification of a complex set of processes, Figure 5.1 summarizes the formal recursive model that is implied by the foregoing discussion. It embodies the following propositions:

- The incumbent party's relative management competence rating is: negatively affected by unemployment, inflation, interest rates and taxation; positively affected by rising aggregate personal retrospections; and positively affected by 'favourable' television coverage of economic news.
- 'Favourable' television news coverage is related negatively to unemployment, inflation, interest rates and taxation, and positively to rising aggregate personal retrospections.

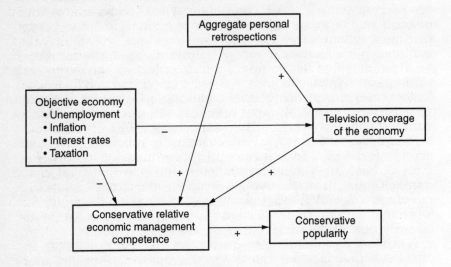

Figure 5.1 Simple recursive model of public opinion, summarizing the hypothesized relationship between personal retrospections, the 'objective' economy, television coverage, Conservative economic management competence and Conservative support. Negative signs (−) indicate a predicted negative relationship, positive signs (+) indicate a predicted positive relationship.

Operationalization: the variables and their measurement

The data that we employ in this study combine weekly opinion poll data on political preferences and economic perceptions, modified monthly data on the objective condition of the economy, and weekly data on television coverage of economic news derived from a content analysis of news broadcasts. The data cover the period from 17 November 1993 to 29 November 1994, giving a total of 54 weekly observations (resource constraints prevented us from sampling a longer period). Given that the data are time-series, we sought to ensure that all of the variables analysed were stationary prior to statistical estimation.

The opinion poll data were taken from the weekly breakdown of Gallup 9000 polls. Conservative support was measured by responses to the standard voting intention question: 'If there were a general election tomorrow, which party would you support?' The Conservatives' relative economic management competence was based on responses to the question: 'With Britain in economic difficulties, which party do you think could handle the problem best – the Conservatives ... or Labour?' The competence index was constructed by subtracting the percentage specifying Labour from the percentage specifying Conservative. As noted above, our measure of aggregate personal retrospections was derived from the question 'How does the financial situation of your household now compare with what it was twelve months ago?' by subtracting the percentage of respondents whose situation had worsened from the percentage whose situation had improved.[3] Dickey–Fuller tests showed that, for the time period under analysis, all three of these variables were stationary. They were accordingly entered into the subsequent analysis in undifferenced form.

The 'objective' macro-economic data were rather more complicated to deal with. Unemployment, inflation, interest rates (Bank of England base rate) and taxation[4] are generally measured on a monthly rather than a weekly basis. Converting interest rates (IR) into weekly form was relatively straightforward because base rates are changed on a specific day and it is therefore easy to determine the precise weeks in which changes took place. Although week-by-week variations in unemployment (UN) and inflation (INF) are impossible to determine, changes in unemployment and inflation are announced on specified, known dates. Using these dates, it was possible to determine the precise weeks in which knowledge about a change in either unemployment or inflation entered the public domain. Changes in unemployment and inflation were accordingly counted as having occurred from the time of their announcement. This strategy did not seem appropriate with regard to the taxation index (TAX), however.

The taxation index, as such, is not officially published and in this sense changes in it do not enter the public domain on a specified date. Accordingly, the taxation index was simply recorded in its monthly form, giving the variable a step-like quality. Dickey–Fuller tests on the level versions of the unemployment, inflation, interest rates and taxation variables showed that they were all non-stationary. Since the UN, INF and IR variables were genuinely measured on a weekly basis, first-differencing was a legitimate and easy route to achieving stationarity. UN, INF and IR were therefore first-differenced to produce variables we called dUN, dINF and dIR respectively. For TAX, however, first-differencing produced a distorted series in which change appeared to occur only in the first week of each month. We therefore calculated the monthly, rather than the weekly, first difference in TAX, which successfully produced a stationary series, dTAX.

The primary data for the study were derived from a content analysis of the economic coverage on the two principal UK weekday news programmes (BBC *Nine O'Clock News* and ITN *News At Ten*) between November 1993 and November 1994. The coding regime draws on and develops the work of Page *et al.* (1987), Gavin (1993), and Sanders *et al.* (1993), in the sense that the emphasis is placed on what is said by presenters, correspondents, experts and commentators. We did not code the comments of politicians: these may be significant in setting the public agenda, but were excluded on the grounds that, as partial and interested voices, they were unlikely to have an impact on the public's political perceptions. This is firmly in line with evidence from psychology on the contingencies of persuasive communication (Gergen and Gergen, 1981; Severin, 1988). The coding strategy, in addition, had to be tailored to the distinctive way in which UK television handles news about the economy. Unlike the editorializing of the press, the BBC and ITN are under a statutory obligation to present impartial and balanced news. This tends to give the presentation of the economy a very distinctive style. If we exclude what is said by politicians, there is little judgemental commentary on the rights and wrongs of particular economic policies. Instead, there is a great deal more on the ups and downs of the economy. The economy on television is often presented as a linear phenomenon, with coverage focusing on the upward and downward trends in a variety of different indicators (inflation, unemployment, wages and so on). Commentators regularly concentrate on what this means for the likely trajectory of the economy and for its overall health. The coding strategy reflected this: the emphasis was on the form that these economic trends took as well as their predicted trajectory (i.e. did the news present inflation as trending upwards; was unemployment seen to be going down; did the news suggest an increase in interest rates was imminent?).

We chose to focus on 11 economic news sub-themes. These concerned the issues of: inflation and prices; taxation; jobs and unemployment; sales and spending; wages, pay and disposable income; balance of payments and foreign trade; short-time working; interest rates; state borrowing and PSBR; and the housing market. A final broad category encompassed the 'economy generally' (the last including news about recovery and recession, production, investment and growth, as well as references to the general health of the economy).[5] The general aim was to produce a set of measurements that could be aggregated to give a reasonable overall picture of the coverage of the economy – see Gavin and Sanders (1996) for the analysis of the impact on public opinion of particular economic sub-themes, and for a focus on headline news alone. The main, all-encompassing aggregate measure that we employ is 'Allnews'. This composite variable takes all the thematic codes for the whole of a particular story and calculates whether there is a positive or negative balance (i.e. was it, on balance, a 'good' news story or a 'bad' news story, taking into consideration all the themes included?). A typical weekly period would have three or four such stories on either channel. If three of these were 'good news' stories, and one a 'bad news' story, the overall media coverage indicator would register +2 for that week's observation. The justification for this tactic is that, while errors might throw up the occasional mis-specified code for a specific item of news, it is extremely unlikely that they would unbalance the overall coding for an entire news story.

In addition to the overall coverage measured by 'Allnews', the analysis that we report here makes use of the four 'sub-theme' coverage measures which correspond to the four main 'objective' macro-economic factors that previous research has identified as being connected to UK party support patterns (unemployment, inflation, interest rate and taxation). Dickey–Fuller tests revealed that these four sub-theme coverage measures – as well as the composite Allnews measure – were stationary. As with the opinion poll data, therefore, the variables were entered into the analysis in undifferenced form.

Empirical results

A series of lagged-endogenous-variable ordinary least square (OLS) models was estimated using the general-to-specific econometric methodology advocated by Hendry and Doornik (1994). Cointegration methods were not deployed on the grounds that, with a time period of just over one year, the idea of specifying a long-term equilibrium relationship among the constituent variables in any given model (Harris, 1995) was inappropriate. The initial specifications all contain a series of 'event' dummy variables designed to correct the parameter estimates for any possible distortions deriving from the two most prominent political events which occurred during the time period analysed: the death of the Labour leader, John Smith, in May 1994, and the subsequent election of his successor, Tony Blair, in July. All of the exogenous variables except those relating to television coverage are entered at up to three lags, to reflect the possibility that the effects concerned may take up to three weeks to work through. The coverage variables, however, are entered only at (t) and $(t-1)$ in recognition of the sheer transience of 'news': if the effects of news do not act quickly, they are likely to be rapidly overtaken by the tide of 'new' news that follows them.

Column 1 of Table 5.1 reports a simple model of Conservative support (CON) for the 1993–94 period. The model is estimated merely to confirm that Conservative support is primarily a function of voters' perceptions of Conservative versus Labour economic management competence (CONM). The results indicate that only CONM has a significant (positive) effect on Conservative support. As anticipated in Figure 5.1, the remaining variables – overall coverage (Allnews), aggregate personal retrospections (PRET), unemployment, inflation, interest rates, taxation and the event dummies – all fail to exert a significant direct effect on CON: any indirect effects of these variables are clearly mediated through CONM.

Column 2 of Table 5.1 reports an equivalent model for Conservative economic management competence (CONM). The results here are rather more positive and go some way to confirming the causal structure outlined in Figure 5.1. Although personal retrospections and most of the objective macro-economic measures fail to provide significant coefficients, changes in interest rates (lagged 3 weeks) do appear to exert a significant and (as predicted) negative effect on CONM. The pattern of coefficients on the event dummies shows that although the Conservatives' competence ratings dropped briefly ($b = -3.92$) in the week of John Smith's death, they recovered by almost the same amount the following week ($b = 4.37$); the ratings dropped again with Tony Blair's appointment ($b = -3.11$) – though this effect (like all the others) discounted rapidly at the rate of 0.60 per week, the coefficient on the lagged dependent variable. Most importantly, however, the column 2 model shows that the Allnews variable, lagged one week, has a significant, positive coefficient ($b = 0.17$), indicating that voters' perceptions of the Conservatives' managerial competence are indeed influenced by the overall tenor of television coverage of economic news. What is particularly important about this finding is that the estimate of the Allnews effect controls both for changes in the 'objective' economy and for the level of personal retrospections (i.e. the public's subjective and direct appreciation of its economic circumstances). Television news coverage appears to influence competence perceptions independently of any effects on those perceptions that might derive either from voters' perceptions of their own economic circumstances or from external, 'objective' economic forces.

Column 3 of Table 5.1 reports the results of our preliminary efforts to specify the major direct influences on television news coverage. The results show that neither personal retrospections nor any of the event dummies (nor most of the measures of the objective economy) appear to exert any effect on the overall weekly balance of coverage. The only exogenous variable that produces a significant coefficient is the change in unemployment, lagged three weeks. These results offer an intriguing insight into what might seem like the somewhat arbitrary nature of television coverage of economic news (a point to which we will return later). The unemployment issue excepted, overall coverage seems to bear little relation either to what is going on in the 'objective' economy or to voters' personal experiences of the economy over the previous year. It is important to acknowledge, however, that the dependent variable here (Allnews) relates to the combined output of BBC and ITN. While these organizations strive to produce balanced and impartial coverage, they have no obligation to make their combined output reflect the ebb and flow of economic turbulence. With this in mind, the obvious next step was to isolate the news output from the respective news programmes and ascertain the nature of the relationship between their coverage and measures of subjective experience of the economy (as well as 'objective' economic indicators).

The results are reported in Tables 5.2 and 5.3. Table 5.2 shows the consequences of re-estimating the Table 5.1 'Allnews' model using separate measures for BBC and ITN coverage as dependent variables. The lagged unemployment terms continue to figure significantly in the BBC model, which also indicates a significant effect for changes in interest rates. The ITN model, however, yields no significant coefficients whatsoever. Table 5.3 reports the consequences of relating each of our major 'objective' macro-economic measures – unemployment, inflation, interest rates and taxation – to the corresponding *news* coverage sub-theme: objective measures of unemployment are used to predict the character (positive or negative) of news coverage about unemployment; objective inflation is used to predict inflation coverage; and so on. The results again suggest very little correspondence between objective macro-economic changes and coverage. Only the unemployment equation (column 1) yields a significant (and negative) coefficient: increases in unemployment were systematically associated with negative unemployment news coverage. This obviously raises the issue – though it is not one that we can even start to address here – of the criteria that news editors do in fact employ when they decide (1) to run a particular story and (2) to put a particular construction upon it (though see Harrington, 1989; and Gavin and Goddard, 1998).[6]

What all of this indicates is that, unemployment apart, television coverage of economic news is unrelated to short-term changes in objective or subjective economic conditions. This does not necessarily imply, however, that news editors were wilfully ignoring either 'the real economy' or voters' concerns. It is important to note that, throughout the period analysed, unemployment was consistently ranked – and by a very large margin – as 'the most urgent problem facing the country at the present time'.[7] In this respect, the fact that news coverage was clearly related to changes in unemployment could imply that editors were actually quite sensitive to the most important economic issue of the day in determining the character of the news coverage that they presented.

Table 5.1 Models of Conservative support, management competence and television coverage

Independent Variable	Column 1 Conservative support$_t$ (CON$_t$)		Column 2 Conservative management competence$_t$ (CONM$_t$)		Column 3 Overall balance of television news (Allnews$_t$)	
CON$_{t-1}$	+0.38**	(0.19)				
CONM$_t$	+0.73***	(0.16)				
CONM$_{t-1}$	−0.21	(0.22)	+0.57***	(0.19)		
PRET$_t$	−0.07	(0.1)	+0.02	(0.12)	+0.02	(0.29)
PRET$_{t-1}$	−0.07	(0.12)	−0.04	(0.16)	−0.21	(0.36)
PRET$_{t-2}$	−0.06	(0.12)	−0.12	(0.15)	+0.25	(0.35)
PRET$_{t-3}$	−0.06	(0.1)	−0.07	(1.3)	−0.29	(0.30)
Allnews$_t$	+0.10	(0.07)	+0.06	(0.09)		
Allnews$_{t-1}$	+0.04	(0.07)	+0.17*	(0.08)	+0.11	(0.18)
dUN$_t$	−4.58	(4.39)	+6.64	(5.44)	−15.85	(12.59)
dUN$_{t-1}$	−3.85	(4.41)	−6.24	(5.45)	+9.71	(12.58)
dUN$_{t-2}$	−0.78	(4.00)	+0.31	(5.12)	−8.79	(12.09)
dUN$_{t-3}$	−3.56	(4.38)	+3.22	(5.59)	−25.82*	(12.07)
dINF$_t$	−1.83	(1.80)	+0.71	(2.31)	−4.81	(4.65)
dINF$_{t-1}$	+0.62	(1.84)	+0.30	(2.32)	−3.31	(5.28)
dINF$_{t-2}$	+0.05	(1.25)	−1.50	(1.57)	+3.06	(3.73)
dINF$_{t-3}$	−1.02	(1.21)	+0.69	(1.53)	+0.34	(3.69)
dIR$_t$	+2.27	(1.79)	+1.20	(2.27)	−3.64	(5.10)
dIR$_{t-1}$	−2.03	(1.78)	−1.05	(2.25)	+5.91	(5.29)
dIR$_{t-2}$	+2.18	(2.05)	+1.85	(2.52)	−2.09	(5.92)
dIR$_{t-3}$	−0.96	(2.42)	−7.87**	(2.57)	+2.68	(6.13)
dTAX$_t$	+3.11	(5.63)	+0.48	(7.24)	−19.58	(16.80)
dTAX$_{t-1}$	−7.19	(5.42)	+8.13	(6.71)	+0.43	(16.22)
dTAX$_{t-2}$	−3.76	(5.25)	−3.70	(6.49)	+1.15	(15.13)
dTAX$_{t-3}$	−4.97	(4.89)	−5.59	(6.03)	+7.29	(14.46)
Smith$_t$	+1.97	(1.51)	−4.42*	(1.65)	−2.59	(3.92)
Smith$_{t-1}$	−0.62	(1.81)	+4.07*	(2.11)	+0.69	(4.12)
Smith$_{t-2}$	−0.30	(1.41)	−1.81	(1.76)	+0.17	(4.24)
Blair$_t$	−0.56	(1.32)	+0.80	(1.62)	+3.84	(3.77)
Blair$_{t-1}$	+2.07	(1.31)	−3.04*	(1.52)	−0.67	(3.67)
Blair$_{t-2}$	+1.64	(1.44)	−0.24	(1.81)	−5.60	(4.04)
Constant	+2.59	(3.86)	+8.29	(4.35)	−8.08	(6.22)
Corrected R^2	0.63		0.81		−0.27	
Durbin–Watson	1.48		2.32		2.19	
LM(6) serial correlation	17.85 [p=0.007]		12.50 [p=0.05]		5.38 [p=0.50]	
Ramsey's RESET	4.55 [p=0.033]		0.24 [p=0.63]		0.24 [p=0.63]	
DF unit root in residuals	−5.49		−8.59		−7.64	
N	50		50		50	

Table 5.1 (*Cont.*)

Estimation by OLS. Standard errors in parentheses, probability values in brackets. *** signifies estimate is significant at the 0.001 level; ** at 0.01; * at 0.05. Sample is 1 December 1993 to 29 November 1994.

Reduced-form versions of each model, dropping all non-significant predictors, were estimated, with the following results:

[1] $CON_t =$ 6.36^{***} + $0.16^{*}CON_{t-1}$ + 0.60^{***} $CONM_t$ + u_t
              (1.75)   (0.08)   (0.07)
Ctd R^2 = 0.66 DW = 1.81   LM(6) serial corr. = 6.75 [0.34]   RESET = 0.31 [0.57] ARCH (6) = 2.95 [0.81]

[2] $CONM_t$ = 9.46^{***} + 0.60^{***} $CONM_{t-1}$ + 0.16^{**} $Allnews_{t-1}$ − 6.83^{***} dIR_{t-3}
              (2.00)   (0.08)   (0.06)   (1.67)
− 4.35^{***} $Smith_t$ + 3.90^{**} $Smith_{t-1}$ − 3.14^{*} $Blair_{t-1}$ + u_t
              (1.25)   (1.30)   (1.25)
Ctd R^2 = 0.66 DW = 2.28   LM(6) serial corr. = 9.89 [0.13]   RESET = 0.00 [0.97] ARCH (6) = 4.50 [0.61]

[3] $Allnews_t$ = -1.38^{**} + 0.16 $Allnews_{t-1}$ -15.30^{*} dUN_{t-3} + u_t
              (0.48)   (0.14)   (7.83)
Ctd R^2 = 0.06 DW = 2.09   LM(6) serial corr. = 10.98 [0.09]   RESET = 0.69 [0.40] ARCH (6) = 5.75 [0.45]

Key:

Allnews	Overall balance (positive versus negative) of television news coverage of the economy
CONM	Conservative versus Labour economic management competence
CON	Conservative support
PRET	Aggregate personal retrospections
dUN	Weekly change in the percentage rate of unemployment
dINF	Weekly change in the percentage rate of inflation
dIR	Weekly change in interest rates (BoE base rate)
dTAX	Monthly change in taxation index
Smith	Dummy on Smith's death (May 1994)
Blair	Dummy on Blair's accession as leader (July 1994)

Table 5.2 Models of BBC and ITN coverage of the economy

Independent Variable	Dependent variable			
	Column 1 BBC overall coverage		Column 2 ITN overall coverage	
BBC_{t-1}	+0.10	(0.19)		
ITN_{t-1}			+0.24	(0.19)
$PRET_t$	−0.03	(0.17)	+0.05	(0.16)
$PRET_{t-1}$	+0.02	(0.21)	−0.26	(0.19)
$PRET_{t-2}$	+0.08	(0.20)	+0.19	(0.19)
$PRET_{t-3}$	−0.13	(0.17)	−0.12	(0.16)
dUN_t	−4.27	(7.22)	−12.75	(6.70)
dUN_{t-1}	−7.62	(7.15)	−0.34	(6.74)
dUN_{t-2}	−2.92	(6.93)	−4.43	(6.46)
dUN_{t-3}	−13.27*	(6.92)	−12.23	(6.42)
$dINF_t$	−1.99	(2.67)	−2.89	(2.52)
$dINF_{t-1}$	−0.93	(3.00)	−2.11	(2.87)
$dINF_{t-2}$	+0.59	(2.13)	+1.18	(2.00)
$dINF_{t-3}$	−0.62	(2.11)	+1.00	(1.97)
dIR_t	−5.82*	(2.92)	+2.57	(2.72)
dIR_{t-1}	+4.55	(3.15)	+0.87	(2.81)
dIR_{t-2}	−2.47	(3.44)	+0.91	(3.15)
dIR_{t-3}	−1.14	(3.56)	+1.05	(3.24)
$dTAX_t$	−9.94	(9.64)	+9.64	(9.12)
$dTAX_{t-1}$	+5.53	(9.19)	−6.98	(8.48)
$dTAX_{t-2}$	+8.39	(8.86)	−6.74	(8.04)
$dTAX_{t-3}$	+5.26	(8.45)	+2.39	(7.88)
$Smith_t$	−0.81	(2.25)	−1.38	(2.09)
$Smith_{t-1}$	−0.52	(2.36)	+1.48	(2.19)
$Smith_{t-2}$	−0.38	(2.42)	+0.28	(2.30)
$Blair_t$	+2.98	(2.17)	+0.74	(2.00)
$Blair_{t-1}$	−1.55	(2.13)	+1.21	(1.94)
$Blair_{t-2}$	−5.25*	(2.33)	+1.23	(2.15)
Constant	−2.46	(3.53)	−5.14	(3.41)
Corrected R^2	0.01		−0.24	
Durbin–Watson	2.16		2.26	
LM(6) serial correlation	3.34 [p=0.70]		13.53 [p=0.04]	
Ramsey's RESET	2.88 [p=0.09]		6.34 [p=0.01]	
DF unit root in residuals	−7.57		−8.32	
N	50		50	

Estimation by OLS. Standard errors in parentheses, probability values in brackets. *** signifies estimate is significant at the 0.001 level; ** at 0.01; * at 0.05. Sample is 1 December 1993 to 29 November 1994.

Table 5.3 Models of the objective economy and television economic news themes

	Dependent variable			
	Unemployment coverage	Inflation coverage	Taxation coverage	Interest rate coverage
Constant	+0.09** (0.31)	Constant +0.29 (0.17)	Constant −0.53** (0.14)	Constant −0.20 (0.14)
dUN_t	−7.41* (3.87)	$dINF_t$ +0.32 (1.22)	$dTAX_t$ −4.41 (3.23)	dIR −1.50 (1.27)
dUN_{t-1}	+1.94 (3.89)	$dINF_{t-1}$ +0.74 (1.21)	$dTAX_{t-1}$ +5.21 (3.02)	dIR_{t-1} −0.61 (1.27)
dUN_{t-2}	+2.02 (4.34)	$dINF_{t-2}$ +0.80 (1.23)	$dTAX_{t-2}$ +3.00 (3.02)	dIR_{t-2} −0.61 (1.27)
dUN_{t-3}	−1.39 (3.89)	$dINF_{t-3}$ −0.21 (1.13)	$dTAX_{t-3}$ −0.34 (3.02)	dIR_{t-3} −1.50 (1.27)
dUN_{t-4}	−1.58 (3.87)	$dINF_{t-4}$ −0.41 (1.14)	$dTAX_{t-4}$ −1.58 (3.07)	dIR_{t-4} −3.03 (1.69)
Ctd R^2	0.00	−0.09	0.03	0.02
DW	1.86	2.00	1.46	1.52
LM(6) serial				
Correlation test	5.15 [0.52]	10.6 [0.10]	7.37 [0.29]	6.18 [0.40]
RESET test	0.12 [0.72]	0.53 [0.46]	4.77 [0.03]	0.03 [0.86]
ARCH test	2.33 [0.87]	9.92 [0.13]	8.74 [0.19]	5.14 [0.53]

Estimation by OLS. Standard errors in parentheses, probability levels in brackets. ** signifies estimate is significant at the 0.01 level; * at 0.05. $N = 49$. Sample is 8 December 1993 to 29 November 1994. Variable definitions for predictors as in Table 5.1. The coverage variables refer to the overall balance of positive *versus* negative stories within the specified sub-theme.

Conclusions and discussion

What has the preceding analysis shown? First, we have established that economic news on television (and, for that matter, the 'objective', 'subjective' or event variables) has no discernible direct impact on government popularity. Popularity is, however, influenced by perceptions of the government's economic competence. Second, and more importantly, the results suggest that television news *is* related to perceptions of government economic competence and can affect government popularity through this indirect path. The model of government competence that includes television economic news is also robust. When objective and subjective measures of economic 'experience' are entered in the model, all but the interest rate variable failed to achieve statistical significance.[8] In this context we can be relatively confident in ruling out an alternative reading of the connection between news and public perceptions of government economic competence – that news simply and faithfully represents the lived experience of the public, and that it is this experience, rather than television representation, that informs views of government competence, and, in turn, helps to drive government popularity. When we turned our attention to modelling economic news we found it unrelated to subjective experience of economic turbulence. This was the case when we looked at the total output of news and at the separate coverage from the two respective channels. A few 'objective' measures do appear to be related to news output (a feature that was evident in the modelling of Allnews; the coverage of BBC output, and BBC's output directly on the topic of unemployment).

The model we have outlined does suggest that economic news has a stable and consistent effect on public opinion (albeit of modest proportions). Yet this formal model cannot tell us a great deal about the subtleties of the individual decision-making processes involved (Gavin, 1997). We may have to look elsewhere for these. An intriguing glimpse of the processes involved *can* be seen in the focus group work reported in Chapter 1. It is hardly surprising that the deluge of economic news has a relatively modest impact, when the audience is occasionally confused by the technical detail involved or loses interest in (and, therefore, engagement with) coverage it does not understand. Equally, the modest impact is less of a mystery if we appreciate that viewers are capable of reinterpreting the news to suit their own political predispositions or ignore it because of its perceived political biases. In this sort of context it is hardly surprising that the news on television has no profound effect on public opinion. However, one thing is clear. In future, economic news ought (in the UK at least) to be a significant additional consideration when specifying models of public opinion on the economy (over and above the conventional inventory of 'subjective' and 'objective' variables). Although this is likely to prove difficult (given the lack of archived news transcripts and the time-consuming nature of its analysis), it is an aspect of the dynamics of public opinion that can no longer be ignored or excluded.

We would also suggest that our results have some bearing on the way in which the political science community understands the decision calculus reflected in formal models of public support for the government. Here our conclusions are, inevitably, rather more tentative and speculative. The way one reads the results is contingent on how the respective variables are conceptualized. We felt that the personal retrospective measure in our analysis should pick up the public's direct experience of any (or all) of the aspects of economic turbulence that Downsian theory considers important (from the experience of rising interest rates, to the public registering the upward creep of prices; from people seeing the impact on their families of tax rises, to their direct experience of periods of family unemployment). This might be conceptualized as a direct reflection of lived experience of the economy. However, in the event, this factor did not show up as a determinant of perceptions of government economic competence (or, indeed, of economic news).

On the other hand, 'objective' economic variables often seem to be conceptualized as a fairly accurate (and, somehow, more 'real') reflection of economic turbulence, and it is in this context that they figure in many models of public opinion (Paldam, 1981; Nannestad and Paldam, 1994). However, these are, essentially, statistics about the economy (often derived from government sources), and it is important to remind ourselves that these are aggregated, weighted, averaged and adjusted (Marsh, 1989; Horn, 1993). In this sense, they are at least one stage removed from the economy that people experience. They are not directly or unambiguously 'real' in any sense (if by 'real' we mean unambiguously related to the public's experience of the economy).

There is, however, one sense in which these statistics are directly and tangibly real: in their manifestation as televisual representations of the economy. In this connection, it is very important to note that our news measures were a numerical summary of coverage which more often than not reports a complex and interrelated array of economic statistics. Coverage is often stimulated by the release of official figures – it is often about the 'objective' or 'real' economy. It is this televisual reality (measured, however roughly, through content analysis) that appears to have an impact on the public's perception of governmental competence (while objective and subjective measures largely fail to register). This conceptualization opens up the possibility that we may misinterpret the results from models of public opinion that incorporate only economic statistics. If a relationship emerges, this may be a function not of the impact on public opinion of the 'objective' economy *per se*, but of the coverage of that economy. This brings into sharp focus the problematic nature of the distinction that is often drawn between 'objective' or 'real' variables and their subjective counterparts. It has been assumed in the past that Downsian explanations gave substance to statistical models that linked the objective economy and public opinion, and that the information that the public use to frame decisions revolved around their direct and lived experiences of the economy. In the light of our results, this assumption looks more shaky than it did. Our results offer a potentially different explanation of how these different elements hang together, and highlight some of the ambiguities that enter our conceptualization of what the different variables actually measure.

Our results also shed some light on the practice of relating news coverage variables to measures of the 'objective' economy (Blood and Phillips, 1995; Goidel and Langley, 1995). It is extremely important to note, however, that in the past researchers working within the media studies tradition have been criticized for suggesting that government statistics offer a clear and real approximation to the objective reality of economic conditions, against which televisual representations can be judged. Harrison (1985, pp. 26–46), in particular, criticized the Glasgow University Media Group (1980) for judging televisual representations against official statistics, suggesting that:

It is futile to look for it [television news] to conform to the reality of official statistics, both because the statistics themselves are by no means a pure distillation of reality, and because despite its naturalistic style television news is neither a sample survey nor a cross-section of reality. (Harrison, 1985, p. 43)

If there is an element of truth in this, it is, in fact, rather surprising that *any* of the objective economic variables should prove significant (as they did) when we modelled the determinants of economic news. However, it is plausible to suggest that they figure there as a function of journalistic news value criteria (as figures emanating from official, accredited and self-authorizing sources), rather than as a reflection of the 'realities' experienced by ordinary citizens (again, it should be noted that subjective perceptions of the economy failed to achieve statistical significance when entered in the same model). This re-emphasizes the danger of taking official statistics as an unambiguous reflection of lived experience of the economy, or suggesting that they might or should figure on news irrespective of normal journalistic news values. In this respect, we do not suggest (as Harrison does) that relating news to the 'objective economy' is futile; only that we need to be careful in interpreting the results – especially where there is doubt that the official figures simply and faithfully reflect or represent the public's lived experience of the economy. Instead, we suggest that the results need to be interpreted in the light of a fuller understanding of editorial considerations and newsroom practices.

Appendix

The coverage was divided by theme for the purpose of coding. There were 11 themes, including the following.

Prices

Under this heading were stories concerning: the price or cost of goods; inflation; reference to cheaper or more costly goods; bills, charges or fares; and discounts.

Tax

This grouped references to: tax, VAT and national insurance; and duties, tariffs, excise, levies and customs.

Jobs

Under this heading came items on: closures and companies going 'out of business', 'bust', 'to the wall' or 'shutting'; jobs, jobless, redundancies and (un)employment; staffing and posts; and axing and lay-offs. Increases in part-time, seasonal or women's as opposed to men's jobs were not coded.

Consumption

This included news on: buying, shopping for, or purchasing goods; the sale of, or spending on goods; consumption, and benefit for the consumer; and demand.

Disposables

This category was reserved for news on: living standards; pay, wages, income and earnings; wealth; and consumer confidence.

Foreign trade

This included references to: the deficit, imports and exports; the trade balance or surplus; trade figures; and the balance of payments.

Short-time work

This included references to night shifts, short-time working, holiday truncation, and shortening of the working week.

Interest rates

All references to interest rate, base rates, mortgage rates, loan and lending rates were coded under this rubric.

State borrowing

Under this category were classified references to PSBR, public borrowing, government borrowing, and government or public debt.

Housing

A separate category was set up to include: house prices; house buying, purchasing, selling and turnover; and the housing market.

General economic

This large and catch-all category included general references to: the economy, trade, business, and industry; recovery, upswing, upturn, 'boom' and prosperity; and recession, downturn, slow-down, slump and 'bust'. Also included were references to production, output, growth and GDP. Finally, this category included references to invest(ment) and business confidence.

The tagging of these pieces of news coverage proceeded as one might expect: more jobless coded negative; sales down negative; interest rates down positive, etc. The exception to this was the prices/inflation and pay coding. In the former case it was noted that prices rarely if ever decrease. So, there was a danger of any mention of inflation being negative, when, in fact, much news on inflation was positive. It was decided to code as negative if inflation was 'rising', 'going up', 'coming back' or 'starting up'. On the other hand if inflation was 'steady', 'stable', 'slight', 'low', 'unchanged' or 'zero', this was coded positive. The same was done with references to inflation 'decreasing', 'falling', 'threatening to turn negative', 'down' or 'slashed'. On pay a similar sort of coding strategy was applied. If pay was 'declining', 'diminishing', 'being squeezed' or 'reduced' it was coded as negative. If pay was rising, but at a lower rate than inflation, this too was coded negative (likewise, if pay was 'static', at the 'same level', or 'not rising'). A positive code was registered for references to pay 'increasing' or 'getting better'.

Acknowledgement

This research was funded through the generous support of the Economic and Social Research Council (Ref: R000221336).

Notes

1   The year 1991 was the first in which data on relative economic management competence were collected on a regular monthly basis. The competence index employed here uses responses to the question: 'With Britain in economic difficulties, which party do you think could handle the problem best – the Conservatives ... or Labour?' The index is constructed by subtracting the percentage specifying Labour from the percentage specifying Conservative.
2   Gallup Poll, December 1994, reported in the *Daily Telegraph*, 12 December 1994.
3   Because this question was asked only in the first two weeks of each month, it was necessary to interpolate the values of the personal retrospections variable for the third and fourth weeks of each month.
4   The taxation index is constructed by subtracting the Central Statistical Office's monthly inflation measure from its monthly tax and price index.
5   The guidelines for identifying each of these themes are described in more detail in the Appendix.
6   These topics are touched upon in Chapter 8 where economic journalists from the UK and Sweden discuss their experiences.
7   Gallup Political Index (various months) 1994–95.
8   This finding is not particularly surprising. Interest rates have a direct, tangible and immediate impact on the public (through credit and mortgage commitments). Moreover, raising interest rates is visibly the act of the incumbent Chancellor, and in this context the government's capacity to deflect the associated blame is diminished.

6
Between state and market: the economy in Swedish television news

Bo Mårtenson

Introduction

The increasing impact of economics has characterized social and political development in the 1990s. The general market prerogative, the internationalization of financial business and European integration have led to ongoing restructuring and redefining of the economic realm. The role of media exposure in general and news journalism in particular is a central, yet problematic, aspect of this process, since it affects the understanding of 'the economy' as a public area of national and political debate. In this context, enquiry into the performance of popular, broadcast economic journalism in Sweden produces some specific observations. The transition from welfare politics and Keynesian economics to deregulation and neo-liberal theory hardly makes the country unique in a European context. Nonetheless, considering the starting position and the rapidity of the process, the Swedish 'shift of system' provides a quite distinctive case. In a relatively short period of time, changes in the political and economic spheres have been paralleled by obvious changes and reformulations at the discursive and rhetorical levels (Boréus, 1994; Hugemark, 1994).

In this chapter, I intend to identify and briefly to discuss the dominant and typical ways in which national economic topics are presented in the news reports of Swedish television. The focus is on the specific characteristics of broadcast journalism in relation to a subject highly marked by abstractions, symbols and expectations. The study deals with the economic news reports of the three main Swedish television newscasts around the presentation of the national budgets in 1994, 1995 and 1996.[1] My general aim is to map out the televized media reports in terms of their contribution to 'the economy' as a public issue (Corner *et al.*, 1990). I will show that the study of content and form suggests that particular journalistic strategies and their consequent forms of representation (and of addressing the audience) give a specific character to economic reporting on Swedish television. The strong tradition of public service broadcasting is a key factor, but so too are its reformulation and adaptation to a new situation. An emphatic future orientation is evident, with expectations, outlooks and forecasts dominating; and market reactions and the international scene are now highly important elements. Just how the media represent a growing autonomy of the economic sphere (see Jensen, 1987) has important consequences for its definition as a public issue, and also affects citizen identities (Dahlgren, 1995).

Sweden: a changing economy

In Sweden, as in other countries, economic journalism in general has expanded over the last decade, in print as well as in broadcast media. Defined broadly the field of 'economic journalism' now comprises a whole range of media output, from specialized business and financial journals to television talk shows. Journalism about economic phenomena, 'with a public interest', is not confined to matters of economic policy or macro-economics alone. That the mediated economy is now present in a variety of media and journalistic genres is clearly a significant factor in explaining audience reception and citizens' perceptions of economic matters. However, even if this is admitted, news reporting is still the core and origin of economic journalism, and the obvious primary object of study.

Parallel to the growing level of media coverage, the area of the economy itself has undergone important and noticeable changes in Sweden. Following deregulation and privatization measures and periods of turbulent bank and real estate crises in the late 1980s, the Swedish welfare model was meeting increasing challenges.[2] With the liberal-conservative parties forming a government after the 1991 parliamentary elections, this process was reinforced. The crisis of government finances, above all the large budget deficit and the rapidly growing national debt, became the leading economic topic of debate, in which the media were urged to help create a public 'crisis consciousness'. So, viewed on a general level, the formerly relatively stable and optimistic view of Swedish economic politics as that of allocating the benefits of economic growth in a collective and fair manner, has turned into its reverse. During the whole of the 1990s, the issue has become one of allocating the burdens, the cuts or 'savings' of public economy, and of the possible defence of the welfare system. In the Swedish case, this reversal is often debated in terms of awakening to a harsh reality. The backwardness of the former idyllic isolation is contrasted with the need to adapt to the laws of the international economic community. The interplay or conflict of the state versus 'the market' summarizes the core issue concerning the Swedish economy in the 1990s.

During the same period, the Swedish media system has also been restructured significantly, with deregulation measures particularly affecting the broadcast media. With the opening up of commercial television channels in 1989, TV3 and later TV4 have been added to the national television scene, influencing and challenging the Swedish Television Corporation channels, TV1 and TV2. Although adaptation to the new competitive situation has been clearly noticeable in the traditional channels, the public service ideal still determines most television news reporting (Dahlgren, 1995). As I will show in the case of economic news, this involves a popular educational ambition to 'explain', approached through partly conflicting strategies by journalists, and with a certain emphasis on consensus. This is to be found in TV1 and TV2, as well as in the commercial TV4.

The economy in the media

Economic issues have a number of characteristics which carry implications for journalistic treatment. These also affect the way in which different economic events are placed or defined within a wider public context of the economy, or within the narrower contexts of industry, markets or unemployment. In the Swedish case, the following characteristics seem relevant to an understanding of the contribution of broadcast television news.

The term '*the* economy' corresponds in economic theory to a concept of the totality, or the accumulation of material and financial activities, measured as gross national product or income. However, in a cultural perspective 'the economy' also has the quality of reification. This notion implies a certain independent action or power assigned to it, which has to be understood or interpreted (Emmison, 1983). Both the economic and cultural connotations of 'the economy' are relevant in the processes of reporting economic matters. Moreover, the systemic character of economic issues is also a basic characteristic (Emmison, 1983; Corner *et al.*, 1993). On the general level, the system contains a number of components of the macro- and micro-economy, interrelated in a complex manner, primarily growth, inflation, employment, investment, public spending and state borrowing. These components function as indicators, and grasping or reporting 'the economy' always involves a selection of indicators and an implicit or explicit understanding of the relations between them. One may talk of a hierarchy of indicators, where the rank order is not self-evident. This aspect is crucial to economic theory and naturally affects the news value of economic events and processes.

It is also important to recognize the symbolic side of the economy. Admitting that the material economy is always in one sense symbolic, one could argue that the economic sphere is growing more symbolic. This trend is largely explained by the growth of the financial sector and the international exchange markets. Economic information serving the markets makes up an increasingly important part of economic activities, also affecting the demand for economic news among ordinary citizens. Additionally, there is a growing 'commodification of symbolic values', pointing to the increased marketing of rights, formulas, licences, etc. Generally, with the growth of markets and financial activities, expectations, forecasts, judgements and even sentiments now seem more important to the economy. This symbolic advance has implications both for the functions of the international and national economy and for the journalistic reporting of it.

As a static or synchronic system, the economy can appear complex and difficult to grasp for any citizen. In reception of economic news, factors of comprehension and systemic or 'technical' understanding are more important than in most other issues (Höijer, 1989). Diachronically, however, the economy often emerges as being relatively uncomplicated. The constantly moving nature of the economy is a significant characteristic, and this process paradoxically often appears or is reported as a fairly simple or one-dimensional one (involving variously 'balance', 'growth' and 'recession'). Simplicity depends on a reduction in the number of indicators, and the establishment of fixed or presupposed causal relations between a limited number of components. This corresponds, of course, in economic theory, to the necessary 'modelling' of the economy. However, in a communicative and cultural perspective, it has important implications for the reporting of economic change, seen as the narratives, or stories of the national economy, underlying most economic news reports. The relation of common-sense understanding with expert knowledge provides areas of 'non-knowledge', where elements of myth cannot be disregarded. Television journalism, with its need for pictures and brief, 'punchy' speech, is especially open to this 'mythic' dimension (Silverstone, 1981, 1988).

On a general level, the increased impact of economic events and perspectives in society and the growing importance of the economy as a public issue may be discussed in terms of a process we might call 'economization'. It is manifested by the tendency of the economy to dominate over politics, above all through the superiority of economic policy over other political areas, an increasing share of the political agenda being discussed in economic terms. Also, the expansion of formerly private economic phenomena affects the collective political and economic public sphere. And we can see further tendencies concerning the growing influence of economic aspects and perspectives on other areas of society, notably culture, arts and sports. On the media level, economization is manifested by the expansion of economic news reporting and its more dominant positioning in the media. Equally visible is a strong tendency for economic events and perspectives to be treated in other journalistic and quasi-journalistic genres, such as talk shows and infotainment. Here, one factor to take into account is the generic hybridity of much television today, the general move towards a 'blurring of boundaries' (Nichols, 1994). Economization concerns the definition of society in economic terms, or the definitional power of the economy. However, its impact on the media is difficult to assess. Will the increased number of genres or formats lead to economic events and processes being represented or constructed in different or alternative ways? Should we expect uniformity or variation? What will be the consequences for the formation of public knowledge of the economy (Neuman *et al.*, 1992; Corner, 1991)?

Television news and the Swedish economy

The performance of economic news journalism in Swedish television will be illustrated and discussed in the following five steps. First, the economic issues are described through the respective budget news of 1994, 1995 and 1996. Second, the totality of economic news of a crucial September week of 1996, including the opening of the parliament on Tuesday and the budget presentation on Friday, is presented, with the emphasis on content themes, actors and journalistic strategy. Third, a narrower focus is placed on the problem of representational form in economic news. The two final sections then deal with 'the market', an important feature of Swedish economic news, and with the question of how the audience is addressed.

The news programmes studied were *Aktuellt* of TV1 and *Rapport* of TV2. These are the two original non-commercial public service channels. The third newscast is *Nyheterna* of TV4, a commercial channel, but operating in accordance with public service.[3] In all three cases, the main evening news was chosen, *Aktuellt* at 9 p.m., including its appending financial newscast *A-ekonomi*, and *Rapport* and *Nyheterna* at 7.30 p.m. The three programmes show some distinctive differences in terms of their respective news formats. In *Aktuellt*, there is a policy of giving priority to longer news features and analyses, while *Rapport* acts more conventionally, mostly with shorter news items. *Nyheterna* in TV4 has introduced or marketed itself as a different and unconventional news programme, with a policy of reporting news with a more personal and tabloid approach, appealing to a younger audience.

The 1994–96 story

The three consecutive budgets of the study were presented to the parliament in January 1994 and 1995, and in September 1996.[4] This period constitutes an interesting phase in the development of the national economic issue of the 1990s. After the elections in 1991, the liberal-conservative government was expected to reinforce its proclaimed 'only-way' policy of reducing the public economy, cutting back on expenditure and lowering taxes. However, after the currency crisis in the autumn of 1992, the finances of the state, the growing budget deficit and the national debt soon became the overshadowing problem, together with rising unemployment.

1994: Recovery and optimism

In January 1994, finance minister Ann Wibble presented the last of her three liberal-conservative budgets, characterized in the media as 'weak', 'cautious' and 'without surprises'. The tactical, pre-election budget attempted a balance between marginal measures against unemployment and fairly modest cuts, or 'savings', in public expenditure. In the finance plan, attached to the budget, the government presented an optimistic forecast of a 4 per cent growth in GNP, which, it was alleged, would reduce unemployment by half by 1996.

The 'halving' of unemployment was a recurrent forecast in the three budgets under study, and also one of the themes of the news reports throughout the whole of the 1994–96 period. The dual content of the budget presentation (on the one hand, the actual proposed budget *measures* to be put before the parliament; on the other, the assessment and forecasts of the finance *plan*) provides an interesting choice for the news editor. Not surprisingly, the economic journalists gave greater news value to the finance plan than to the actual budget in 1994. The 'optimism' was heavily commented on, although not questioned, and visually constructed through, for instance, metaphors of a sunrise. This preference is partly explained by the media logic of news selection, but also has something to do with the enhanced symbolic side of economic functions in general – forecasts, evaluations and judgements being more important. The tendency holds for the news reports of the budgets of 1995 and 1996, where the topic of the forecast economy is a dominating feature in all three programmes.

A second observation of the news reports of the 1994 budget is the general downplaying of the unemployment problem, compared to the budget deficit issue. This evaluation corresponds to the government's interpretation of the economic situation. Of the two evils, the financial problems were more compatible with the liberal-conservative programme of reducing public expenditure. On the whole, the budget news reports of *Aktuellt, Rapport* and

Nyheterna point to the source dependency of economic journalism. The three newscasts presented a fairly homogeneous picture of the economy, in terms of content emphasis and bias, leaning heavily on the government's finance plan calculations. This homogeneity is countered by a diversity in the use of presentational form and visualization techniques. Common to all three programmes was an explicit treatment of the political 'play and tactics' of the budget, most obvious in *Nyheterna*, where the framing of the budget issue is accompanied by the moving graphics of a computer game. A definite irony is discernible.[5]

1995: Financial crisis and uncertainty

Experimentation with visualization and representational form also dominated much of the news reporting of the second budget under study, that of January 1995. This can be traced to a possible uncertainty by journalists, facing new kinds of economic problems, and lacking established ways of covering the issue of the Swedish economy. In September 1994, the Social Democratic party regained power and formed a minority government, after an election campaign which foregrounded the welfare system and reducing unemployment. Somewhat paradoxically, the new finance minister, Göran Persson, was brought forward as the one capable of enacting the 'sharp' measures needed to get the now overwhelming financial budget problems in order, the general impression being that only with a Social Democratic government could the necessary cuts in public expenditure be carried through. Consequently, the budget presentation in January 1995 (in the parliamentary speech and in press conferences) was marked by seriousness and a crisis atmosphere: 'Cuts to the tune of 22 billion. A European record.' The minority situation called for support from other parties in order to get the harsh budget measures through parliament.

All of the reports in the television coverage of the 1995 budget conveyed, in different ways, the almost war-like crisis interpretation of the government. *Nyheterna* placed the emphasis on the injustice of the budget measures – reporting a strike mentality among hospital nurses, and letting *them* judge the budget. Apart from that, the reports concentrate on the forecasts of the finance plan. *Aktuellt*'s lead was on the 'paradox' of the 'hard savings' as opposed to the forecast growth in private consumption, questioning the calculated withdrawal of household savings for purchasing capital goods. In *Rapport*, the budget issue was presented as a matter of guessing the future. Accompanying a constructed visualization of a female fortune-teller with a crystal ball, a three-times repeated quotation from Göran Persson's statement at the press conference frames the report:[6] 'It looks extremely bad for us, with the kind of national debt we have, and we really have to understand that in this country!' The reporter's introduction was as follows: 'Now it's time again. This year's budget proposal from the hands of the Chancellor. Long-term forecasts. An attempt to tell the fortune of the national finances 18 months in advance.' However, in *A-ekonomi* (the financial newscast of *Aktuellt*), the lead item took a more scientific approach to the question of future prospects, using the same type of visualized framing – the crystal ball. The report was a critical assessment of the government's forecasts in the finance plan and presented a competing alternative.

Market reactions and business judgements on the critical Swedish economic situation and the proposed budget measures were also salient in the news of the 1995 budget presentation. In *Rapport*, negative reactions were reported from three different sources. 'But it's not enough' was the quote of the managing director of Skandia, a large insurance company. Later, an analyst at the Midland Bank in London was urged to give the same judgement ('The need is really for twice as much'), and the markets 'at home' were reported to have found 'nothing encouraging' in Persson's budget. In *Nyheterna*, the financial market response was given the same weight, although the reported reaction was more positive: 'It's not a failure. We got what Persson promised, maybe a little more.'

The overall tendency of the budget news of January 1995 was a clear orientation towards future expectations, sentiments and financial judgement. The government's interpretation of the economic situation and the arguments for budget cuts were on the whole accepted, paralleled with a general concentration on the financial side of the budget. In one way, the budget was reported with a more 'serious' and certainly more pessimistic approach than was the case in 1994. On the other hand, there was much of the same extended play with visual metaphor, giving some of the leading reports a definite tone of uncritical naivety.[7]

1996: A dual picture

Eighteen months later, in the budget presentation of September 1996, the approach in the news reports of *Aktuellt*, *Rapport* and *Nyheterna* was different. The new social democratic Chancellor, Erik Åsbrink,[8] presented a budget within the context of a radically improved economic situation. By then, the bulk of the necessary expenditure cuts and savings had been implemented and the solution of the unemployment problem was under way, through an earlier government 'package' of employment measures. Leaning once again on the finance plan, the optimism was manifested by a shrinking budget deficit and a two-year forecast of the national debt beginning to decrease after 1998.

The media, following the pattern of concentrating on the

forecasts of the finance plan, now focused on the unemployment problem. The government's assessment of the prospects for state finance development was largely adopted, in contrast to the general scepticism towards unemployment. *Nyheterna* took the clearest position, in constructing the now familiar phrase 'halving unemployment by the year 2000' into a lead item about broken promises and fraud.[9] The example illustrates the impact on economic news values of statistics about future developments. The issue was about the conditions for reducing unemployment down to 4 per cent (the 'half') after four years. By questioning these figures, *Nyheterna* presented the case for accusing the government, announcing a debate on promises and deceit.

The news items of *Rapport* also focused on the unemployment prospects, and termed the actual budget proposal 'poor news'. In *Aktuellt*, the approach was more towards analysing the budget measures, and foregrounded women's perspectives on the unemployment situation. Too little was being done for women employees in the public sector, and the reporter reminded the viewer of the explicit ambition of the Social Democrats to 'let equality permeate every aspect of government policy'.

The financial markets formed a key actor in all three programmes. Compared to the 1995 situation, the reported response was now reversed. 'And the market trusts Erik Åsbrink' was the introduction to the news items on financial reaction in *Nyheterna*. In *Rapport*, a definite causal relation was established: 'Financial markets received the budget positively. The Stockholm stock exchange index turned upwards and rose by 0.6 per cent.'

In the news of the 1996 budget presentation, a second external 'judging' factor was introduced: the European Union (EU), centred around the convergence criteria for a 1999 involvement in monetary union. Both *Aktuellt* and *Nyheterna* reported positive European reactions. In the studio, commentators predicted a situation of 'applauding' EU finance ministers at the weekend Dublin meeting, cheering the successful managers of the budget deficit crisis. Obviously, this illustrates the changing European setting of the issue of the national budget.

Finally, a significant feature of the September 1996 budget news was the way in which all channels focused and commented on the distribution of the budget documents, which were being put on a CD-ROM disk and on the Internet.

The budget week economy

The newscasts of *Aktuellt*, *Rapport* and *Nyheterna* were studied through the whole of the budget week, 16 September to 22 September 1996. The week contained several important events in government, politics and the economy. On 17 September, the parliamentary session (of the Riksdag) was opened and included the prime minister's speech about the government's aims. On 18 and 19 September, government bills concerning culture and defence were presented, and on 20 September, the national budget. At the weekend, the Dublin meeting of EU finance ministers took place. While not being a typical week, these days definitely represent an interesting and significant period for looking at the reporting of the economy in television news. The objective here is briefly to present a picture concentrating on thematic aspects and on journalists' strategy.

The weight of economic news

The profile of the economy in news programmes can be judged by the importance ascribed to it by news editors. Using a narrow definition, including only budget-related and economic policy news, 37 longer news items out of a total of 152 (or roughly 25 per cent) dealt with 'the economy'. The share of economic reports is somewhat smaller in *Aktuellt*, while 30 per cent of news reports in *Nyheterna* and *Rapport* were about economy and economic policy. The budget day on Friday produced only marginally more economic news than the average day, the economic news being equally distributed over the week.

Themes and topics

The 37 economic news reports, including the coverage of the budget and finance plan, belong to a fairly fixed set of thematic categories. The following are the themes of the September week economic news on television, ranked in quantitative order.[10]

1. The welfare state, questioned or under threat: items under this heading include reports on public sector cuts and 'savings' and their consequences for the fair allocation of burdens, or, alternatively, they concern the need for responsible sacrifice.
2. Unemployment: this category comprises economic news mostly concerned with reporting the consequences of unemployment, often in the form of case interviews. One important feature of this news is analysis and features about the causes of and suggested solutions for unemployment.
3. Market reactions: news of financial market activities and, mostly, reactions to the national economy and economic policy.
4. The market perspective: news reports with an explicit market or economic efficiency perspective on economic policy.
5. State and government finance: reports with the financial aspects dominating.

6. The European issue: reports concentrating on the national economic consequences of the EU or of monetary union.
7. The economic theory perspective: a distinctive group of economic items, confronting economic policy problems with answers or solutions. The category includes the expert interview as well as the independent journalist analysis.

Actors

The participants in the economic news reports in *Aktuellt*, *Rapport* and *Nyheterna* were identified and classified into five broad categories of actors:

- political parties   16
- journalists (acting independently)   15
- citizens   7
- economic experts   5
- organized interests   4

Seen in this way, economic news reporting in the September week revolved around journalists and politicians – at least in terms of visual presence and speech and commentary appearance. Somewhat surprisingly, the role of experts is a rather minor one. Only one academic economic expert was interviewed, Erik Dahmén, a well-known retired professor, who warns the government against stimulating demand. The remaining four participating expert voices are all business and bank economists. Organizational representatives are main actors in no more than four news items in this week, and 'citizens' in only seven.

Journalists as main actors

The independent activity of participating journalists and reporters in the economic news involved a double strategy. Of the 15 items in which the journalists were the main actor, 10 represent the familiar studio commenting format. During the week, and especially in the budget-related news, this journalistic in-house-expert strategy was a recurrent feature in all three newscasts, and probably corresponds to the relative absence of academic economists. This type of 'secondary reporting' included both personal reflections and authoritative as well as sweeping judgements, but was not the only case of independent journalist action. Although the distinction may be blurred, it is still apparent that an important part of journalistic 'primary reporting' of the economy functions in a similar way to studio expert commentary. The origin of the report is not a 'real' event or a source activity. Instead, this type of news, amounting to five of the economic news items of the week, seems to build entirely on journalist initiative, and works through extensive choice of topic, perspective and sources. It now represents a more common journalistic practice, and it might be labelled 'investigative' – restricted as it is by the canons and conventions of media practice. Its application to the reporting of economic expectations and abstractions may produce particular difficulties.

This practice of journalist initiative can be exemplified during the week by a longer news report in *Nyheterna*, which confronted economic theory with the observation that the salaries of industry workers rose by as much as 8 per cent, due to wage drift. The studio reporter introduces the report:

At present in Sweden, business shows low profits. Unemployment is high and there is almost no inflation. Normally, according to all economic textbooks, that should mean that salaries would keep almost still. But reality doesn't seem to have studied economic theory.

The reporter's analysis implies that industry workers are responsible for the low employment. The succeeding part of the report was a journalist's interview with the leading economist of the LO (the Labour union federation), in which the latter took a defensive position. The impression is that he yields to economic theory. The example certainly points to some of the complications of journalistic initiative in this area.

Another example is the leading item of *A-ekonomi* (the financial newscast of *Aktuellt* on budget day). Leading on from an announcement that the budget was now being distributed on a CD-ROM, and reporting the Chancellor's subsequent claims of having achieved an 'availability revolution', the reporter drew a direct parallel with the annual reports of business corporations to shareholders. The reporter stressed the rights of every citizen to one copy of the full budget proposal. Confronted with implicit accusations of concealing information, Erik Åsbrink rejected the critique. While this is an interesting further case of a market perspective on the public economy, the reporter could well be said to have used a highly problematic analogy.[11]

This is not to say that reporting with a clear journalistic strategy of initiative and independence is dubious, or that television journalists in general are insufficiently competent in economic matters. However, across the 1994–96 budget news reports there were indications of media discourse growing more contained, and thus enhancing the initiative of journalists. And the fact that in 15 out of 37 economic reports during the September week journalists were main actors (while experts, citizens and organizational interests were far less well represented) may call for a discussion and problematization of journalistic action and initiative.

Budget day reports

By taking a closer look at the specific budget news of 20 September 1996, we can see the thematic focus more clearly. All three newscasts studied used roughly the same amount of time for coverage of the budget, 40–45 per cent of total time. The budget issue was also the leading item in all programmes. A common structure was used to present the issue, involving the mixing of a number of smaller news items with longer reports together with studio and closing comments, to construct a block of budget news. *Aktuellt* showed the largest number of individual items and covered a somewhat broader field than *Rapport* or *Nyheterna*. In total, 42 minutes of budget news were transmitted in the three main newscasts of the evening. The visual framing of the budget news block was conventional in all three newscasts, involving the personification of the budget – a pleased finance minister, this time, however, with a CD-ROM in his hand.

The 'double-sided' nature of the journalistic focus – on either the proposed budget measures or on the longer-term evaluations and forecasts of the finance plan – is indicative of an alternative thematic dimension in much economic news. A concentration on the finance plan means a focus on the economic system rather than on parliamentary politics and on the future rather than on the present, and in one sense, on the symbolic aspects as opposed to the material. As was shown above, the finance plan (originally a complement to, and a basis for the budget proposal) has received greater attention in recent years.[12] It will have greater news value in popular economic reporting, but its functions are also more vital to the real economy today than formerly. In the Swedish case the focus on the forecast prospects of the finance plan may also be explained by a national sentiment of uncertainty, and of an economy lagging behind in recession. Not least, one has to bear in mind that the future orientation certainly originates from the government. Showing future prospects, rather than present difficulties, is an important political ploy.

From the budget news on 20 September the overall impression is that, regardless of which topic is chosen for report (unemployment or government finance), the future orientation of the finance plan will dominate. A basic question, underlying most of the budget news, often latent, but in several cases explicit, was about the prospects and conditions of the national economic situation: 'What is necessary in order to preserve the welfare state?', or, alternatively, 'What does the economy need?' *Nyheterna* presented the clearest future-oriented approach to the budget issue. As noted earlier, about one-third of the news was devoted to the question of a disputed government 'promise' to reduce unemployment by the year 2000. The lead item in *Rapport* was a more neutral reporting of the optimism of the Chancellor, presenting the forecast statistics for the finance plan. *Aktuellt* put a definite 'equality' perspective on the budget in its lead story, foregrounding the prospects for women employees in the public sector. The macro-economic forecasts were presented later.

The unemployment question was dominant in all three newscasts. It overshadowed the national finance issue, a reversal from the budget news of 1995. Both the unemployment and finance issues were reported with a strong future emphasis, and were based on the same source. Yet the two indicators of the economy presented a dual picture. The optimism of the evaluation of government finance, and the notion of national debt beginning to decrease after 1998, were not questioned in the news reports. This contrasted heavily with a marked pessimism and scepticism concerning the forecasts of future employment and economic growth. This pessimism was further countered by the reports of market reactions, in which sentiments of approval and optimism prevailed. An impression of the economy as divided and contradictory emerges from these budget accounts, when they are taken together.

Representations: speech and image

The verbal and visual representational forms used in economic reporting are, of course, crucial. In this section, I will point to some of the most typical expressions of Swedish economic journalism, and show the way in which they were applied to the budget news of 1994-96. Initially, the example of *Nyheterna*'s budget story of the government's 'promise' is illustrative of the power of the future orientation.[13] The fact that a promise was made was established by the reporter with no reference to real changes in unemployment. A more accurate terminology would have concentrated on a change of 'objectives' or 'ambitions', which in itself (but not so easily) could have been interpreted as a 'deceit'. In reports of forecast economic developments, it is interesting to note which tenses were used. One example is the recurrent expression in commentary speech about the state finances: 'The budget deficit *is* gone in 1998', 'unemployment *is* on the same level in the year 2000'. In this way, the future tends to materialize as the present in language use.

A characteristic of Swedish economic news is the use of the word 'savings' (besparingar) as an alternative to 'cuts' or 'reductions' in public expenditure. In the course of the recession and crisis of the 1990s, this term has been one of the most frequent in news reports. The preferred terminology carries a positive connotational value, which explains its political use. The obvious problem of its dual and contradictory meaning has, however, rarely been recognized by economic journalists – in the 1996 budget news 'cuts' seemed to replace 'savings' to signify public sector reductions.

In the budget news of September 1996, there are several examples of another language feature – the recurrent use of the 'winners and losers' dichotomy. This binary device served to illustrate the consequences of various expenditure 'savings' or tax adjustments, and was often followed up by case interviews. The device has explanatory value at the apparent cost of a high degree of simplification and seemed to be utilized by journalists in a rather arbitrary way. *Aktuellt* used the dichotomy in the 1996 budget to show the equality aspect of the proposed measures. The report contrasts the effects or consequences for men and women, e.g. reduced widow's pensions (affecting older women) against tax cuts for driving a company car (more of a concern for active younger men). In another budget-related item in *Aktuellt* the same day, about the growing household income gap, a 'victorious' or 'winning' group was identified (pensioners in general), and also the 'losers' (young people and families with children).

Connected to the effects of the cuts and savings of economic policy are notions of 'the wallet' and 'belt tightening', frequently used to signify a general level of citizen affluence. The latter expression was a key element of popular Swedish economic journalism during the whole of the 1990s, and functions as a metaphor for 'crisis consciousness' and the need for harsh measures ('the politics of a tight belt')[14]. In their journalistic use, both the 'wallet' and the 'belt' could be said to carry connotations of solidarity and consensus, implying commonly shared sacrifices. *Rapport*, in January 1995, extends the 'belt' metaphor to a visualization, in one of the framings of its budget news block.[15]

The edited structure of the budget news blocks (which is similar in *Rapport*, *Aktuellt* and *Nyheterna*) is an important consideration when discussing the visualization of the budget. The budget items are edited and structured as narrative, a convention now in television news. This means that almost all external interviews, predominantly with the Chancellor or with the opposition, are broken up, dispersed and mixed with visual representations. This technique is most obvious in *Nyheterna* but it is a characteristic also of *Rapport* and *Aktuellt*. The editing reveals a journalistic initiative, and it may be significant to note that the traditional form of live studio interviewing in the budget news is used exclusively to present comments from fellow reporters.

The statistical graphs and figures in the budget news represent the traditional, and still dominant, type of visualization. While economic figures serve the purpose of summing up and informing, they also function as images, and in that sense they have connotational value. The interplay and clash of graphics, along with the use of a range of images (from documentary depictions and conventional metonyms to visual or reconstructional metaphor), make up much of the present Swedish economic news on television. An overall impression of both arbitrariness and over-visualization is hard to avoid. The budget news of 1994–96

presents typical examples. Apart from the documentary visualization of the budget event, the budget walk, the CD-ROM or the
parliamentary speech, depictive or illustrative visualization was a
common strategy in all three newscasts. This included images of
physical settings or events standing for components of the budget:
petrol stations, supermarket and bar interiors, etc., signifying tax
increases or other proposed budget measures. These images
function as conventional metonyms. It is interesting to note that
the image of bundles of bank notes and heaps of coins is still the
most frequently used visual metonym in Swedish economic
journalism.

The general problem of visual news, that of representing
abstractions (Corner, 1995), is increased in economic news.
Metaphor as well as narrative come into play in visualizing
abstractions of the economy, future prospects, optimism or trust.
The optimism of the government's evaluation in 1994 was visually
constructed through images of nature, such as sunsets and the sea.
The uncertainty and crisis atmosphere of 1995 was accompanied
by mini-narrative filming of the crystal ball and the fortune-teller, to
give an arbitrary 'guessing' character to economic analysis
(*Rapport*[16]). The image of a 'piggy bank' also recurs in news about
recession, cuts and savings.

The market

Probably the most significant single aspect of Swedish economic
journalism in the 1990s is 'the market'. In economic reports, it was
established as the representation of an anonymous, but influential,
financial actor on the national economic scene – particularly in
connection with the financial currency crisis in the autumn of
1992. Since then, market reactions have been essential elements of
any larger economic policy issue. The typical news report uses
market reaction when judging economic policy measures, often
indicating an unambiguous rejection or approval. It is interesting
here to connect the appearance of the 'market response' to
strategies of journalistic action or initiative. A market response
angle has become a convention of present economic reporting on
Swedish television, and the visualization of financial brokers at
work, in a hectic computer-dominated environment, accompanies
almost every report.

This observation should not overshadow the obvious fact that
the status of state finances and the national currency value have
become crucial, and now condition and set the limits for the
government's economic policy and expenditure. In recent years,
market judgements have also been complemented by 'European
reaction', particularly as a consequence of 'conditions of convergence' criteria for entry to monetary union.[17] This international
factor now equals the importance of market reactions, and is also

dominant in news reporting. Market and European reactions are factors behind the shift of focus of the economic issue towards forecasts and expectations and are analogous to the corresponding future orientation of the budget itself. At a general level, it can be considered as a manifestation of the economy becoming more symbolic.

In the budget news of 1994–96, all newscasts used the format of asking for market judgement of the government budget. The chosen wording is often to 'mark' or 'grade' the economy, the terminology belonging to economic discourse, but also implying an unequal student–teacher relation. In 1994 and 1995, the budgets and financial situation were generally judged negatively:

Good, but not enough. That is the way to sum up the financial markets' judgement of government's budget today. Interest rates went slightly up (during the day), following a renewed statement from head of Skandia, Björn Wohlrath, that Skandia will *not* buy Swedish bonds. (*Rapport*, 10 January 1995)

In 1996 a definite positive market reaction was reported and commented upon:

Financial markets received the budget positively. The Stockholm stock exchange index turned upwards and rose by 0.6 per cent. (*Rapport*, 20 September 1996)

The market trusts Åsbrink. The budget lowered the interest rates significantly and the Krona increased its value. Tonight there will be more cheering in Dublin, when the Chancellor meets his EU colleagues. But what about the voters? Well, they will not be convinced until the promises are felt in their wallets. (*Nyheterna*, 20 September 1996)

Yes, we will continue to talk about the content of the government's budget, which made the stock exchange shares rise and interest rates fall today. (*Aktuellt*, 20 September 1996)

Market grading of the economy is also a routine element of daily news reporting. Three indicators of the market are foregrounded: the changes in the stock exchange index; the value of the national currency; and the market interest rates. These elements of economic news now concern an increasing number of the population. In this sense, it *is* of public interest. However, on a different level it also has implications for the wider *political* issue of the economy, as a complement or commentary to the news reports. When made explicitly, the limited choice of these indicators as a measure of national economic performance certainly appears biased and crude. The visualization aspect is crucial. In *Rapport*, the voice-over graphics and statistics of stock exchange index, currency and interest rates are complemented with large marked arrows, having only three possible positions, to indicate either stability or upward or downward movement. In visual reception, the constructed trichotomy is informative, but highly simplified.

The lack of coherence and causality in market information (see also Jensen, 1987) contributes to impressions of an apparent 'short-sightedness'. The day-to-day movements show an interesting contrast to the long-term future orientation of budget reports. To financial markets, the year 2000 is relevant primarily as it informs present judgement or action.

Addressing the audience

I want to make a final observation here on the strategy of addressing the audience in the reporting of economic news in Sweden. The historical context of public service television is relevant to the point. This affects both the news format and the positioning of journalists, giving a particular identity to the broadcast news. In the economic news of the three news programmes studied, two different and contrasting ways of addressing the audience are easily recognizable, each indicating an assumed relation between reporter and viewer. One is the 'ordinary citizen approach', on the surface characterized by journalist uncertainty, lack of expert knowledge and honest scepticism, in treating economic issues by asking 'the ordinary citizens' questions. Apparent here is the intended 'inclusion' of viewers and the non-distancing of address. This strategy, being fully compatible with active or even provocative reporting, was evident in all three newscasts studied. It was used in at least some of the interviewing of experts and financial representatives, but is not frequent in interviews with political representatives.[18]

The second strategy of address is its opposite – the 'expert approach'. This was equally common, most often in studio dialogue between anchor and commentator, but was also applied in voice-over film reporting and interviewing. The chief character-istic is self-assured judgement, in which facts are established, and cause and effect are connected – using little or no reference to authoritative sources. The studio dialogue is a double strategy in terms of audience address, the anchor often taking the citizen approach and the commentating reporter the expert approach. Together these create an educational context, one journalist being ignorant, the other producing the answers. The outcome and problematic is similar to the appearance of expertise and common sense in participatory programming (Livingstone and Lunt, 1994). All three programmes used the dialogue format in the budget news on 20 September 1996, placed at the end of the respective budget blocks. The following are some brief examples, showing intro-ductory questions from the studio anchor (ordinary citizen) to commentator (expert), and short quotations from commentary speech, indicating the main perspective adopted and the direction of expert evaluation or judgement. The first is from *Rapport*, the second from *Nyheterna* and the last from *Aktuellt*:

Studio Anchor
So, what are the prospects? [referring to the pessimistic forecasts for employment for young people]

Commentator:
They are as bad as before, since there were no new proposals on unemployment ... The goal of 4 per cent by 2000 will not be reached, and not even the main alternative, 5.7 per cent ... However, the government has succeeded with state finance. The budget deficit is gone. But so is purchasing power.

Studio anchor:
There will be brighter times?

Commentator:
Yes, it may sound like it ... with state finance getting in order, and international confidence returning.

Studio anchor:
Will there be new savings?

Commentator:
There will be no new shock packages ... Surely we will be hit by more savings, but these would already have been agreed to in the Riksdag.

Studio anchor:
What do you think will be the marks in Dublin for Åsbrink's budget?

Commentator:
Well, he's very likely to pass ... there will be praise ... pats on the back. But not quite from the voters ... There is no common policy for jobs.

One observation is that old-style 'neutral reporting' is in decline, and that the chosen address mode of economic reports tends to fall into one or other of these dialogic categories. The subsequent audience impression of journalist competence, and viewers' confidence in the news, are definitely affected. Both of these strategies, however, can be viewed in the light of the continuing public service tradition of Swedish broadcast media, one important aspect of this being that society is 'explainable' to all citizens.

The legacy of Gunnar Sträng (for a long time Swedish Chancellor) may be influential too. As late as the early 1970s, budget presentations were made on television by the Chancellor himself, having full control over the government's priorities. Political ambition being obvious the popular Chancellor's presentations concerned the allocation of the gains of economic growth, Sträng announcing new reforms and advances of the welfare state. Today, the public service ambition involves an attempt to make the complex economy explainable by visualization and narrative. Both approaches work with a strong idea of consensus, of common understanding, which conflicts with recognition of division and conflict.

Conclusions

To summarize, the study of Swedish budget news on television between 1994 and 1996 shows a general thematic bias towards the forecasts and expectations of economic development. Media focus on the state finance problems in 1994, which was enhanced in 1995, turned into a concentration on the unemployment issue in 1996, with a definite sceptical and pessimistic edge. The Swedish case points to several general characteristics of televised news reporting on the economy (its visual and verbal forms), but also reveals distinctive national features:

- The 'future' orientation of Swedish economic news is significant, and is analogous to a growing media interest in the symbolic economy.
- The strategy of foregrounding journalists as independent actors is of particular interest with regard to popular broadcast news on the economy. Generally, a stronger journalist initiative is seen in Swedish economic news, economic reporting becoming more confined to the speech of journalists.
- 'The market' is a new and now recurrent feature in Swedish television economic news, appearing in two aspects. The most obvious is the response report, with the market judging economic policy. The day-to-day reporting of developments in the share and currency markets also produces a condensed image of a reactive short-term economy.
- Strategies of addressing the audience are crucial to the public service aspect of economic reporting, and often involve the journalistic technique of the 'citizen and expert' dialogue. However, the notion of consensus is problematic for these forms of address.

The observations from the study of Swedish television news reports on the national budget may contribute to a general discussion of how to define the public issue of the economy. One factor to take into account here is the nature of the interaction between economic journalism and the political and economic spheres. Following the enhancement of the financial and symbolic side of the economy, the reporting of forecasts, prospects, expectations and the psychological dimensions of optimism, trust and confidence are a more prominent part of economic journalism. In this capacity, economic news reports are becoming more important to the workings and functions of the economy itself. Whether they concern market reactions or questions about the external judging of the national economy, impressions and perceptions are today central factors of the national economy, far more important than before. Economic news seems increasingly to confront a 'second audience', separate from the political, democratic objective of informing citizens. One impression is that the government's old presentation of the budget is now managed and staged with both 'audiences' in mind.

Markets need information, not only about business developments, but also (and increasingly) about the productivity and financial prospects of nations and states. There is an interchange of symbolic values between the two spheres – with economic news reporting as a key mediator. If 'economization' during the 1990s in Sweden is largely about a changed relation between the political and economic, it could be seen as a displacing of the economy from the public sphere, in the sense that the economy is increasingly conceived of as autonomous from political control. The consequences of such a shift for public knowledge and democratic participation could be great.

Notes

1 This study is part of an ongoing research project on Swedish economic journalism throughout the period 1970–98 (Journalism on the Economy 1970–98) undertaken in the Department of Journalism, Media and Communication (JMK) of Stockholm University and funded by the Bank of Sweden Tercentenary Foundation, to which thanks are due. I also wish to thank project members at JMK, Håkan Lindhoff and Kjell Nowak and the researchers of the Liverpool Public Communication Group, for productive comments on earlier drafts of this chapter.
2 The press coverage of the activities of Swedish banks during the deregulation period has been studied by Hadenius and Söderhjelm (1994).
3 TV4's franchise for transmitting involves a commitment to fulfil certain content criteria, corresponding to public service broadcasting.
4 Traditionally, 10 January has been the date on which the finance minister (the Chancellor) presents the Swedish national budget to the Riksdag (parliament). From 1997 the fiscal year corresponds to the calendar year, so the latest budget was presented in September 1996.
5 A more detailed account and discussion of the constructional elements in the news of the 1994 budget is presented in Mårtenson and Lindhoff (1995).
6 The extended quote, as well as several other examples of Swedish television news (and the full transcripts from the UK focus group screening sessions) can be viewed at the Liverpool University

Politics Department web site. The address is:
http://www.liv.ac.uk/~polcomm/polhome.htm

7 Three of the most frequently used representations in popular economic news all show up in the evening's news: the pig and the piggy bank, 'the wallet' and the 'tightening belt' – the last is a common metaphor for 'crisis consciousness'.

8 Göran Persson was elected party leader of the SAP, and became the prime minister in the spring of 1996.

9 See note 6.

10 Items are classified by 'theme' according to their respective dominating 'story element'. Although the classification is problematic and in a few cases subjective, it may still be helpful to illustrate the relative weight and bias of content. Frequencies are left out, in order to indicate the necessary 'relative reading' of the listed themes.

11 See note 6 for access to the full-length quote.

12 The terminology used by journalist is sometimes a problem. Generally, the issue is referred to as the 'budget', regardless of focus.

13 See note 6.

14 Translation is problematic. The Swedish word is 'svångrem'. Being an old expression, no longer used in its original meaning, it is a 'dead metaphor'.

15 In web site; see note 6.

16 See note 6.

17 See note 6 for access to extended quotes from *Rapport* 1995 and 1996.

18 The London Midland Bank report in *Rapport* on 10 January 1995 is one example. See note 6.

7
Economic journalism in the 1990s: the 'crisis discourse' in Sweden

Håkan Lindhoff

Introduction

When reflecting upon the main traits of the system of capitalism in the first chapter of *A Journey Through Economic Time* (1994), the Harvard economist John Kenneth Galbraith stresses the two sides of the dynamics of capitalism, i.e. economic growth as an innate aspiration of the system, and the tendency to severe instability. The former is taken as a given by any economist, but according to Galbraith the latter is not. In the USA during the nineteenth century, periods of slow or even negative growth were called 'crises' or 'panics'. As those terms might create fear, with accompanying negative effects on business morale, they were replaced by the milder term 'depression'. Later, when these expressions became associated with the hard times of the 1930s, 'recession' was substituted for them. However, when 'recession' also came to have unpleasant undertones, the term 'growth accommodation' superseded it. The latest expression is more complex: 'sustained equilibrium with under-employment'. For economists, this covers the European predicament of the 1990s, Sweden included.

This history of terminology can be read as a story of the discursive struggle against the crisis. Besides economic measures, economists and politicians evidently needed linguistic means, too, to paraphrase or cover up the symptoms of crisis. Those linguistic remedies were often in vain or did not last for long, as this review suggests. However, the economic policies brought forward must be launched through some linguistic or symbolic means, and to be effective must be used or supported by the various economic actors. Some policies even require that the great mass of actors (the consumers, savers, citizens and tax-payers) accept the policies through their economic behaviour. Also, the public may have to be educated about the necessity of the crisis measures (by raising its 'crisis consciousness').

The crisis perspective

The story of crises in Sweden makes it obvious that we should look at Swedish economic journalism from a 'crisis' perspective. However, an attempt to interpret the crisis discourse from the mass of economic news stories raises a number of difficult issues. What are the characteristics of economic reporting when trying to cover and explain a crisis? How is a crisis to be grasped and comprehended, making it part of common public knowledge on economic matters? These are important issues for the economic journalists and for the other actors taking part in the public dialogue on economic crises. For the researcher, it is a challenge to evaluate the role played by the media in this context. Using materials from the Stockholm newspapers *Dagens Nyheter* and *Expressen*, this chapter will analyse the crisis discourses of current Swedish economic journalism. A survey of newspaper texts from the years 1992–96, aided by a full text database, aims to look at the nature and extent of the use of economic and crisis terms.[1]

The Swedish public is used to hearing and reading about 'the crisis'. Evidence presented below will show that it is likely that the literate Swede will, in the first instance, see 'the crisis' as an economic problem and not as a political one. The concept of 'crisis' has an ancient Greek origin. In the terminology of Hippocrates it means the turning point of a disease, when the patient either dies or recovers. With this meaning of the concept of 'crisis', it may well be used as a metaphor for a specific and acute economic problem of the state or society. However, there are two objections that may be raised here. A state seldom dies or goes bankrupt. And recovery should not necessarily mean shifting from one disease to another, i.e. from one crisis to another. Neither should the crisis process be everlasting – as it seems to have been in the Swedish economy and in economic discourse over the last seven years or so.

As early as the early 1920s, when the real estate market fell, savings banks went bankrupt and a spiral of deflation followed, the notion of 'crisis' was used accurately. The recovery from the crisis was quick. In the 1930s the term 'depression' was used. But when the slump began, it was described in the Swedish press in crisis terms. Later, the recessions of the late 1970s and early 1980s were discussed in terms of 'crisis'. Such reflections on the 'prehistory' of the current Swedish economic crisis discourse are not definitive or exhaustive, and it is difficult to assess the extent to which the terms became part of public comprehension of the economy. However, this is the background to the economic discourse of the 1990s.

The economic crises of the 1990s

Over the last ten years or so Sweden has experienced a system shift of its economy which, in many respects, still continues. This has been accomplished in spite of (or through) a series of economic crises. The period commenced with the deregulating reforms of the mid-1980s and late 1980s, starting in 1984 with the abolition of foreign exchange restrictions and the prohibition of direct state borrowing on the exchange markets. The financial sector was deregulated through the abolition of credit restrictions for banks and by making it easier to start a finance company. Tax reform was launched in 1988 and came into effect in 1990. This reduced taxes – especially for those on higher incomes. The late timing of the tax reform added significantly to the boom. However, the plea by the Conservative leader, Carl Bildt, for a 'system shift' on the eve of the election of 1988 failed. Only two and a half years after the murder of Prime Minister Olof Palme, the electorate was not prepared to accept a new system based on neo-classical economic theory, inspired by Milton Friedman's ideas and by the practice of President Reagan and Mrs Thatcher. So, the system shift was still a task for the Social Democratic government under Prime Minister Ingvar Carlsson.

The old model this replaced was a traditional Keynesian one. Both the Social Democrats (1932–76 and 1982–91) and the Liberal-Conservatives alike (1976–82) had practised full employment policies despite the inflationary consequences. This was especially the case in the 1970s and in the early years of the 1980s. In the context of recession and crisis, the rising demands of the welfare state were met by taxation, public spending and – if necessary – budget deficits. Devaluations were also used, on several occasions. Consequently, inflation was high, in some years reaching 10 per cent.

In the debate among Swedish economists this old model began to be criticized, starting in 1976 in the new journal *Ekonomisk Debatt* (Hugemark, 1994). During the 1980s this critique went public on radio, television and in the newspapers, along with contributions from neo-liberal politicians and the rightist Social Democrats. It also surfaced in reports from commissions and parliamentary committees. The leading morning newspaper of Sweden, the liberal *Dagens Nyheter*, was an important forum for this economic debate, as was the growing economic and financial press (*Affärsvärlden, Dagens Industri, Finanstidningen, Veckans Affärer, Privata Affärer*). The launching of this new economic and political discourse in the newspapers and in the Swedish parliament has been studied by Boréus (1994) who investigated the language used in ideological disputes. The title of the book (*The Shift to the Right*) summarizes her conclusions, and she describes in detail how neo-liberal ideas about the economy and the public sector came to be established.

Hadenius and Söderhjelm (1994) have also studied the way in which the deregulation of the banking sector up to 1990 was mirrored in the popular Swedish press, the elite press, the specialized economic journals, and the *Financial Times*. Their conclusion must have been a disappointment for those believing in a free and critical fourth estate: Swedish economic reporters led the demands for deregulatory reforms, but without looking critically at the consequences of the reforms or warning of the market boom that might follow. The most important exception to this trend were reports in the *Financial Times* – a newspaper more detached from the Swedish scene and more aware of the experiences of the UK deregulation offensive.

The deregulation campaign was very successful, in the short term at least. The boom peaked with an enormous credit expansion from the exploding finance sector at the end of the 1980s. In the prevalent climate of deregulation, the state authority that supervised the finance sector did little to control the expansion of lending, apart from changing its name – from Bank Inspection to Finance Inspection. Real estate prices rose quickly to a high level until the crash of the real estate market. Consequently, in 1990 the financial sector started to contract, as did parts of the construction industry, partly due to rapid deflation. Real estate speculation had developed into a finance boom, where the actors believed in an ever-rising price spiral. The finance companies, lending on the basis of this spiral, were the first to be affected. Many of the smaller ones went bankrupt, but the traditional banks were shaken, too, as they had floated the finance companies with capital. And, of course, the stock exchange was also affected.

Of the six Swedish big banks, only one was largely unaffected by the real estate and finance crises (Svenska Handelsbanken). The others suffered varying degrees of credit loss – between 1 and 40 billion Swedish krona. Without measures taken by the government under Carl Bildt (1991–94), at least two other banks would have gone bankrupt. A new Bank Support Authority was introduced, serving three banks with state credits and letting the fourth be bought by the fifth. The latter happened to be the state-owned bank Nordbanken, which suffered the most from credit losses. Putting its credit loss aside, the aim was to reconstruct Nordbanken with the help of 40 billion Swedish krona from parliament.[2]

As a consequence of deflation and the banking crisis, and with the banks trying to recover through cancelling credits to the industry, many small and medium-sized companies had to dismiss personnel or quit the market completely. During the first years of the 1990s, around 300,000 industry jobs disappeared, creating an unemployment crisis as well. The total effect of the multiple crises of the real estate sector, the finance and banking sectors and small and medium-sized industries was enormous. Together with the bad timing of tax reforms, this reduced the state income considerably. The bank support costs, unemployment measures and the reduced tax income strained the state budget heavily, creating a budget deficit that grew from 1992 onwards. Added to this, a currency crisis exploded in the autumn of 1992, when confidence in the Swedish krona fell to its lowest level due to the multiple crises. Attempts to defend the ECU fixed exchange rate of the krona failed after two months of struggle, costing around a further 20 billion Swedish krona. The aim was to demonstrate that Sweden had left behind the old model of devaluation, but it still ended in November 1992 with a floating krona and *de facto* devaluation. With a deficit of about 200 billion Swedish krona, the cost of financing the deficit rising, high and rising interest rates on the market and the low confidence in the krona, the budget deficit crisis was now definitely on the agenda.

To raise confidence during the currency crisis, the Bildt government entered into two crisis agreements with the Social Democratic opposition and launched a set of 'crisis packages'. These consisted of remedies to raise temporarily the tax on higher income and to cut public spending (social costs, pensions and unemployment benefits) as well as public investment. Public sector jobs in child care, in schools, in hospitals and in the care of the aged were lost. This, of course, added to the unemployment crisis. With a total unemployment rate of 10 per cent, it was easy for the Social Democrats under Ingvar Carlsson to win the election of September 1994. Despite the fact that most of the leading Social Democrats (and all the neo-liberals of the Liberal and Conservative parties) supported a 'yes' vote in the EU referendum of December 1994, it was quite hard for the 'yes' side to win the day, due to the Euro-scepticism of the Swedes.

By the mid-1990s, the budget deficit crisis seemed to be over, at least according to the September 1996 government projections for 1997, and still more so according to the corresponding statement for 1998. Following a series of mergers, the big banks had recovered, and six of the biggest were now reduced to four.[3] Real estate prices are also reported to have risen slowly through 1997.

The system shift has continued through further cuts in the public sector – especially in medical care and medical benefits. Public dental care insurance is all but abolished. The many now bear the burden. The 'only' acute crisis still evident is the extremely high level of unemployment. Twelve per cent of the workforce are now outside the labour market and Sweden is now adapting to the high unemployment rate of many countries in Europe and the EU.[4] On the other hand, inflation is reduced to zero and from November 1996 to March 1997 was even transformed into deflation. The stock exchange market has also performed well –

rising 40 per cent, on average, during 1996 – and the problem of the over-rating of stock is a current issue. Is another (new) financial boom under way, and a stock market crisis or crash imminent? The answer will probably not to be found in the Swedish market alone, as financial speculation has grown into a highly international business. One solitary stock exchange is hard to protect against developments in the other big markets (see Kask, 1997; Reinius, 1996; Hamilton and Rolander, 1993; Eklund, 1993).

Processes of 'economization' and 'crisis-ization'

Parallel to the processes of system shift within the Swedish economy during the last decade, one can also readily observe the tendencies towards 'economization' of social reality and journalism. 'The economy' as a public realm or public issue has been extended, affecting and increasingly dominating traditional political and cultural domains. In addition, this tendency is paralleled by an increased media interest in economic matters generally. This can be observed as an enhanced economic bias in the overall content of different media. News media, television talk shows as well as new hybrid genres and pure fiction are affected (Neuman *et al.*, 1992; Corner, 1995; Lindhoff and Mårtenson, 1996a, b).

The increased impact of 'the economy' may be discussed in terms of a two-level notion of 'economization'. On one level, *real* 'economization' is manifest in the tendency for economics to dominate over politics, above all through the superiority of economic policy over other political areas. Also, the areas of the market and of private economic initiative expanded as a consequence of the system shift and at the expense of political decision-making in the public sector. Sport, the arts and culture generally (as well as the media) are all affected by this. On another level, *media* 'economization' is manifest in the growth of pure economic news reporting and its increasingly dominant editorial position in the media (see Hvitfelt and Malmström, 1990). This can also be seen in the increased use of discursive notions like 'the economy', 'the market' and 'unemployment'.[5] An intensive analysis of three Swedish newspapers during an ordinary week in November 1995 showed that about 40 per cent of the articles touched on economics as an important dimension (Lindhoff and Mårtenson, 1996a, b). The greater use of numerical presentation and quantification in news coverage in *Dagens Nyheter* has also been demonstrated (Ekecrantz and Olsson, 1991) and is typical of economic news more generally. The economic dimension in news about politics (as well as sport, the arts, culture and entertainment) is more prominent in both print and broadcast media, and outwith the specialist economic newsbeat. Equally important is the tendency to deal with economic events and processes outwith the news and current affairs genres, in talk shows and infotainment (see Nichols, 1994; Dahlgren, 1995).

There is a parallel tendency within Swedish economic journalism of the 1990s (within the news genre, as well as in commentary and chat shows) towards increased talk of 'the crisis'. It seems that media 'economization' goes hand in hand with a process of media 'crisis-ization'. These tendencies towards 'economization' and 'crisis-ization' will be demonstrated below, but a few words should be said first on the materials and methods used.

Materials and methods used

The media content surveyed in this chapter is taken from two Swedish newspapers, *Dagens Nyheter* and *Expressen*. These are both edited in Stockholm, are independent and liberal and belong to the biggest media conglomerate of Sweden – owned by the Bonnier family. In the newspaper business this family controls about 25 per cent of total Swedish circulation. *Dagens Nyheter* (founded in 1864) is the leading national mid-market morning paper (circulation: 363,000, January 1997) and in many respects sets the agenda for the political and economic debate of Sweden. For this reason it carries a regular section called 'Dagens Nyheter Debatt', where leading figures in the political or economic arena are invited to introduce their ideas or proposals, and where leading experts may explore and dispute fresh ideas.[6] On the other hand, *Expressen* (founded in 1944) was for many years the leading popular afternoon paper. However, in terms of circulation it has been outstripped in recent years by the social democratic paper *Aftonbladet*. *Expressen* used to be the biggest newspaper of the Nordic countries, with half a million copies, but its circulation today is a mere 352,000.

Another reason for using these two newspapers (other than their respective positions) is the availability of a useful, quick and easily used full-text database for both the titles (from 1990 for *Expressen* and 1991 for *Dagens Nyheter*). Since 1995 this 'Press-Text' database has been available to researchers at low cost. PressText is more user-friendly than most library databases. All text is accessible (captions included) although photographs are not; and diagrams can be searched on another database. In total, the database of *Dagens Nyheter* and *Expressen* consists of about 100,000 text units for each year. This comprises all written articles in the two newspapers within all the sections – with the exception of advertisements.

The PressText database presented the opportunity to follow different aspects of the discourses on the economic crisis in two newspapers quantitatively over five years, from 1992 to 1996. The analysis of the frequency of particular discursive terms can be superficial and sometimes lacking context (and, therefore, hard to interpret). However, it can be used to indicate what the discourse is about and flag changing trends over the course of the five years. Such analyses will be combined, here, with a more qualitative approach, interpreting specific cases and using subsets of text units identified through searches in the PressText database. Through the analysis of citations and the exploration of the main characteristics of news and commentary on the economic crisis, the aim is to interpret some of the important dimensions of news constructions, as well as of content themes.

Indicators of 'economization' and 'crisis-ization'

The PressText databases of *Dagens Nyheter* and *Expressen* were searched for all newspaper articles containing at least one mention of the following terms: 'the economy', 'politics', 'the market', 'the crisis', 'the depression', 'the budget deficit' and 'unemployment' (searched for in the *definite* form). The results are plotted in Figure 7.1 below. Of course, these must be judged only as an indication of terminological use – no control has been made for the *context* of use (or for the frequency of use *within* each article). Still, the figures may be used to illustrate the extent to which the terms referred to are deployed in the two most dominant Swedish newspapers. Comparisons over time of the use of a specific term can tell us about discursive tendencies. In Table 7.1 comparisons may be made between the concepts of 'economy' and 'politics' (in the *in*definite form), as well as between those two terms used in compound wordings.[7]

Table 7.1 The terms 'economy' and 'politics/policy' in *Dagens Nyheter* and *Expressen*

	1992	1993	1994	1995	1996
Economy	4125	3899	3960	4243	3966
Politics/policy	7124	6953	7930	6816	6426
Economy +	11,295	10,997	10,848	10,414	9831
Politics/policy +	11,161	11,202	12,282	11,549	10,881

Note: cells contain the number of articles containing the term at least once; the '+' refers to the use of the term in different forms, or in compound wordings.

Several conclusions can be drawn from Table 7.1. Of course these are, of necessity, tentative since we know little about the exact wording or about the contexts in which the terms have been used. However, the figures are a clear indicator of the number of text units containing the specific themes. If the figures in the third and fourth rows of Table 7.1 (economy+ and politics/policy+) are interpreted as indicators of 'economization' and 'politicization' respectively, we might say that the two trend in a similar way, although over the period articles involving the term 'politics/policy' outnumbered those deploying the term 'economy'. This suggests, however, that between 10 and 12 per cent of all news texts in the two papers over this period used some form of 'economy' notion, although there is a slight tendency for the use to decline over time. When looking at the term 'economy' alone, the level is 4000 text units per year, while for the term 'politics' the level is higher: it is used at least once in 6000–7000 news texts per year.

However in the *definite* form (see Figure 7.1) 'the economy' is deployed at about the same frequency as 'politics' (1600 to 1900 news texts per year as opposed to 1500 to 1700). It should be noted that the tendency to use 'the economy' seems to diminish in 1996. This is also the case regarding the indicators of 'the market', 'politics, 'the crisis' and 'the budget deficit'. However, it should be noted that the problem of Sweden's budget deficit is on its way to being solved and the acuteness of the crisis symptoms were less obvious in 1996 than in 1992–93. It is harder to interpret the other trends in Figure 7.1. Two indicators moving upwards between 1995 and 1996 were 'unemployment', strongly, and 'the depression', weakly. That might be said to reflect changes in Swedish economic reality, with unemployment figures reaching the European level. 'The market' seems to be the most prominent of the terms compared here. This may indicate a stronger tendency to use 'the market', rather than the other terms, as a systemic and reified notion.

Is 'the crisis' economic?

Comparing the use of the term 'the crisis' with the use of 'the economy', 'politics' and 'the market', we can see from Figure 7.1 that for the years 1992 and 1993 'the crisis' is used about as often as 'politics'. This is not the case for later years, where the use of 'the crisis' in news clearly diminishes. One explanation might be that at the beginning of the period Sweden was struck by several crises at the same time, so there were many reasons to talk of crisis. Later in the period studied, the need for a discourse of crisis weakened as the real economy strengthened.

What was meant by 'the crisis' when the term was used? Can we be sure that the news texts point at the economic crisis and not at some other crisis? Without looking at each case independently, we can use some other indicators. We will compare the use of the term of 'economic crisis' with terms for some other forms of crises: political crisis, crises of confidence, crisis of identity, military crises, etc. (see Table 7.2).

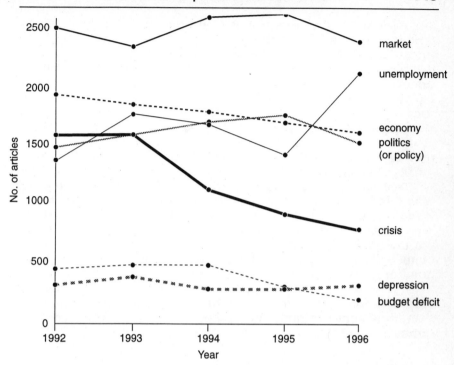

Figure 7.1 Seven discursive terms in *Dagens Nyheter* and *Expressen*, 1992–96

Table 7.2 Crisis terms in *Dagens Nyheter* and *Expressen*

	1992	1993	1994	1995	1996	Total
Economic crisis	534	603	384	311	237	2069
Political crisis	93	120	95	87	56	451
Crisis of confidence	53	51	48	64	48	264
Crisis of identity	31	25	26	40	28	150
Military crisis	32	24	17	25	16	114
Education crisis	20	15	15	8	8	66
Care crisis	4	4	3	9	15	35
Social crisis	9	8	3	7	4	31
Medical care crisis	1	0	3	4	5	13
Cultural crisis	3	2	1	0	0	6

Note: cells contain the number of articles containing the term at least once – in the *definite* form.

With the differences as large as those demonstrated in Table 7.2, one can be quite sure that the use of the term 'the crisis' points to 'the *economic* crisis'. It figures in around two-thirds of all the cases. The next most numerous reference is to 'the *political* crisis'.[8] The other crisis terms tested are rather less frequent. Also, the use of 'the economic crisis' diminishes over time, confirming the similar tendency for 'the crisis' in Figure 7.1. In 1996, when all but the unemployment crisis appeared to be over, it was only half as prominent as in 1992 and 1993. Does this suggest that the unemployment crisis is not as severe as the other crises – as far as news portrayals are concerned (cf. Figure 7.1)? Such a suggestion necessitates a closer look at the form and content of the respective news items. Before moving on to this form of analysis we can use numerical indicators to describe the distribution of the different *kinds* of economic crisis terms. Table 7.3 details this breakdown.

It seems that, with the exception of 1995, the crisis term is associated more with unemployment than with the 'banking crisis'. However, in practice 'banking crisis' and 'finance crisis' are notions used for talking about the same underlying issue. So, it is clear that the unemployment problem is less salient in the news than the finance and banking crises. Besides that, it should be noted that the number of news texts on the unemployment crisis diminished, while the unemployment *rate* (and, therefore, the actual unemployment crisis) remained high. The newsworthiness of unemployment evidently diminished over time, which may be a symptom of getting accustomed to the higher rates.[9]

Table 7.3 Economic crisis terms in *Dagens Nyheter* and *Expressen*

	1992	1993	1994	1995	1996	Total
Real-estate crisis	86	45	30	26	23	210
Finance crisis	151	184	117	99	45	596
Banking crisis	99	172	81	114	37	503
Unemployment crisis	110	205	99	65	72	551
Currency crisis	146	61	23	47	21	298
Interest rate crisis	66	16	40	18	7	147
Budget deficit crisis	38	36	29	20	6	129
Debt crisis	18	17	32	11	5	83

Note: cells contain the number of articles containing the term at least once – in the *definite* or the *in*definite form.

Table 7.4 'Crisis+' with 'economy+', 'politics+', 'market+' in *Dagens Nyheter* and *Expressen*

	1992	1993	1994	1995	1996	Total
Crisis+/Economy+	785	851	544	465	352	2997
Crisis+/Politics+	163	195	122	127	85	692
Crisis+/Market+	52	39	25	37	21	174

Note: cells contain the number of articles containing both terms at least once, in the same paragraph of the unit; '+' refers to the term used in different forms or in compound wordings.

Confirming the results of Table 7.2, Table 7.4 indicates that in the news texts examined, the connection between 'crisis' and 'economy' is made more than four times as often as is the case with 'crisis' and 'politics'. Table 7.4 also confirms that the use of the term 'crisis' diminishes over time – even when we looked at its connection with the two other terms. It is striking here that it is rare for the term 'market' to be linked to 'crisis'. It seems that crises are much more to do with the systemic concept of 'the economy' than with the corresponding concept of 'the market'. Discursively those two differ significantly, a point we will return to below.

Characteristics of economic news on crisis

In contrast to the broad, but narrowly quantitative, description of the use of economy and crisis terms, we now move to a closer look at the form of crisis news. A number of stories from *Dagens Nyheter* for 1992 were isolated for closer analysis. The choice of year is appropriate, as commentaries on the crisis in Sweden were particularly prominent in this period and the reporting of crisis increased in the spheres of banking and finance, currency and interest rates. Moreover, the budget deficit was high and rising and unemployment began to increase. We will start by analysing the specific discursive features of the news selection and move on to look at the embedded economic crisis discourse. The focus here is the 'Labour and Money' section of *Dagens Nyheter*.[10] From this corpus of news text, articles were isolated in which the terms 'economy' and 'crisis' (in any form) appeared at least once within the same paragraph. Altogether, 103 news texts were found, carrying at least one paragraph dealing with 'economic crisis', with 'economy' and 'crisis' or with 'economics' and 'crisis'.[11] These are useful in illustrating the kinds of news constructions used in economic coverage and allow an insight into the discursive features of crisis reporting. A number of issues will be dealt with. This is also done in an effort to contextualize the 'crisis talk' of the news stories. First, some plain descriptive features will be introduced; second, a typology of news constructions will be used to categorize the news texts; third, some of the thematic dimensions that were typical of economic crisis news stories will be analysed as a step towards understanding their discursive features.

Descriptive features

It should be noted, first, that about 10–15 per cent of the texts analysed were introduced as 'commentary', 'analysis', 'background' or 'summaries'. These were mixed with the more common news texts, although they did not have a specific placement within the layout of the page and, so, may be treated by the reader in a similar way. The commentaries carried opinions as well as news, trends, comparisons and predictions. Many of them had the same author, Johan Schück, who was also the most frequent economic reporter and was responsible for 14 texts. The rest (i.e. the bulk of the 103 articles) were ordinary news stories, the majority of which (about 70 texts) were written by *Dagens Nyheter* reporters. In total, 37 *Dagens Nyheter* reporters contributed, most writing between one and three articles. Less than 15 stories were constructed from news agency copy, mostly from the Swedish agencies TT and Direkt. Below, we will focus on the whole corpus of 103 articles.

Only 31 actors and sources, in total, were cited or referred to in the news texts – 20 of those were Swedes, and of the rest six were Finns, with one each from Norway, the UK, Ireland, Italy and Russia. Looking at positions and occupations of this whole group, not surprisingly the economists were the most frequently represented (14), with the politicians the next most prominent (9), followed by managing directors (4), state officials (3), and one 'ordinary person ', who, in this case, was an unemployed woman. Looking at gender, it should be noted that only another two women appeared – the female party secretary of the Swedish Social Democrats, Mona Sahlin, and a newly appointed female head of the Finnish central bank, Sirkka Hämäläinen. So, the economic crisis news of *Dagens Nyheter* seems to be a male affair, as is the economic sphere itself. However, among the 37 *journalists* responsible for the news texts, there were seven females who wrote 10 of the stories – mostly on labour, family and international economic news.

Geographically, the focus of crisis news was, of course, primarily on Sweden, but less so than might have been expected. Around half of the stories (54) dealt principally with Sweden, 13 with Finland and four with the rest of Scandinavia. Another 10 concerned Western European nations outside Scandinavia, especially with the UK (8). Eight dealt with Europe in general or the EC, the ERM or the EMU, and ten with Eastern Europe, especially Russia. Two dealt with Japan, one with the USA, and one with the UN. The attention paid to Finland was considerable, possibly because its symptoms of crisis and the processes involved paralleled and preceded those of Sweden. Except for the news stories on Europe and European organizations, only 11 news texts explicitly compared economic crises in different countries or connect Sweden's crisis to economic slumps or crises elsewhere. The most frequent cases were relations between Sweden and the USA (4), and Sweden and Finland (4). Looking at the whole corpus of news stories, one may still conclude that during 1992 *Dagens Nyheter* took some interest in contextualizing the Swedish crisis news – connecting it to crises in the surrounding European countries, especially Finland. This seems to be in contrast with mainstream economic news, where the dominance of Swedish stories is more pronounced (see Lindhoff and Mårtenson, 1996a).

News constructions of economic crisis

Having pointed at some descriptive features, we will continue introducing and applying a typology of news adapted from Ekecrantz and Olsson (1994). They developed a typology of four basic (or ideal-type) news constructions. They took a corpus of 500 Swedish news articles, selected from a longitudinal study straddling the twentieth century (with focal points at 1910, 1935, 1960 and 1990), and analysed them according to their function and their relation to sources and readers (as well as to prevailing journalistic practices). The resulting typology generates four basic ideal-type text constructions: the case description, compound representation, narrative and concerted action. The authors found that compound representations were ever-present in news journalism and that concerted actions were typical of 1990s news (see also Ekecrantz, 1997; Ekecrantz and Olsson, 1991).

Two earlier explorations of this form of typology (Lindhoff and Mårtenson, 1995, 1996a,b) confirmed the findings of Ekecrantz and Olsson and informed the categorization of our 1992 corpus of 103 economic crisis news stories. A differentiation was first made between reports focusing primarily on economic events and circumstances ('primary representations') and those focused primarily on the accounts of economic actors, including the attribution of blame, the advancing of 'solutions' and the investigative work of journalists ('secondary representations'). A further differentiation was made between broadly diachronic and broadly synchronic accounts. Allowing for some overlap, this gives us four basic categories in the typology. The results are outlined in Table 7.5.

It should be noted that the *main* points of the respective news stories have been the focus when applying this system of classification. So, for instance, when time is more crucial to the news construction of an item than space, it will be referred to as 'diachronic'. Or when the journalistic strategy of the item seems to be dominated by 'primary representations', the assignment of an article to a category will not be the same as those instances where forms of 'secondary representation' predominate in the strategy of the news item. The latter was often the case where the reporter used many sources and voices.[12]

In the present application of the analytical model to the study of economic crisis news, two types of news constructions dominate and the results are consistent with those derived from earlier studies. First and foremost, there are compound representations, based on financial accounts, on inquiries into current economic and crisis states of affairs, on recent forecasts of economic

Table 7.5 Constructions of crisis in *Dagens Nyheter*'s 'Labour & Money' section

	Time–space orientation	
	---	---
Journalistic strategy	Diachronic	Synchronic
Primary representations	*Narrative* (8 items) Unemployed woman Crisis of the 1920s Finnish budget crisis	*Case descriptions* (7 items) Expositions of celebrities Businesses in bankruptcy Particular national economies

Secondary representations	*Concerted action*
	(39 items)
	Remedies/claims from:
	  Government
	  Bank of Sweden
	  Economists
	  Business
	  Trade unions
		Compound representation
		(49 items)
		Financial accounts of firms
		Inquiries into economic affairs
		Inquiries into the state of crisis
		Recent forecasts and plans

indicators, or on plans of economic actors (49 of the 103 news items). Second, the reader would find various forms of concerted action: on specific economic crisis initiatives, from the government, the Bank of Sweden, the business community, committed economists, trade unions or other actors. The most conspicuous concerted actions are those launching Swedish 'crisis packages' to counteract the currency and budget deficit crisis of the autumn of 1992 (39 news items).

Less frequent among the media texts on the economy are diachronic *narratives* (eight items) and synchronic *case descriptions* (seven items). Narratives occurred, for instance, when telling the story of a woman becoming unemployed as a result of the crisis (or when people draw on family experiences of Sweden in the 1920s and 1930s, or crises in Denmark, Russia or the USA). Examples of a grand narrative of crisis also recur in the material, for example, in relation to the Finnish budget crisis. The most typical case descriptions apply to comments about certain economic and political celebrities, business companies on the brink of bankruptcy or other nations currently in crisis, such as Estonia, Ukraine, or Norway.

Applying the time–space dichotomy to economic news may resolve the obvious paradox pointed out by the Public Communication Group, Liverpool University (1995) – that the economy and the economic crisis appear, in reality as well as in the news, simultaneously as an extremely complex system of interrelated variables and as an apparent narrative over time. The paradox may be seen as a tension between the synchronic complexity of space-oriented economic news constructions on the one hand, and, on the other, the diachronic clarity of time-oriented news constructions – in the form of episodes or stories. The results, when applying the ideal typology to the crisis news, show that the news items are evenly distributed along the time–space dimension. However, the diachronic episodes that might help the public with concrete illustrations of the complexity indicated in compound representations are dominated, instead, by 'concerted actions'. This means that they are formed as journalistic events, mostly from source initiatives, with few narrative representations. And as regards the synchronic news constructions of crisis, primary representations (in the form of concrete case descriptions) are not frequent either (see Corner (1995) on news narrative in relation to news exposition).

Discursive features of 'the economic'

We will now look more closely at the issue of characterizing some of the discursive features of economic reporting. In dealing with media discourses it has been common to concentrate the analysis on linguistic and rhetorical aspects, in order to make it clear how certain discursive traits are formulated in the media texts (see Fairclough, 1995; van Dijk, 1988; Fowler, 1991). Here we concentrate, instead, on those important dimensions of discourse which primarily concern economic and crisis content, i.e. the particular topics, biases, themes and perspectives that dominate or are absent from the news texts under analysis. This is an avenue of investigation into the discourse of economic news that has been pioneered in the studies of Emmison (1983), Jensen (1987) and Rae and Drury (1993). Our focus, then, is on the thematic side of the economic crisis news reporting. What are the focal points and predominant features? We are looking, first, for 'the economic' of economic crisis discourse. The survey below focuses on a few economically relevant dimensions and stresses the systemic character of the economy. However crude, these have been chosen as being sufficiently defined within the economic system or within economic thought itself (see Huge-mark, 1994; Parsons, 1989). This approach also seems to be productive when discussing media discourse on the economic crisis in relation to surrounding or neighbouring discourses, i.e. professional or political ones.

When looking into media discourse, the economy may be viewed as a system of complex components or indicators that are related, empirically as well as theoretically – for example, inflation, unemployment, budget deficits, exchange rates, interest rates and savings. Taken together, these components constitute a synthetic state or position (Corner *et al.*, 1993). Such a holistic view is consistent with the idea of 'the economy' as a reified notion – appearing as an independent social force (Emmison, 1983). The same may hold for the notion of 'the economic crisis' that appears in the newspaper texts under analysis here.

One way of determining substantive features of the economic crisis discourse would be to focus on the hierarchy of (and the relationship between) important economic components or indicators. The analysis in the preceding section was a rough attempt to classify the whole news corpus of *Dagens Nyheter* and *Expressen* in the period 1992-96 (Figure 7.1 and Tables 7.1, 7.3 and 7.4). Complementing that strategy, the main objective now is to look at the general and economically relevant dimensions of the economic crisis news in our corpus. First, the dominant time perspective of the articles will be established. Second, the news reports will be discussed in terms of their focus on material or symbolic components of the economy. Third, a distinction is made between the 'micro' level and the 'macro' level. Finally, the 'market' dimension of the economy will be commented upon.

The time focus of the economic crisis items has been categorized either as oriented towards historical trends, current affairs and situations or oriented to the future. Often two or more time perspectives may be present in a news story; in most cases we have noted only the main focus of each item. In 25 cases, however, a secondary time perspective has been noted as well. When judging the time focus one has to disregard the syntactic verb forms, as the predominant habit of journalism is to collapse the past as well as the future into the present through the tense of verbs – thus making anything a current topic of interest irrespective of the actual time focus. So, one has to look for the temporal meaning of an utterance or a statement.[13] By these criteria, half of the news stories are dominated by a future focus (53 items). Historical perspectives hold for 28 items, while the current focus was valid for 22 items only. When we include the secondary time perspectives of the news texts as well (in 25 items), the 'futural' focus is a little less dominant. This is similar to the balance found in an earlier study of all economic news stories in *Dagens Nyheter* (as well as two other Swedish dailies) during one week in November of 1995 (Lindhoff and Mårtenson, 1996a).

So it seems to be typical of the economic media discourse to talk of the future. However, this should not surprise us, considering the importance of expectations and predictions in market economic systems. The frequency of historical parallels (and of reports on the financial accounts and reports which form the basis for predictions) makes the historical category a substantial one. The fact that the news items studied here concern economic crises does not diminish our interest in looking for future solutions or historical analogies for the crises. It may be added that the tendency of written journalism of the

1990s to make current news out of future eventualities has been observed also in a longitudinal Swedish study of all kinds of news journalism (Ekecrantz, 1997).

News reports also vary in their level of focus on material or symbolic components of the economy (see Lindhoff and Mårtenson, 1996a). We explored our selection of 103 news items for this material–symbolic dichotomy and found a predominance of *symbolic* perspectives on economic crisis (65 news items).[14] Only 38 items were devoted to material aspects of the crisis economy. The economy of today is still oriented towards production, the labour force, fixed capital assets, financial accounts, results and concrete money. These are all material components. However, to an increased extent the economy deals with and is becoming dependent on symbolic assets, components and transactions. The financial side of the economy is growing fast, and with it the importance of expectations, professional guessing, forecasts and predictions, estimates of risks, speculation and planning for the future (cf. Lash and Urry, 1994). Obviously those aspects are connected to the question of time perspective too, i.e. to the important role played by 'futural' perspectives. However, the symbolic dimension of communication plays an increasingly important role within the economy, through advertising and commercial channels, through e-mail and the Internet, but also through common talk and utterances via traditional journalistic media. This is especially the case within the financial sectors of the economy, where electronic networks are used for trading, while similar networks constitute on-line media reporting and commentary on transactions. Actions taken, as well as word-of-mouth, may influence expectations and, with them, market behaviour. As market forces expand, those tendencies towards a symbolic economy strengthen. Obviously, this holds for news reports on economic crises too – like guessing the consequences of the crisis or speculating on ways out of it.

When looking at the micro- and macro-dimensions that are embedded in the economic crisis news, we find that these notions are used in a way that corresponds to traditional forms of economic analysis. 'Micro' here refers to the structure of markets and the behaviour of actors, while 'macro' implies an analysis at the societal or national level. When looking at the economic crisis news, the macro-level was predominant (71 out of the 103 items). The rest may be assigned to the micro-level. Of the latter, about a third cope with branches or sectors of business (sometimes referred to by sociologists as the 'meso' level), while 21 items concern individual actors, mostly within particular companies. Concrete reports of crisis conditions in specific companies were more rare in our selection than general news stories about the societal crisis state. One possible reason for this may be the criteria for news item selection. On the other hand, it seems quite probable (and reasonable) that *Dagens Nyheter* concentrated on the macro-economic crisis during 1992. This was a year in which Sweden experienced several crises – in the areas of finance, currency, the budget deficit, and unemployment.

Turning to those areas and actors which were not frequently represented in the crisis news stories, there are some interesting features worth mentioning. Just one item talks of regional crisis and only four items are concerned with the problems of local communities. There were only eight articles, in total, quoting or referring to trade unions, and seven dealing with or mentioning individuals as citizens or members of a household. It should be added that in these cases the macro-level perspective dominates. This means that the stories are rarely concrete and substantive. In conclusion, it is evident that the crisis news items from the 'Labour & Money' section of *Dagens Nyheter* very seldom report the ways in which the economic crisis hits the private economy of, for instance, wage earners or the unemployed. The resulting psychological crisis that can arise from this sort of trauma is dealt with on only two occasions (and the unemployed woman mentioned earlier figures in one of them).

It is also striking that the market is not often used in those articles in our corpus where the economy-in-crisis is covered. About 20 instances of the term were found. Half of these signified the labour market and the others referred to the market(s), market forces, the market economy, market interest rates, the credit market, the furniture market, etc. Instead, 'the market' is either represented in subordinate parts of the news stories or is presupposed to be important. It looks as though 'the market' and 'the crisis' do not meet each other in the body of the economic news discourse, although the market must be considered as crucial for the current crisis discourses.[15] A possible interpretation of this discursive trait can be found in the notion that 'the market' is neither hit by 'the crisis', nor is it the cause of 'the crisis'. However, the labour market is left as an exception – unemployment is touched upon in 13 news items, for instance. It is quite often presupposed that 'the market', while not part of the problem, is still part of the solution to 'the crisis'.

Conclusion

In this chapter we have made an effort to study the main features of economic crisis reporting within Swedish newspaper journalism. Without trying to apply specific criteria, we found it possible to combine analysis of the real economy of the 1990s with a quantitative examination of discursive terms embedded in news, and a more intensive interpretative focus on a limited number of news texts. This allowed the identification of some discursive patterns that are characteristic of economic crisis news. Certainly, an even more intensive and detailed analysis of contexts would be necessary to fully validate the results. However, some important conclusions can still be sketched out. We will start with the descriptive and quantitative analysis of economic terms.

The economic term most widely use in Swedish journalism of the 1990s seems to have been 'the market' (Figure 7.1). Irrespective of the development of crises, it is very frequent. The extent of 'economization' of newspaper journalism is also manifest in the fact that 'the economy' is as frequently deployed in news coverage of 1992–96 as is 'politics'/'policy'. We have also demonstrated that the notion of 'the crisis' in newspaper coverage stands for 'the economic crisis' rather than any other crisis (although political crises may, in some specific instances, be an exception). According to our analyses, it is reasonable to assume that these terms are being reified – the terms live a life of their own within the newspaper texts, often without being defined.[16]

The 'budget deficit' and 'unemployment' are terms indicating specific types of economic crises. On one hand, during the first three years of the period the budget deficit was one of the most severe crisis problems and consequently the coverage in the newspapers was more visible than in the following two years. On the other hand, it seems that 'unemployment' has been allowed to develop as a more prominent term in 1996, although problems in the labour market started to appear as early as 1993. Does this mean that 'unemployment' is not as closely connected to 'the economic crisis' as other crisis factors? The prominence of the term 'the crisis' has declined over the years, while the corresponding trend for 'unemployment' is rising. Also, the impression given by our intensive analysis of news texts is that the unemployed seldom get a voice – at least within the 'Labour & Money' section of *Dagens Nyheter*.

The analysis of co-occurence of two reified terms verifies the notion that the 'economy'-and-'crisis' combination is four times as prominent as that of 'politics/policy'-and-'crisis'. Perhaps more surprising is the fact that in the same coverage the combination 'crisis'-and-'market' is rather infrequent. Evidently, the notion of 'the market' does not signify a crisis problem. Nor is it portrayed as an explanation for the crisis or used as a symbol of the consequences of the crisis. When we look more closely, it is obvious that the term 'the market' is used, but not in the context of discussion of the crisis. Alternatively, it is assumed to be an appropriate solution to many of the crises afflicting the economy.

The term 'the economy' is approached from a 'futural' perspective and is dealt with in symbolic terms that touch on thoughts, hopes, expectations, predictions, considerations, plans, etc. Usually, this is done from a 'macro' rather than a 'micro' perspective. Journalistically, compound representations and concerted actions abound – many of them highly dependent on particular sourced voices. However, these individual actors (and sources) were not often visible and named (only in a quarter of news texts). When this did happen, expert economists constitute half of these actors, and politicians another third.

Further work on this material is currently under way, with attention being paid to the representation of causes, consequences and solutions for 'crisis'. Results so far indicate a significant absence of historical perspectives and explanations (in contrast to the UK mass media, see Gavin and Goddard, 1998). There is also some indication of tension between a discourse of market forces (the 'active economy') and (neo)Keynesian discourse (the 'active policy'/'passive economy'). One important task for future research will be to map the complex interrelations of these two discourses.

Notes

1   This is part of continuing research on economic journalism in Sweden, carried out at JMK, Stockholm University. It is funded by the Bank of Sweden Tercentenary Foundation, to which thanks are due. I would like to thank Bo Mårtenson and Kjell Nowak, members of the research group in Stockholm, for their comments on earlier drafts of this chapter. Thanks are due, as well, to the members of the Public Communications Group of the University of Liverpool for a fruitful exchange of views.

2   In February 1997 the Swedish bank sector was recovering; they all report high profits from 1996 (25–30 billion Swedish krona in all), with Nordbanken in the lead, according to *Dagens Nyheter*, 18 February 1997.

3   Having recovered most of the state's crisis support via profits and the selling of shares, the finance minister is now planning to privatize Nordbanken.

4   This figure should be reduced to half by the year 2000. This was the aim of the new Social Democratic prime minister Göran Persson, when entering his office in March 1996.

5   Tunstall (1996, p. 354) has made similar observations with regard to the expansion of financial journalism in the UK press.

6   During the period from 1992 to 1996 about 10 per cent of the contributions to the debate in this section dealt with economic matters. During peak periods, this proportion could rise to 30 per cent. The ordinary letter-to-the-editor section is for ordinary people, and although probably much read by the audience, is considered to be a less important part of the paper.

7   In Swedish there is no difference between notions of politics and policy, or between notions of economy and economics. The context decides. In compound wordings the parts stick together as in 'ekonomipolitik', meaning economic policy.

8   When Tunstall (1996, p. 297) indicates that 'crisis' is a significant issue within UK journalism – most often to do with governments experiencing political crisis.

9   We might also note that Figure 7.1 shows 'unemployment' and 'the crisis' trending in different directions.

10 According to an earlier study of *Dagens Nyheter* economic news in 1995, about half of all economically relevant news items were

found in the section on 'Labour & Money' (Lindhoff and Mårtenson, 1996a).

11 Of course, the 103 articles are just a subset of all those texts in *Dagens Nyheter* representing 'the economy' and 'the crisis' or 'the economic crisis'. This is obvious when they are compared with the data introduced in Tables 7.2 to 7.4 above. For instance, many texts on 'the banking crisis', 'the finance crisis' or 'the currency crisis' may not contain paragraphs which conform to the criteria we have chosen here for isolating articles.

12 An alternative application would have been to judge each paragraph of a news story separately, assigning it to one of the ideal-type news constructions. If news stories had varied strongly in their structure, this procedure might have produced a different result.

13 A historical focus is typical of statements concerning what happened long ago (or some time ago) or of compound representations based on final accounts of companies or of historical comparisons. A current focus holds for descriptions of a state of affairs, of present conditions, of recent occurrences, and of recent utterances about the future (when being recent is more important than the futural aspect). A future focus may also be identified by the tense of the verb, but more often through various expressions of prediction, speculation, expectation and planning. Moreover, expressions concerning process or talk of the possible effects of current trends, etc., have been judged to have a future focus.

14 It should be noted that this dichotomy is used here to encompass the economy/crisis content or reference to news on the economic crisis.

15 A similar tendency was observed at the more general level, as shown by the categorizing of the whole of the news corpus in Table 7.4.

16 The exception is the case of the term 'depression'. Although used infrequently (only five times out of 103 articles), it is always in a context indicating possible future depression, e.g. 'at the risk of ...', 'warning of ...', 'developing into ...', 'transforming into ...' depression.

8
Journalistic practice and economic reporting

Economic news and the dynamics of understanding – a response

Evan Davis

It is not uncommon for academics in different areas to discuss their subject in a style, a tone and language far removed from those used by day-to-day practitioners in related professions. That tendency is apparent in Chapter 1 of this book, although I am pleased to report that the gulf between the language of the university-based commentators and those of us working in the media is not as wide as I suspect it is in some other disciplines. Nevertheless, it has to be said that much of the chapter reads, to me, a trace naively. For example, the first part of the paper provides a relatively mundane description of economics news pieces – observing that they contain pieces-to-camera, graphics, and pictures that are loosely related to the subject being discussed. It does this in a language unfamiliar to the normal broadcast journalist (e.g. 'core depictive material'). It is almost reminiscent of the aliens describing mashed potato in the specialized space-man jargon of the Smash advertisements of the 1970s. This aside, the conclusions of the chapter – and, in particular, the emphasis on audience comprehension – are well supported and believable, although they are by and large not very surprising. But can we understand the process of reporting the economy better by looking at the day-to-day pressures on those reporting the economy? While I do not think we should be uncritical of the way in which we do things, I think the answer to this question is yes. So let me describe some of those pressures.

For one thing, the most pressing constraint on journalists is the need to provide a one- or two-minute report that conforms to the usual grammar of television news. That means that one has to have several voices in a piece (and they cannot usually be shorter than eight seconds, or longer than 25 seconds without sounding strange). One has to have pictures. One has to devise a script that 'talks to the pictures', i.e. that refers to the 'thematically supporting visual stimuli' in a direct and relevant way. One usually has to have a peg – a reason for reporting for whatever is being reported, in terms of events that have passed on the day in question. One might question whether these requirements are truly as necessary as journalists and editors sincerely believe they are. But it is generally true that items that deviate from this form significantly distract viewers and attract the criticism of 'being a bit weird'. The BBC is keen to promote alternative forms of presentation – the feature, for example – but there is a limit to how much of this one can do without changing the perceived character of the bulletin in a very significant way.

The pressure to conform in style constrains the subject matter and the ability to explain economics. One cannot be abstract – other than in pieces-to-camera – because that involves deviating from pictures. One cannot cover some issues, because no-one talks about them (the affairs of private companies often fall outside of broadcast news for this reason). One cannot dwell on a careful explanation of some phenomenon, because that involves too much time on a particular picture sequence. One cannot always provide a logical explanation, because supporting sync (external voice) may not fit with the explanation being offered. Then there is the second pressure, to provide a reasonably comprehensive coverage of the issue in question. Balance between different points of view often detracts from comprehension. At its most extreme, there is the sequence of three-party sync – where different spokespeople from the political parties each talk in meaningless terms for 12 seconds or so to counter the view provided by the Chancellor, who is often the person who makes the decisions being reported. Often, there is perceived pressure to do justice to all aspects of a story, in order that no facet is left out. That may involve piling on details – or statistics – that are obviously extraneous to the ordinary viewers' needs. There is the related problem that there are a number of different audiences for any news piece, so that one has to help both the 'new readers' who start knowing nothing about the story so far, and the established viewers, who know a good deal of the plot already. We have to take account of those viewers who need interpretation, and those who just need the facts.

An additional problem is the fact that bulletins – unlike the BBC's other output – cannot run repeats too often. There is a need to keep reporting the economy – and sometimes, quite frankly, it is hard to think of interesting new things to say, unless one wanders into more subtle territory, away from the mainstream facts about the obvious variables. Finally, in reporting the economy, one has to take account of the fact that the mood-swings of those whose job it is to understand and comment on the economy are often more substantial than one would like them to be. If the markets – supported by economists – change their mind over the course of a week, and if they do so in a newsworthy way, then it is not surprising that those who report the economy change their tone over the week as well. That is just the way the material being reported comes in. It is possible to argue that it would be beyond the bounds of journalistic licence to hide the changing perceptions from the public, any more than weather forecasters should hide changing forecasts from the public.

I mention these pressures not as excuses, but as explanations. However, overall it should always be remembered that the main goal is to broadcast something on time – and that pressure is often the one that is decisive in shaping the output. We often look at our pieces and could think of ways in which they could improve on one criterion or another. But complete comprehension of all viewers would not be the only criterion by which to judge them. Often, what may look like quite a bad piece may in fact be an astonishing triumph of endeavour – given the time available to prepare it, the voices on offer to speak in it, the pictures ready to be pulled together, and the needs of a particular audience to whom the story most directly matters.

In addition, as an apology for what we do, I would say that we should really be judged not on the basis of individual reports – important as they are – but on the basis of the general pictures painted over time. Those producing bulletins are conscious of their need to provide what one might call 'long-term balance', and are more conscious of the difficulty of providing a comprehensively representative picture in any one report. It is a bit unfair to apply too much weight to any one report. For example, at the time of writing the pound is high, and that is hurting exporters. One way of getting this across would be to run an explanatory report on this issue. That would score well. But it is not the only way – one might alternatively mention the issue in a more peripheral way in a number of reports. What matters, surely, is that over the course of a few months, people should have 'picked the right impression up'. Indeed, the risk of relying on one sweeping report to get that point across is that a large swathe of viewers will miss it. Then, to ensure balance, you have to run repeats of the report, or run mentions of the subject in other economic reports.

But enough of the apologies and excuses. Let me offer a few musings of how we might improve things. Undoubtedly, by releasing some of the constraints under which we work, one might improve the output. This involves decisions that affect the whole format of news and current affairs. But, for example, I am sure we could be more imaginative in the formats we adopt – have more illustrated monologues; have lengthier graphic explanation (not of the figures, but of the abstract relationship between variables); allow sync to run far longer sometimes; or use one witness in a piece several times, rather than insisting on several different voices. All of these would break the rather stagnant and constrained form in which we force ourselves to explain and report. Personally, I would also be inclined to report rather less of the day-to-day economic news, particularly the less important figures. We should be willing to either let them pass unreported, or we could just mark them with a mention, as a matter of record for those who are interested. And I think, in general, we need to be far more willing to run themed-type current affairs items on the bulletins, and only the most tenuous of daily pegs. We should probably keep a playlist of interesting themes in mind (from the obvious to the obscure – from globalization to changing patterns of retailing) and we should run items on these when an excuse offers itself.

Finally, I also think that we are pretty weak at finding tasty angles to business and economic stories. Of course a lot of it is dry, but it is possible to find drama, personality, tension and other interesting devices to make the news more interesting. I would be unashamed about trivializing the news, as long as the trivial item contains an uplifting and challenging element. It is interesting that the 'Ken and Eddie show' (Chancellor and Bank of England Governor) has proved much the easiest and most palatable route to coverage of the dilemmas of monetary policy. Not, indeed, just for the audience of Radio One, but also for Radio Four and the city sections of the daily broadsheets. We would have been mad not to have availed ourselves of the opportunity to personalize debates about interest rates, and if we had never followed the Ken and Eddie route, we would simply have covered interest rates less. We should aim to find that kind of drama in other stories too. Our function is to open a door to some heavy themes – the door obviously has to be enticing.

I offer this list not as a coherent manifesto for change, but as a set of loose thoughts that suggest themselves from the constraints outlined. In fairness, at least at the BBC, most of these points are to some extent recognized. There are difficulties in treading new paths, however, and, understandably, progress tends to be slow. Most importantly, confronted with a half-hour to fill, on a slow day, when maybe several crews are out of action for other outlets, do not be surprised if you get news reports that are less snappy than you might like.

Reporting the economy

John Williams

Like most political journalists, I have never been taught economics. It was a Cinderella subject at my school. I know only what I have picked up along the way. All three of the country's top-selling newspapers – *Sun*, *Mirror*, and *Mail* rely mainly on political non-specialists like me to keep their millions of readers informed about the economy. This says as much about the readers as it does about the papers. It says a great deal about our democracy too. The UK has many qualities, but you would not list numeracy among them. There is little demand for economics among newspaper readers; using the political staff is good market economics.

The political correspondent should be as capable of grasping economics as he is able to deal with arms to Iraq, Mad Cow Disease, education policy, crime and punishment, opinion-polling, Tony Blair's hairstyle and all the other myriad topics that a good professional can handle in the course of a day's work. If we have no economic training, we do perhaps have the same gut feel for the underlying truth about the economy as our readers, or so we would like to think. This is not to say that we do not take economics seriously. At the risk of sounding pompous, I am worried about this country taking a decision as large as joining or staying out of the single currency against a background of ignorance, nationalism, hysteria and sheer idleness. Let us be honest about our fellow citizens and admit that few, if any, are boning up on the Maastricht criteria and the stability pact in order to be well-equipped for the fateful decision that awaits them in the referendum some time between 1998 and 2002. The press is doing little to infiltrate some knowledge into the national indifference to this historic choice. Worse, some newspapers are poisoning the public mind. The anti-European press is waging a dirty war against the single currency. Meanwhile, the pro-European press, like pro-European MPs, fails to put a vigorous case for. It is so much easier to rail against than to argue for. If we are not careful, the *Sun* will not only make the single currency untenable for any UK government, but will drive us out of Europe.

Standing up to this dangerous bigotry is not a task for economic specialists. While my lack of economic training bothers me, I am arrogant enough to believe that I can put the pro-European case better than a gaggle of economics graduates. Economics is too important to be left to the specialists. When I wrote a piece saying our fear of the single currency has much to do with the inferiority complex created by Franz Beckenbauer in the 1970 World Cup quarter-final, I was not being flippant. That was a calculated attempt to make the issue understandable to the non-specialist on the terraces, whose lifestyle will be affected more than he or she could dream by the wrong decision on the single currency. The *Sun* and *Mail* present the Euro as if it were merely a 'threat to the pound' and as if the chief consequence would be the disappearance of the Queen's head on our age-old currency, which goes back about ten years in the case of the pound coin. Nobody reading a popular newspaper – indeed, any newspaper outside the financial pages and the better political commentaries – would have much idea of the single currency's implications for monetary policy. Indeed, monetary policy is not a phrase you will read in most newspapers.

One of the main constraints on the part-time economics correspondents like me is the impossibility of using the kind of jargon that the economics correspondent of a broadsheet takes for granted – and a good thing too. Jargon is a disease and the popular journalist the surgeon. We never talk about the PSBR or fiscal drag or the underlying trend. But there is an important question here, which we seldom ask ourselves. By avoiding technicalities, do we simplify or do we censor? Do we skilfully translate econo-speak into English, or do we skim over the surface of complex issues? I sometimes fear we are more inclined to duck issues than decipher the complexities that determine people's lives. For instance, I would always try to avoid a word like 'deficit'. Simple though it may be for the specialist, it is just not a newspaper word. The concept of the government deficit is almost never addressed in popular newspapers. Yet the deficit reduction required by the single currency will have a deep impact on real lives. We do not do enough to explain and prepare our readers for the hard choices ahead. I was very struck by the comments of the focus groups who took part in this project (presented in Chapter 1) and by their fear of economics. This confirms my feeling that, as soon as you mention a jargon word like deficit, readers and viewers switch off. We should not shirk from explaining unwelcome ideas to an unwilling audience. Or is circulation all that matters? This is not a trite question, or new. If the papers had explained the Depression a little better, the country may have elected a more imaginative leadership than the national government of MacDonald and Baldwin.

How do I approach economic reporting? I start from the premise that there is no such thing as objectivity. How can anyone be objective about Ford switching from Halewood, about Toyota warning it might not invest here if we do not join a single currency, about the pre-election falls in unemployment, or about Ken Clarke's interest rate battles with Eddie George? To feign objectivity is to be dishonest. This is my defence of my pro-Labour, pro-European journalism. You know what you are getting and you can discount my attitude if you like. Having said that, even subjective reporting should avoid deception. How often do the anti-European newspapers point out how little the Social Chapter contains? The *Mail* carried a piece about a businesswoman who was threatening to move her firm to Morocco if we signed the Social Chapter. The piece did not point out that, since she employed only 450 people, she would not be affected by the works councils required by the Social Chapter, because they apply only to firms employing 1000 or more.

But, then, does any of it matter? There is some evidence that none of our fine words are read at all. There could hardly have been more coverage of Gordon Brown's pledge not to raise income tax. Yet, a month later, Labour focus groups were reporting nil public recognition of the no-tax pledge. Newspaper coverage of tax is even more pernicious than coverage of Europe. If politicians lie about tax, it is because we make them. It ought to be obvious to anyone that tax might sometimes go up, as well as down. But the Conservatives have created a culture in which the public willingly suspends its disbelief in the reality about tax. They talk as if any rise in public spending, however small, is a threat to the basic rate and journalists connive at this distortion, especially broadcasters ('But where is the money coming from, Mr Brown?'). Labour has no choice but to play the Tory game. If Tony Blair had pointed out, like the economic forecasters, that Ken Clarke's sums were so tight that taxes were likely to rise under either government, he would have been taken apart.

What is the picture that most readers get of the economy from their newspapers? In February 1997, they read that unemployment is down; inflation is up a bit, but not dangerously, though interest rates may have to rise to curb it. We never explain how higher interest rates curb inflation. We write about interest rates purely in terms of mortgages, because mortgages interest our readers. If our readers have registered the recent rise of the pound, do they realize this could be good for their holiday but bad for their jobs? We leave our readers adrift on a sea of unconnected facts. I hate to be a pessimist. But I cannot imagine how the electorate of this mature democracy makes its choices in the fog of indifference and misunderstanding to which people are condemned by our innumerate education system, newspapers and politicians. Or could it be that the voters somehow discern the larger shapes without being distracted by detail? One of the great pre-election mysteries was why the voters seem so unmoved by the economic recovery to which all the conventional indicators point. Was this a result of poor public understanding of economics? Or was it that the public understands the fundamentals far better than the specialists and realized the recovery was not as real as the figures suggest? Was the government failing to make its economic message clear through the fog, or was the public making an instinctive, real-life judgement that is more valid than the opinion of any number of economists? I hope so. I do hope the public has a gut feel for the single currency decision. Otherwise, if the country makes the wrong decision, the public is going to turn round in the early 21st century and say – why did nobody tell us this was going to happen? It is a terrifying thought and we all – politicians, journalists and economists – have a responsibility to ensure that whatever mistakes this country makes are made knowingly.

The unexplainable explained, or pure guesswork as 'truth'

Peter Malmqvist

On 17 March 1997, the Swedish bond interest rates went up by 20 points in one day. That was a huge jump and worrying if it represented the start of a new trend. Memories of 1993–94 came rushing back. At that time, the interest rate rose suddenly and continued to do so for half a year, until the level had been doubled. 'Incomprehensible', many had thought. So, when the rate of interest increased in March 1997, the question was inevitably, why? In fact, the answer is not terribly interesting. It is more important to try to follow the event through the various media during the day. That can tell us more about why economic journalism, in particular financial journalism, in Sweden has been buffeted in the climate of the last few years.

Time has become the one and only competitive factor. The choice between 'fast and fairly correct' or 'slow and really correct' is not practical for today's economic reporters. Speed is decisive. When the interest rates jumped on 17 March, the following chain of events occurred. The reporters within the digital, on-line media – being at the front of the news chain – were obliged to find out *why* quickly. Their computer pages must not flash empty (in their advertisements, 'efficiency' is measured by how much faster, in seconds, they have been than their competitors on big news events). To perform their research, they need an extensive network of sources among the actors in the financial market. A large number of calls must be made, since several sources will be at meetings, travelling or 'unavailable'. Telephone research does yield results, however. In this case, comments by sources were put together for a news story of the event, and then were quickly transmitted to the computer network. The length of the story was about 20 lines. The citations from financial sources made by the news agencies are almost always without names ('according to an analyst'). The reporters of the on-line media probably have to promise anonymity to be able to develop a large network of useable sources. These vague citations should have had low credibility, but they did not.

Then the following is likely to have happened. Those reporters on newspapers, television and radio who were assigned to research the interest rate jump after their morning meetings started by looking at the commentaries of the on-line media. This computer approach, supported by intricate search functions, helps make capable reporters fully up-to-date, at the outset, on the answers that will be given. This is not the whole story, however. The news text of the on-line media is also the basis of the work of the more specialized financial reporters who write the commentaries. Some newspapers go one step further, bringing the total market commentary of the news agency into the next day's edition of the paper. Within broadcast media, the frame is narrower. Here, the aim is to find one or two sentences that would constitute an explanation and put them into a short clip, usually at the end of the news programme. A really big news event will become a story on its own, of course, but financial news is normally not given high priority.

It is easy to see that the original research carried out by the reporters in the digital media had a large impact on people's comprehension of what had happened 'in the market' in March 1997. When newspapers and broadcast media started looking for complementary explanations, another wave of telephone research with the market actors was started. The answers given were probably influenced by what the actors had read on the computer screens, when connected with the news agencies. That is natural, as we are all looking for explanations of events even when they may appear unexplainable. Then everybody makes use of everybody else, and in reality the explanations are more like collective guesses. Furthermore, no market actor wants to get too far away from the average view, as that might be interpreted as being insufficiently informed. There is an obvious risk that the combined effects of the market and reporting processes, interdependent as they are, could strengthen each other and establish a self-fulfilling chain of events.

Much of the reporting above would have been harmless if the explanations had not been related to the political field. The headline of one of the first computer pages was: 'Prime Minister Göran Persson forces up the interest rate strongly'. The source of the anxiety was apparently an article in a Social Democratic journal, in which Göran Persson had made statements which were seen as detrimental to the interest rate, according to the cited anonymous market actors. It was then that the merry-go-round started. The finance minister had also been cited on the computer screens earlier, implying, not very sensationally, that the current finance policy would remain in place. In such course of events, the temperature will always rise when the finance minister comments in public upon an unexplainable financial event (in effect this is what he did, indirectly, by the mere statement). Furthermore, the statement might have been interpreted as the finance minister attempting to soften what the prime minister had said in the article.

The matter was likely to have been compounded for the newspapers and broadcast media. The printed media often prefer to put editorial comments in the news columns. This is becoming a more common practice. Big news events – not only economic events – are commented on by individual journalists. The original role, as unbiased reporter, is gradually replaced by the journalist *actively* contributing to the public debate. This is a problem, as only a few reporters have sufficient experience, time and knowledge to be able to make a real contribution. In the worst case the same reporter writes the current news account too. So it will hardly be surprising if the commentary rattles off the same guesses as those earlier put out on the computer screens. Furthermore, the commentary is often spiced up with a prediction of what will happen next. In the worst cases, editorial comments will be put on the front page of the newspaper. Here the objective may be laudable – to create a personal connection with the reader. But assuming that many of the readers will never read on to the more detailed account, there is a risk that the commentary will replace more balanced journalism. At this point, the merry-go-round is usually at full speed, the interest rates moving up and down and the politicians getting all the more involved.

In editorials on the day following the rate rise there was talk of 'the dictatorship of the market', and of 'time to listen to the market'. Certain politicians expressed their disgust, while others gave their approval in popular afternoon newspapers. Some of these were spiced up with a double page on 'How the rise of interest rates will affect you.' Such turbulence usually lasts for a couple of days. The course of events is sometimes put on the agenda of some talk show on television, and, a few days later, the weekly business magazines will give their commentaries. However, by that stage, the heat is off.

Why, then, did the interest rate rise on 17 March 1997? This we do not know (and we never will), but the picture in most people's minds is that 'Göran Persson said something that the market didn't like', and that picture will damage economic journalism. Basically, nobody knows what brought about the rise in the interest rate. Short-term financial movements cannot be explained. They just happen, not least because strong individual investors can influence Swedish market fluctuations on a short-term basis. So it gives a distorted picture if a turbulent market is described as if, for instance, thousands of decision-makers were selling in panic or in rage because of an anxious reaction to a political statement. The changes of the interest rates should not be interpreted as the result of an 'opinion poll'!

The financial actors of today are powerful beyond the formal political sphere, the business sector and the trade unions. Reporters have learnt to scrutinize these three players critically. This does not yet hold for the financial actors, though, so a greater sensitivity and awareness is needed to cope with those factors which might influence financial trends and changes. Also, a broader examination of possible causes is necessary. Anonymous citations should be avoided. Furthermore, media managements need to realize that not all reporters are fit – i.e. not all of them have sufficient integrity and competence – to write editorial commentary. If economic journalism does not apply these basic rules, there is an obvious risk that it will be considered as an ally of the financial power that it should scrutinize. Recurrent criticisms of today's Swedish economic journalism must be interpreted with this in mind.

It's the economy, stupid!

Erik Fichtelius

Sports is politics. Culture is politics. Everything is politics! But what about economics? For many years economics was something extraordinary, a field played only by the experts. 'Never touched by human hands', could very well be a slogan used by the leading economists during the prosperous years of booming post-war European economic development. 'Let the experts handle the economy, and we will distribute at least some of the fruits to our electorate', said the politicians. Most of them were unknowing or even afraid of the more complex, nitty gritty details of economics.

Reporters in popular media would never dream of even getting near such a dreadful and dull subject as macro-economics. Those days are gone, forever. When Bill Clinton first ran for president of the USA, he and his aides put up signs in all the offices of the campaign headquarters which read, 'It's the economy, stupid!' That was a reminder to everyone about what really mattered. Sweden has for decades solved its economic problems by devaluation, inflation and borrowing. This has been the responsibility of governments of all colours. It finally came to a halt in the early 1990s. 'It's the economy, stupid!' could be a valid statement in Sweden too.

But macro-economics is hard to understand. The line between cause and effect is not always completely clear. Why was the economy suddenly in such bad shape? Why should we have to abandon all the good things that we have allowed ourselves for so many years? Who killed the Swedish model? For a politician seeking or holding office it is more rewarding to distribute wealth than cutbacks. In that respect the political orientation of the office-holder does not matter. Economics is definitely a part of politics, but it took some major crises for everyone to understand this. Now economics is even part of journalism. It is no longer confined to 'the experts', but is part of everyday journalistic assignment life.

For many years I was Executive Editor and Head of News Department of the Swedish National Radio. In the spring of 1993 I decided to go back to reporting and took a position as Senior Political Correspondent with *Aktuellt*, the news department of Swedish Television's Channel One. Until then I had done lots of reporting in other fields, but never as a political correspondent lobbying the halls of government. So how could I prepare myself to start reporting on politics? As former Head of News I had good contacts in the political and economic spheres, so I simply spent some time refreshing and rebuilding a network of sources on the beat. I called them, met them and asked them – what are the most pressing political issues to report on today? Almost everyone I asked in government, political parties, and the academic and business worlds said the same thing – it's the economy, stupid! If I was to be a political reporter to be reckoned with, I must understand economics. Many of my sources had been quite specific in trying to sort out the priorities – 'if you are to report on politics, you must start with the structural budget deficit'. I started reading on the subject. But there was an obvious problem for a new television reporter – where do I go to shoot it? In television I need images. Bo Mårtenson shows this clearly in his report in Chapter 6. But where can I take pictures of the structural budget deficit?

This issue was of no concern to my sources. They had enough problems *dealing* with the deficit and could not really engage themselves in my predicament. But this is exactly the dilemma facing the economic or political television reporter. How do I make myself clear? How can I visualize the great problems facing our nation? If the structural budget deficit is the most urgent issue on the political agenda, I have a responsibility as a political correspondent to address it in my reports. This is crucial to our democracy. The people have a right to know what the *real* issues are, the *real* problems being discussed and hopefully solved by our elected representatives. The newscaster in a democracy has a dual obligation in this sort of context. We are the fourth estate and represent one of the pillars of power in a democracy. We should scrutinize and criticize the powers of government and business. The media have an important role as controller, balancing other powers in society. But the media should also give the citizens means and tools to function as citizens in this democracy. We should give access to the halls of government and let the general public hear and see for itself. In that sense, the media also play an educational role.

So how do I report on the structural budget deficit so the people really learn and understand what it is all about? When I started as political correspondent in *Aktuellt* I volunteered for my first assignment. The first day on the job I sat down in one of the team cars with photographer Paolo Rodriquez and simply told him – drive, we are going to shoot the structural budget deficit. Amazingly, Paolo knew exactly where to go. He knew something that all the political and economic experts I had been talking to for months clearly did not understand. Television works magic! The well-established political metaphor for the Swedish welfare society is 'Folkhemmet'. It translates as 'the people's home', a symbol introduced by the Social Democratic premier Per-Albin Hansson in his budget speech in January 1928 and implies that society and the welfare state should offer its citizens the warmth and care of the good family home and be the home of all the people. Now what the structural budget deficit is doing is threatening to destroy this beautiful home. When interest payments on the loans the state has taken out are paid, there will be nothing left for housing, education and Medicare. 'The people's home' will fall into ruins. Paolo

Rodriquez drove to an area just south of Arlanda airport outside Stockholm. It is called Rosersberg and it is a training ground for Swedish civil defence forces. There are burned houses, wrecked stone walls and demolished streets. It looks just like Mostar in former Yugoslavia. Or, if you like, it is the way 'the people's home' will look if we do not start dealing with the structural budget deficit. I agree that it might sound a bit far-fetched, but it looked all right on television that night. At least it gave some people a feeling of where we could be heading.

The budget deficit became the most important issue during the 1994 election campaign. Instead of only promising new reforms, the political contenders had to answer questions on how they were going to finance all the good things they promised. They had to be precise as to where they were going to make the cutbacks, what taxes they were raising and who would be affected in what way. Of course, they did not give all the answers, as they desperately tried to avoid any specifics on taxes and cutbacks. But at least they had to address the issue in a more direct and honest way than before. It was a collective effort from political and economic reporters and commentators from all sorts of media to force the politicians to stay on track.

As the study by Bo Mårtenson in Chapter 6 shows, the media (and, especially, television) have a difficult task. We have to find the metaphors that explain and make people feel and understand the problems we are talking about. Sometimes this leads us into the traps of populist journalism. When all sorts of special interest groups (or 'ordinary people') are protesting this or that, and the media do not put it into context or give a perspective, then we are leaving our audience behind. It is very easy to produce good-looking television when the local military is protesting against the closing down of a regiment, or when doctors want to maintain the level of resources for their local hospital. Such reporting often disregards the total picture, overlooking the fact that the Berlin Wall is gone or that Sweden as a nation has built more hospitals than it can really use effectively. If you want to eat, you have to pay. We cannot sustain a welfare state on loans from our children. Economics is politics, and finally that has dawned even on journalists. We are learning and we are shaping our instruments (our tools of trade) to help involve the general public in the intricacies of macro-economics.

9
Economic news research in retrospect

Questions of research design in news reception analysis

John Corner

Most of the problems which we encountered in carrying out the Liverpool-based research were ones we had expected to face, but the experience of discussing them over a year of data collection and analysis has given me a sharper sense of the research design issues attending a study of this kind.

Although ostensibly structured in the form of two conventional kinds of enquiry combined – a news analysis with a reception study (in this sense, mirroring the 'classic' work by Morley as well as many more recent projects) – our study was in fact awkwardly, but I think usefully, different in two important ways. First of all, the study of news programmes was not designed with a hypothesis about 'distortion' or 'bias' or even about significant differences from other accounts. In this it differs from those studies of industrial relations, environmental issues, crime and health where (rightly) some attempt to plot the thematic transformations which the news prism introduces has been the centre of concern. By contrast, our work sought to look more closely at how news handled a topic so abstract and complex as the economic system over a stretch of time. The emphasis was on communicative organization, on exposition – how were stories about the economy told? How were the 'ups' and the 'downs', the 'good' bits and the 'bad', signalled through the use of language and image? This is in many ways a 'quieter' research aim than versions of the news distortion thesis. Despite the detailed examination of news formats which we obtained, I found myself wishing for a major economic 'drama' of some kind (along the lines of the 1992 ERM withdrawal) which would put all the news resources under pressure and generate, for a while at least, a range of intensive, sustained and conflicting accounts for analysis. What we have instead is largely a case study of 'normal-time' reporting, an ongoing national story sustained by the narrative interplay between short-, middle- and long-term change.

Our use of the respondent group method (piloted by individuals before the main study) was simply a consequence of our research questions. If a media researcher wants to explore the sense which viewers make of programmes and the evaluations they make of them (a prerequisite, of course, for any formulations about the processes of 'influence'), then there is only one line of progress – to ask selected people some questions. If the research wishes to explore the way in which particular forms of reportage are received, then, again, there are few practical options but to screen selected material to selected people and ask them questions. Once it has been decided that questionnaires are by themselves an inadequate means to collect the kind of core information sought, the convention of individual and/or group respondents making comments transcribed for analysis becomes almost unavoidable. All the questions of method start here, of course, as the extensive and growing literature suggests (how many groups? of what kind? how formed? how conducted? how employed within the framework of transcript analysis and overall conceptual design?).

The problems become most pressing when research hypotheses directly concern (a) attitudes towards content and (b) differentiation of attitude according to social classification. It is then extremely easy, in a way now extensively acknowledged in the literature, for the respondent groups simply to become representative of the larger social categories about whom propositions concerning difference are to be made. We did not escape problems of generalization and representativeness, as other colleagues note in this section, but the complement to our emphasis on news *exposition* was our equal emphasis on viewer *comprehension*. For this, our baseline requirement was for us to satisfy ourselves that we had conducted sessions with enough groups, controlling as best we could for age groups, gender and occupation, not to give us distortingly untypical indications about how economic reports of varying length, focus and density were made sense of. The results here are anything but startling when expressed as a generalization – lots of people have difficulty with economic news and there is widespread scepticism about statistics. However, the real value of our research lay in opening up both specific terms of economic reporting and then, *in relation to these*, specific terms of viewing. What we have documented, with a volume and density defying full presentation in the book (and finally exceeding the prudent reach of our own analytical categories), are precisely the conditions of the playoff between professional exposition and public knowledge in the economic realm.

Throughout the project, we had difficulty in keeping a degree of analytical separation between our interest in how people responded to economic news on television and people's views on the economy *per se*. Obviously the two are always closely interrelated, but this was not a substantive attitude survey using news as a 'trigger', it was a study in the public communicational process, following the route that two of us had already developed in respect of the issues of unemployment and nuclear power. We had to engage with the specificity of the subject, an esoteric subject field closely allied to national politics, but 'television', not 'economics', was our primary reference. Any future study will need to improve on our approach here, conceptually and in research design, keeping a stronger sense of direction right from the start. In particular it might more clearly identify certain 'non-televisual' factors, including the different sources of popular knowledge which work in combination with television accounts and which are a precondition of any engagement with them. More detailed inquiry into how economic news on television is collected and put together could be a valuable component of future studies, but I am not convinced that it would substantially affect the particular research framing adopted here, with its focus on what happens in front of the screen rather than 'behind' it.

Given my own interests in television form, one of the things I would have most liked to do (following an under-developed precedent) would have been to work with high-quality news simulations, producing a variety of accounts from the same factual core, in which both minor modifications and also quite radical departures from convention were introduced. Feeding this experimentalist material into the research design of a field project like ours could, I think, really open up elements of communicative dynamics only indirectly making an appearance here.

Generalization, reliability and validity in media research

Neil T. Gavin

When the merits of qualitative and quantitative techniques are debated, there can be a temptation to scramble into the methodological trenches and to start shelling those on the other side of No-Man's Land. A whiff of cordite can be detected in the exchange between Rosengren (1996) and Jensen (1996), where the tone has a distinctly abrasive edge. The work in Chapters 1 and 5 raises this sort of temptation, but I want, instead, to look on it as a stimulus to the reconsideration of some of the debates between the qualitative and quantitative schools – particularly where these concern issues of generalization, validity and reliability. I will take Lunt and Livingstone's (1996) study as a platform for this analysis, as it represents a full and lucidly argued defence of focus group research.

The aggregate analysis undertaken in Chapter 5 was based on poll measures whose reliability is considered to be quite strong and whose sampling procedures allow confident generalization to the UK population. The validity of the polls may be contested (although elections pose a regular and fairly stringent test that polls are obliged to endure), but even if we accept that they are not valid representations of public attitudes, the polls are consistent in their measurement, and, therefore, change over time is something that demands analysis and explanation. We looked at television economic coverage as an 'explanatory' factor. The data used are derived from content analysis of the sort of news that reaches the whole population (mid-week, prime-time news on the most watched channels) and there was a systematic attempt to test the reliability of the resultant codes. The results survive a battery of statistical tests, as well as controls on a range of variables that facilitate the exploration of competing explanations. The exposed relationship between media content and public opinion turbulence tends, for a political scientist at least, to place the results in the realm of 'media effects'. It links media output to the mass audience and suggests some form of causal connection. However, the obvious problem with this (as with much quantitative analysis) is that the nature of the *processes* involved is not at all clear (or, rather, not clear at all). So there is a question mark against the validity of the explanations that surround the core model. This is a generic problem with quantitative research, and it has to be fully acknowledged. However, I will argue that focus groups, too, have their problems with explanatory architecture, and that the issue of generalization is still outstanding.

Lunt and Livingstone maintain that focus group research is not analogous to survey work, but is a way of accessing the processes of the social production and reproduction of meaning among naturally occurring groups of like-minded people. They variously describe the data that emerge from focus groups as 'valid', 'ecologically valid', 'rich' and 'believable'. Focus groups, it is suggested, can facilitate respondent expression and simulate the sorts of exchanges and debates of everyday life that are at the root of the production of meaning. They do note, however, that there can be problems with the reliability of the data generated, and the reliability of interpretation of the data, and difficulties in generalizing beyond small-sample studies. Lunt and Livingstone propose what they call two 'weak responses' to the latter point, but these amount to advocating larger numbers of focus groups (a practice that is far from common in media research) or 'triangulation', which is certainly more difficult and fraught with problems than is often acknowledged (Gavin, 1994). The so-called 'strong response' looks very much like a blanket denial of the validity of survey measures on the grounds that they reify the individual and deny the polysemic and context-dependent nature of meaning. Lunt and Livingstone state that 'The study of the media audience is less and less concerned with registering effects at the psychological level in aggregates of individuals, and increasingly concerned with the study of the social processes of communication.' Yet stating that alternative measures and techniques are flawed (which I would all too readily concede) certainly does not 'answer' the problems surrounding generalization (or validity) that surface in focus group research as it is generally practised.

Lunt and Livingstone do elaborate further on the issue of generalization, but their position has a deductive rather than analytical turn:

> it may be as problematic to assume that findings for a particular category of respondent do not generalise to other categories (or other times and places) as it is to assume they do, as both assumptions are comparative; to assume falsely the particularity of one's findings tends to result in an inappropriate analysis in terms of the particular category of person studied. (Lunt and Livingstone, 1996, p. 91)

Yet the point is, surely, that quantitative studies do not assume that their results can be generalized. They deploy a range of systematic techniques (and spend a great deal of time and effort) in trying to assure representativeness. This is not always the case in focus group work, and to assume that results can be generalized is to assume an important problem (and, some would say, an implicit deficiency) out of existence. Lunt and Livingstone argue that, 'different contexts of data collection do not invalidate each other, but rather they illustrate the truism that different contexts generate different kinds of data with different meanings.' This is undoubtedly the case, but to admit this does not compel us to bracket issues of sample scale and sampling technology out of the frame when judging focus group results.

Finally, the exhortation to continue conducting successive focus groups until 'no new stories are told' by group members is, I would submit, not an answer to questions of representativeness. A study situated in a particular locale could, we might plausibly imagine, soon run out of 'new stories'. Yet these stories may be entirely unrepresentative. The fact that we have run out of new stories may simply mean we have stumbled on an idiosyncratic sample – not that we have exhausted the number of stories circulating in the population at large. It is dangerous to assume that the latter, rather than the former, is the case, and the 'new stories' criterion for deciding the number of focus groups is less plausible when viewed in this sort of light.

Issues of generalization would trouble me less than they do if it were not for the fact that there are other outstanding problems with the nature of the data produced by focus groups. Focus group transcripts may, indeed, be 'rich', detailed and 'believable'. But they are certainly not self-evidently transparent, and nor do they offer a privileged and obviously valid window on the processes of meaning production. There are obvious difficulties that arise in using such evidence to describe and explain the precise nature of the mechanisms that underpin the processes of production and reproduction of meaning. Involvement in the focus group research that figures in Chapter 1 has convinced me that the raw respondent talk (or 'data', if you like) and the processes that these reflect are anything but universally transparent (and, by association, 'transparently valid'). What a respondent means by a statement is often opaque, ambiguous and enigmatic. The raw data cannot necessarily be taken at face value and the researcher can be left frustrated and yearning to spirit a group member back, to ask them what they meant by a particular statement or what they were trying to suggest in a particular exchange. This has a bearing on the issue of interpretative reliability between researchers (although Lunt and Livingstone, quite rightly, state that procedures are available for cross-checking). But it is analytically distinguishable from the issue of interpretative reliability (Höijer, 1990); it is entirely possible to combine interpretative reliability and invalid interpretation. This set of issues needs more critical attention than it has usually been accorded, and to my mind this problem is at least as difficult (and may, perhaps, be considered analogous to) those faced by quantitative researchers in explaining the processes underlying the patterns that emerge from aggregate models like those in Chapter 5.

I need to be clear that I am not suggesting that this argument necessitates a reversion to Merton's (1987) position, i.e. that qualitative techniques are secondary (or subordinate) to quantitative data, or only useful in the exploratory stages that precede rigorously scientific (survey or experimental) analysis. I only argue that for much focus group work the issue of generalization is still problematic in a way that it tends not to be in quantitative research, and that the transparency and validity of focus group data are issues that could stand a little more critical attention (in much the same way as the issue of the validity of processual inferences in quantitative studies).

Economic significance, audiences and historical context

Bo Mårtenson

The study of the Swedish budget news in Chapter 6 points to the dominance in news reports of expectations, external judgements and future-oriented aspects of economic events. It also signals the abundant and sophisticated, if also arbitrary, use of reconstructional elements and of verbal and visual metaphors. Further, news about the budget is shown to involve journalistic strategies of 'explanation', utilizing the interplay between the 'ordinary citizen' and the expert journalist (the 'common-sense' approach). A discussion of these characteristic elements of Swedish economic news, including the contextual explanation I have put forward (the specific public service tradition of Swedish television), raises methodological questions of both validity and reliability. These two separate but interrelated problems will be briefly dealt with here.

The first concerns the identification and classification of the *significant* elements of any report. To illustrate, from the September 1996 week of television news, 37 economic reports or items out of a total of 152 news stories were identified. The demarcation of the economic news 'item' is not a simple operation, however. The combination of several items into more or less coherent news 'blocks' is frequent, and the problem of separating these out of a block of news is, of course, a challenge for any attempt at quantification. The 'floating' character of the content units of economic news makes it difficult to establish the relative weight not only of manifest themes, but also formal elements such as 'the interview' or 'the commentary'.

The presence of the news 'block' in Swedish television economic reporting calls for greater analytical attention to the general level of editing, in terms of its strategies of disassembling, mixing, dispersing and reassembling news items or elements. On a concrete level, in making basic comparisons over time, there is a problem in accounting for the contribution of the editing which generates the complex structure of the news blocks.[1] We would have to include some measures of length, mixing, and 'rate of cut' of items, to indicate the pulse or beat of these longer news constructions. The more aesthetic aspects of news need to be brought into the measurement.

This use of 'narrative' editing styles which almost always evoke popular fiction in television news may follow general and international trends in television formats. However, its seemingly increasing frequency in Swedish television news has an interesting bearing on the public service ambitions of economic reporting. Generally, extensive narrative editing can be seen as a manifestation of journalist autonomy, serving 'containment' strategies. Following the special characteristics of the economy as a topic, it would seem that this level of construction is more important to economic news, as a form of public issue reporting, than to other kinds of news. Economic news, with its emphasis on diachronic change and on a constantly moving economy, has a special need for the accessibility which narrative can bring.

It seems relevant here to consider two levels of the news syntagm, both the primary editing of whole news bulletins, showing the context and position of economic news, and the actual news block editing. The quoted extract from the 'crisis budget' of January 1995 is an illustrative case, yet it is obvious that the selected examples and citations in Chapter 6 only give hints of the full news text. A more thorough syntagmatic or narrative analytical approach would definitely contribute to understanding.

The second problem of methodology concerns the journalistic strategies and modes of audience address. I have observed these to be predominantly either the ordinary citizen approach, based on common sense, or the expert role. As in the case of narrative editing, this feature is common to international television news, yet its application to Swedish economic news gives it a specific educational and consensus bias. As has been suggested in Chapter 6, the mode of address is chosen to create an 'educational situation': interviewer to expert, or reporter to commentator. Superficially viewed, the resulting journalistic performance often appears as naive, as an exposed and explicit lack of knowledge. But how these strategies and modes of address should be interpreted or assessed is far from clear. First, any such analytical attempt has to rely on some basic experience and knowledge of both the history and the specific conditions of the Swedish media. Several examples of budget news which are quoted in Chapter 6 may well be interpreted or judged as ignorant, uncritical or weak journalism. In the light of the communicative context of Swedish society, however, they may seem strikingly relevant and appropriate.

The researcher attempting to read as the 'ordinary viewer' might is, of course, not an implicit argument against audience studies. Doubtless, the focus I have put on the constructed relation between journalist and audience of public service television will point to the need to analyse more deeply the viewing strategies too. In the context of a larger ongoing research project on Swedish economic journalism, we have conducted a set of focus group interviews with viewers of budget news. The interview design was influenced by the audience study of the Liverpool Communication Group. Findings from the Swedish interviews have not been included in Chapter 6, since they are both preliminary and difficult to generalize. Interviews were carried out in connection with the budget presentations of 1994 and 1996, and, by engaging the same individuals in both years, the groups have served as a panel or a reference group of viewers. These interviews have produced important initial background knowledge of possible viewer interpretations of economic news. Implicitly, they have also informed and supported our discussion of journalist strategies and audience address. Equally, interviewing and talking to the different audience groups has highlighted some of the various uses of economic news which are possible. This has had the consequence of making the arguments in Chapter 6 less self-assured and the conclusions less one-sided (if also, perhaps, less defined).

Besides incorporating audience studies, continuing research on economic news journalism will include historical accounts and analysis of popular economic news in the Swedish media. To trace origins and follow developments through the 1970s and 1980s, by a selected study of budget news, is not only of historical interest, but should also inform contemporary analysis. Indeed, our final study of 25 years of Swedish popular economic news may provide a necessary perspective, for adequately assessing the themes and forms of news today.

Analysing respondent speech

Kay Richardson

Reception analysis is now a familiar area of activity in media studies. Though research designs differ, the use of focus groups to provide 'qualitative' data is one of its most familiar characteristics, differentiating it from experimental methodologies and from methods involving questionnaire design. Variations include the use of the one-to-one interview and the manipulation of images for comparison with broadcast originals (see Lewis, 1991; Philo, 1990).

It is very easy to follow in familiar footsteps and accept the assumptions behind the 'qualitative' – 'quantitative' dichotomy. Gavin's contribution to this chapter draws attention to some of the problems in this area, from a political science perspective. Here, I want to offer some reflections upon characteristics of the 'data' which are produced by focus group methods and upon the ways in which these data can best be explored and analysed.

One of the objections to the use of focus groups is that they oblige respondents to engage in a non-naturalistic talk activity. Talk generated by and for the research is unnatural and not to be relied upon as indicating anything about the respondents' true state of knowledge and understanding of television texts. The force of this objection, however, can be countered in at least two ways. The assumption that viewers do not talk about their viewing experiences in 'real life' can undoubtedly be challenged. Certain kinds of programmes (soaps, the news) are discussed a lot, and one of the functions of the popular press is to ensure that this continues to be the case. It is important, as well, to challenge the notion that 'artificially' elicited data are of less value than the naturalistic kind. For research purposes, artificially elicited data are not at all 'second best'. They are of more value, not less, than television talk on the sofa or in the pub – certainly for research of the kind described in this volume, focusing as it does upon questions of comprehension. In naturalistic contexts, opportunities to talk about television may be too limited, too subject to the pressures of other agendas, including interpersonal relations, to permit the kind of thoughtfulness that the research context provides. Where questions of comprehension and text–reader relations are concerned, that thoughtfulness is a *sine qua non* of good data.

A further point in respect of focus group talk concerns the ways in which it is accorded meaning and significance in the research. Focus group talk is indeed a particular type of talk, with its own interpersonal dynamics and emergent characteristics. In the Liverpool research this takes on a further dimension when we consider that several groups met with us more than once over a four-month period. Some of the problems here are indeed familiar: the problem of dominant and subordinate group members; of too readily attributing attitudes to groups rather than individuals within the groups; of views expressed 'too soon' in the conversation, pre-empting other responses. But in addition to these concerns, there is another, equally important one, and that is with the danger of taking respondent talk too easily 'at face value'. It is not that I am sceptical about whether respondents 'mean what they say' in the sense that they could be lying. Such a perspective would be a very unhelpful way of understanding matters when respondents initially claim to understand what they have seen on the screen, and then, later, admit difficulties of comprehension. It is, rather, another aspect of our concern for the discourse (discourses) of economics. It is important that attention is given not just to the 'what' of respondent speech but also, and equally, to the 'how'. The respondent who says 'we get more money' as a result of tax cuts, and then follows that with the sentence 'we get more spending power', is, at one level, saying the same thing twice. The referential meaning of each sentence is the same. But the contextual meaning, the 'framing', as it were, is different. As I have shown in Chapter 3, this paraphrase has a particular import in the context where it occurs: it encodes a shift from 'layspeak' into the idiom of mediated economics just at the point where the respondent is drawing attention to what it is, for him or her, that the mediated discourse has failed to explain.

With large amounts of data to explore, and with the obligation to focus upon what is representative for the groups, the question of technique becomes relevant. Future work in this area will be able to benefit from technological developments which have seen the development of computer tools for coding transcripts (the so-called 'ethnographic' software tools such as Ethnograph, Atlas-ti, Nudist) and subsequent sorting exercises. My own preference, however, in working with transcripts, would be to avoid any coding of data beyond that which is involved in producing good transcriptions. All transcription involves the transcriber in decisions about what is/is not significant in the data, with degrees of 'normalization' which elide, variously, characteristics of pronunciation, intonation and volume, as well as repetitions, hesitations, overlaps and other influences. These decisions represent one, unavoidable, level of data coding, even if it is not always explicitly recognized as such. Coding 'proper' is the kind which requires the analyst to provide additional information, relevant to the purposes of the research, by way of annotations to the text. For the sake of flexibility, I am interested in techniques which will work upon 'uncoded' but electronically accessible data. The commercial availability of lexical analysis software which will run on domestic PCs makes it possible to run word searches, produce wordlists and concordances and perform collocation analysis with very little effort, thus revealing patterns in the material which might otherwise remain unremarked or only 'intuited' on the basis of time-consuming close reading. Stubbs (1996) is an excellent introduction to this kind of work, with considerable insight into its potential relevance for social and cultural analysis.

The mediated economy and new technology

Håkan Lindhoff

The changing political and economic climate in Sweden in the 1990s offers challenges to the media researcher who is interested in the media's contribution to the production of public knowledge about economic relations. There are two basic issues to deal with when formulating research questions and developing methodologies for study of 'the economy' in media. The first is the scale and depth of the penetration of economic forces into very sphere of society – when did this start, where, and how? The second is the issue of the extent of the media's basic role in transforming these processes into public knowledge and opinions (through meaning production and in alignment with the public's daily experiences of economic behaviour, in labour, consumption and saving). What implications do these issues have for the choice of approach to the analysis of economic news? Initially, we need a range of basic descriptive studies of the media's role in constructing the economy, and these need to be broad in their scope, as well as historical and comparative. But which media research methodologies are preferred? I would like to include interview-based studies of the production and reception of economic news. The former is exemplified in studies like Schlesinger (1987) and Ericson *et al.* (1987), but also we need basic knowledge of how the economy is comprehended. Focus group interviews, with or without screening sessions, seem to be a method well adapted to this task and one which is less intimidating to informants than individual interviews. However, this method is clearly not applicable when undertaking historical or retrospective analysis of economic news, where estimation of public response will inevitably be more hazardous.

The retrospective analysis of economic news from the more recent past may, however, benefit from the modern technologies available for the storage of media text. It is likely that in future full-text databases will become as common a research tool as the videotape library. These should deliver on-line news agency or newspaper texts. In Sweden some of these on-line resources have been available since the early 1990s. One prerequisite, of course, is a full corpus of newspapers and television programmes, old or new. This is not a problem in Sweden, since all print materials, books, journals, newspapers, etc. have had by law to be handed over to public university libraries since 1661. The same is true for broadcast materials since 1978, when a public archive of sounds and pictures records was established. However, the full-text databases are not yet legally public. Instead, they are supplied to clients outside the media on a commercial basis, some of them through the Internet, some of them direct on-line. Nevertheless they are often supplied at modest prices for research and education purposes.[2]

Through this technology, terms of discursive significance that represent economic or political concepts with a high profile in the current streams of economic thought are easily searched for and sorted. This facility can be used to provide accurate indicators of use and allows comparison within and between media (as well as over time). Also, the co-occurrence of two or more terms within the same news texts (or even within paragraphs) is easily checked. One limitation, of course, is that the specific capabilities of the database system of a newspaper may differ from those of the corresponding system of another title. In this context, comparison can be complicated. Another limitation is the absence of textual contexts: it is usually impossible to reconstruct the newspaper page and the full layout when using texts from a database. There are also limitations with regard to pictures, illustrations and diagrams, etc. These are often impossible to search for. Moreover, where this is possible, it is often through a separate database. As a result, the problem of the lack of textual (or page layout) context can become acute.

However, in spite of these limitations, it is still possible to isolate specific texts from full-text databases which can then be subject to more focused forms of discourse analysis. The random or structured searching of a cross-section of the remaining text which full-text databases allows can then be used to ascertain whether the resultant analysis is generalizable to the larger corpus. This combination of qualitative and quantitative approaches, therefore, offers some real advantages in media research. Such technology may also offer the prospect of international comparisons of newspaper content conducted over the Internet. Moreover, through Internet discussion groups concerned with economic affairs, the interactive strand of on-line media may be researched as well. This would allow various kinds of experimental design with potential for the collection of new kinds of data.

Notes

1   A few typical examples can be seen through the web site already indicated in Chapter 6. The address is:
http://www.liv.ac.uk/~polcomm/polhome.htm
The examples reveal the difficulties in conveying what is actually happening simultaneously on the screen.

2   Of course, an on-line full-text database of current newspaper texts should be looked upon as a type of digital medium that has uses beyond research. These databases can be used to replace the old press records, as well as the press clippings that are used by the editorial staff. They may also facilitate the creation of new on-line newspapers, offering extra readings and interactive options, discussion groups, etc., through the Internet.

10
Conclusions and reflections

Neil T. Gavin

What implications follow from this research? Although each chapter has attempted to assess the significance of the data and their analysis, it might be helpful to close this book with a summary of their most important conclusions and a sense of where they lead. We may begin by considering the relevance of the research for the continuing debates regarding mass media influence.

Influence, like effects, is a troubled word in media research, but that should not stop us from recognizing the degree of informational dependency, and of evaluative trust, which this and other studies indicate (Gavin, 1997). As Chapter 5 has suggested, economic news has an important impact on public perceptions. Politicians cannot afford to ignore its power over the UK public's economic and political attitudes. Although the size of the induced change is modest in absolute terms, its cumulative power is substantial. The influence on public opinion that economic news exerts goes well beyond simply reflecting the 'real economy' back to the public, and thereby somehow awakening them to a reality that they already encounter through the myriad forms of economic transaction experienced in everyday life. At the aggregate level, economic news has an impact additional to that derived from personal or family financial experience. The sort of attitudinal dynamic involved places the journalist (and the television journalist especially) in a rather difficult and invidious position. Public attitudes towards the economy and the government's handling of economic issues are part of an equation that includes the broader range of 'feelgood' sentiments. These have an important position within the interrelated economic and political domains. Buoyant economic attitudes are viewed as both the harbinger of, and, more importantly, the *engine* of economic recovery and development. Conversely, public overoptimism about the economy is regarded by economists as a warning of impending economic overheating –

a situation that will, in turn, require painful corrective intervention by the government. In the face of conspicuous economic recovery or marked economic decline, the public's perception of the government will, in turn, be affected. As a result, where reporters are capable of influencing economic attitudes directly or indirectly, they become, more than ever, almost a part of the economy as well as important, indirect players in a broader political game. They are not simply observers and reporters; they can affect the economy they seek to report and in so doing influence the political landscape.

Economic journalists, then, are perhaps more deeply embedded in the phenomenon they seek to cover than reporters on other domestic and foreign beats, and they face a range of related difficulties and cross-pressures (see Chapter 8). But how are they to describe economic developments to the public? As we document, the task is heavily conditioned by the 'difficult' and abstract nature of the subject. However, it almost goes without saying that economic news does not – nor could it – represent 'the economy' to the public. 'The economy' is not a single entity or 'thing', with elements that can be described with clarity and precision and whose progress can be easily plotted. In a sense, 'the economy' is constructed by the journalist and is constituted in journalists' reports. What emerges from our television screens and from the pages of our newspapers is a construction that involves the conscious choice of some thematic strands over others, the elevation of some explanatory frameworks at the expense of the alternatives, and the focus on particular aspects of the complex whole to the exclusion of others.

Here there is still a need for a better understanding of the role that the broader context of academic, professional and City opinion plays in the construction of economic news. What is defined as economically important at any particular time will be strongly influenced not only by the reporters' sense of what is going on, but by journalists canvassing and assessing opinion in the City or in corporate boardrooms. But in this respect there are important issues that need to be addressed. In the realms of both professional and academic economic analysis, there is perhaps less clarity and confidence than there used to be about our grasp of the processes that drive the economy (Ormerod, 1994). The contested nature of this sphere of knowledge makes the context of economic news sourcing and journalistic framing an important one, for it is here the political themes that permeate economic theory are capable of manifesting themselves – an issue touched upon in Gavin (1992) and Gavin and Goddard (1998). This is especially significant in cases where we are dealing with disputed predictions, projections and interpretations or where news-gathering and reporting are performed by non-specialist correspondents or wire service providers. A fuller understanding of the role and significance of the broader intellectual climate of economic opinion awaits a more detailed treatment of source accessing within the news production process.

The public, it could be argued, needs to be informed about the economy, and the important issue is whether the news is clear enough for the audience to understand – a precondition for any judgement upon its political orientation. In Chapter 2, Kay Richardson notes the degree of distance between the technical discourse of economic news and the language used by respondents. Viewers do not adopt the language of economic discourse, although they may, on occasion, borrow from it. It is also clear that viewers are capable of using very different (and broader) frames of reference in contextualizing their thoughts and discussions on 'the economy' and that they are able to draw on a range of historical and personal experiences which broadcasters would find it inappropriate to articulate in their focused and time-constrained news items. From the focus group research reported in Chapter 1 we can see that the public engages with economic news in a manner that is both complex and ambiguous. The abstract and dense nature of economic news coverage has a negative effect on the viewer's degree of interest and engagement. Furthermore, that chapter also noted the considerable scepticism which was often expressed about the validity of the facts and figures that are the focus or linchpin of many economic news stories. This was brought out most clearly in relation to what was perceived as the management of unemployment statistics, although a more general scepticism was, on occasion, quite evident. As far as comprehension is concerned, it was clear that almost all of our respondents, at one point or another, reported having difficulty with the abstract and technical dimensions of economic news, even where correspondents made strenuous efforts to explicate particular themes through the use of graphics and close explanatory commentary.

This picture of the problematic aspects of the audience's experience of economic news must, however, be balanced against other forms of audience engagement with the news text. It was evident that even where viewers were occasionally confused or baffled by reports, they felt themselves able to appreciate the significance to their own lives of the themes, events and trends reported in economic news items. The news strategy of personalizing national issues – in terms of depictions of the impact of events or trends on 'typical' families – was viewed as accessible and easily understood. This technique was viewed as 'successful' by respondents and was capable of grabbing and sustaining their interest. Even where their own readings took a partisan line, viewers expressed confidence that there was, on the whole, no manifest unfairness in the way in which news represented economic conditions. Moreover, notwithstanding any predilection for scepticism in the face of 'official' information, viewers very often took the statistical or factual elements of the items on trust or as an unchallenged datum for discussion of the significance of particular stories, disputing neither the honesty nor the accuracy of the information. More significantly, as Chapter 1 discusses, it was clear that while viewers often had difficulty with the details of stories, they felt that they had appreciated their overall significance – they reported being able to grasp the 'gist' of what was being conveyed.

In the context of these findings, the future of televised economic coverage in respect both of form and of content deserve the attention of future research. We have analysed how such reportage is presently managed; it would be instructive to consider further what alternative approaches could be adopted for the sake of a better-informed national audience. These might involve, for instance, the regular insertion of 'background' pieces into regular news coverage, and the use of 'question-and-answer' or debate formats for carrying exposition. Journalists are aware of the dangers of condescension as well as of elitist presumption, but perhaps the real requirement is for more practical experiments in parts of the schedule.

As far as content is concerned, we must remind ourselves that the parameters of 'the economic' are subject to change. The extent to which economic coverage adequately informs the public's grasp of events will become more of a pressing issue in the face of the sort of major political and economic developments that are on the horizon, the most obvious of these being the prospect of European economic and monetary union. The latter issue was only just beginning to achieve prominence as the main fieldwork for the UK and Swedish arms of the study were coming to an end. Monetary union is, however, bound to have important economic and political implications for the two countries (for political and monetary sovereignty, prosperity, relative economic development and broader public notions of European identity). This is likely to be the case almost regardless of whether monetary union is a complete or partial success, or, indeed, postponed or turns out to be a failure (see Gavin and Sanders, 1997). The issues that surround monetary union encompass national economies and domestic politics, but they have an implicit and conditioning transnational dimension that is rooted in the complex interplay of international political and economic forces. In this kind of context, journalists will be less able to bank on the public's accumulated knowledge of nationally rooted economic and political background. Television journalists may, in this case, struggle to explain complex issues in a way that the public can understand and relate to. This will be especially important in relation to projections, predictions and the political and economic contingencies surrounding monetary union – precisely the sort of contested 'symbolic' issues referred to in Chapter 6. Explaining and predicting the political and economic consequences of economic union (or, indeed, its postponement or failure) will carry implicit, but potentially important, signals about the likely future state of the national economy and these, in turn, will reflect on the government's competence in handling economic and diplomatic developments.

Bearing in mind the foregoing remarks about the changing character of economic contexts and their reporting, the comparative dimension of the present research can be seen as offering another direction for further study. Notwithstanding the introduction of a European dimension to economic life, national traditions are likely to remain strong and the experience of 'Europeanization' will vary throughout the continent. Comparative analysis will be needed too, to show the differences between countries within and without the European Union as they variously come to terms with the changes now in prospect, since national responses will be affected not only by factors of a political and economic character but also by differences within their respective media ecologies. Such an analysis could usefully be supplemented with comparative work on audience engagement with economic news in different national contexts. At issue is whether different styles of delivery and presentational format (in conjunction with varying national circumstances) foster different forms of engagement with economic coverage. Here the exploration of what precisely people know about the economy ought to be a consideration, as well as an attention to the sources and agencies that illuminate and condition the audience's understanding of economic matters.

Perhaps a final remark might be made about the changing nature of the broadcasting economy. Whether the concern is with foreign or with domestic economic issues, a range of additional and important contextual factors are likely to come into play in the near future. The structure of broadcasting is changing in the UK and Sweden, as elsewhere, with technological development and government deregulation playing an important part. Attempts to cut production costs, rationalize news production structures and maximize audiences are important features of this process and are by no means confined to broadcasting. Channel proliferation, corporate restructuring, competition for audiences and audience fragmentation are likely to affect all areas of news production (Cottle, 1993). Economic news is no exception and, indeed, its complexity, abstract nature and perceived lack of obvious 'entertainment' value may prove a handicap. In this context, there is a danger that economic reports will become truncated, simplified and personalized (where they appear at all). The particular problems which our studies illustrate are likely to be compounded rather than reduced in such emerging institutional settings for broadcast journalism, making it even more important that they are recognized and responded to as soon as possible.

The issues which the book has variously addressed are distinctive ones and deserve to be followed up as such in future research. But they are also part of that much broader playoff between the changing terms of politics and mediation, of the new public information order, which is now the principal focus of much international media research.

References

Anderson, D.C. and Sharrock, W.W. (1979) 'Biasing the News: Technical Issues in Media Studies', *Sociology*, 13(3): 367–85.

Barnett, S. (1989) 'Broadcast News', *British Journalism Review*, 1(1): 49–56.

Bell, A. (1991) *The Language of News Media*. Oxford: Blackwell.

Blood, D. and Phillips, P. (1995) 'Recession Headline News, Consumer Sentiment, the State of the Economy and Presidential Popularity: A Time Series Analysis 1989–1993', *International Journal of Public Opinion*, 7(2): 2–22.

Boréus, K. (1994) *Högervåg: Nyliberalism och kampen om språket i svensk debatt 1969–1989*. Stockholm: Tiden.

Brunsdon, C. and Morley, D. (1978) *Everyday Television: 'Nationwide'*. London: British Film Institute.

Clarke, H., Stewart, M. and Whiteley, P. (1997) 'Tory Trends: Party Identification and the Dynamics of Conservative Support since 1992', *British Journal of Political Science*, 27(2): 229–319.

Corner, J. (1991) 'Meaning, Genre and Context: The Problematics of "Public Knowledge" in the New Audience Studies', in J. Curran and M. Gurevitch (eds) *Mass Media and Society*. London: Edward Arnold, pp. 267–84.

Corner, J. (1995) *Television Form and Public Address*. London: Arnold.

Corner, J., Richardson, K. and Fenton, N. (1990) *Nuclear Reactions: Form and Response in Public Issue Television*. London: John Libbey.

Corner, J., Gavin, N.T., Goddard, P. and Richardson, K. (1993) 'Television, the Economy and Public Knowledge'. Mimeograph, University of Liverpool.

Cottle, S. (1993) *Television News, Urban Conflict and the Inner City*. Leicester: Leicester University Press.

Dahlgren, P. (1992) 'Introduction', in P. Dahlgren and C. Sparks (eds) *Journalism and Popular Culture*. London: Sage, pp. 1–23.

Dahlgren, P. (1995) *Television and the Public Sphere*. London: Sage.

Deacon, D. and Golding, P. (1994) *Taxation and Representation: The Media, Political Communication and the Poll Tax*. London: John Libbey.

Downs, A. (1957) *An Economic Theory of Democracy*. New York: Harper & Row.

Dreier, P. (1982) 'Capitalism vs. the Media: An Analysis of an

Ideological Mobilization among Business Leaders', *Media, Culture and Society*, 4(2): 111-32.

Dunleavy, P. and Husbands, C.T. (1985) *Democracy at the Crossroads: Voting and Party Competition in the 1980s*. London: Allen & Unwin.

Ekecrantz, J. (1997) 'Journalism's Discursive Events and Socio-Political Change in Sweden 1925-87', *Media, Culture and Society*, 19(3): 393-412.

Ekecrantz, J. and Olsson, T. (1991) *Så sant som det är sagt: Källor och konstruktioner i journalistiken*. Rapport nr 1/91. Stockholm: SIM.

Ekecrantz, J. and Olsson, T. (1994) *Det redigerade samhället: Om journalistikens, beskrivningsmaktens och det informerade förnuftets historia*. Stockholm: Carlssons.

Eklund, K. (1993) *Vår ekonomi: En introduktion till samhällsekonomin*, 4 edn. Stockholm: Tiden.

Emmison, M. (1983) 'The Economy: Its Emergence in Media Discourse', in H. Davis and P. Walton (eds) *Language, Image, Media*. Oxford: Blackwell, pp. 139-55.

Ericson, R., Baranek, P. and Chan, J. (1987) *Vizualizing Deviance*. Milton Keynes: Open University Press.

Fairclough, N. (1995) *Media Discourse*. London: Edward Arnold.

Fiorina, M.P. (1981) *Retrospective Voting in American National Elections*. Yale University Press : New Haven.

Fowler, R. (1991) *Language in the News*. London: Routledge.

Galbraith, J.K. (1994) *A Journey Through Economic Time: A Firsthand View*. Boston: Houghton Mifflin.

Galtung, J. and Ruge, M.H. (1965) 'The Structure of Foreign News', *Journal of Peace Research*, 2(1): 64-91.

Gamson, W.A. (1992) *Talking Politics*. Cambridge: Cambridge University Press.

Gavin, N.T. (1992) 'Television News and the Economy: The Pre-Campaign Coverage', *Parliamentary Affairs*, 45(4): 596-611.

Gavin, N.T. (1993) 'Recovery and Recession: Economic Explanation and Expectations in the Near-Term Election Campaign 1992', paper presented at the Political Studies Association conference, Leicester University, April.

Gavin, N.T. (1994) 'Review: Neuman, Just and Crigler, Common Knowledge', *Media, Culture and Society*, 16(4): 702-5.

Gavin, N.T. (1997) 'Voting Behaviour, the Economy and the Media: Dependency, Consonance and Priming as a Route to Theoretical and Empirical Integration', in C. Pattie, D. Denver, J. Fisher and S. Ludlum (eds) *British Elections and Parties Review*, 7. London: Frank Cass.

Gavin, N.T. and Goddard, P. (1998) 'Television News and the Economy: Inflation in Britain, 1993-94', *Media, Culture and Society*, 20(3): 451-70.

Gavin, N.T. and Sanders, D. (1996) 'The Impact of Television News on Public Perceptions of the Economy and Government, 1993-94' in D.M. Farrell, D. Broughton, D. Denver and J. Fisher (eds) *British Parties and Elections Yearbook, 1996*. London: Frank Cass, pp. 68-84.

Gavin, N.T. and Sanders, D. (1997) 'The Economy and Voting', *Parliamentary Affairs*, 50(4): 631-40.

Gergen, K.J. and Gergen, M.M. (1981) *Social Psychology*. New York: Harcourt Brace Jovanovich.

Glasgow University Media Group (1976) *Bad News*. London: Routledge.
Glasgow University Media Group (1980) *More Bad News*. London: Routledge, Kegan Paul.
Goidel, R.K. and Langley, R.E. (1995) 'Media Coverage of the Economy and Aggregate Economic Evaluations: Uncovering Evidence of Indirect Media Effects', *Political Research Quarterly*, 48(2): 313–28.
Graddol, D. (1995) 'The Visual Accomplishment of Factuality' in D. Graddol and O. Boyd-Barrett (eds) *Media Texts, Authors and Readers*. Milton Keynes: Open University Press, pp. 139–60.
Hadenius, S. and Söderhjelm, T. (1994) *Bankerna i pressen, 1984–1990: Bilaga till Bankkriskommittén*. Stockholm: Fritzes.
Halliday, M.A.K. (1992) 'New Ways of Analysing Meaning', M. Pütz (ed.) *Thirty Years of Linguistic Evolution*. Amsterdam: Benjamins, pp. 59–96.
Hamilton, C. and Rolander, D. (1993) *Att leda Sverige in i krisen: Moral och politik i nedgångstid*. Stockholm: Norstedts.
Harrington, D.E. (1989) 'Economic News on Television: The Determinants of Coverage', *Public Opinion Quarterly*, 53(1): 17–40.
Harris, R. (1995) *Using Cointegration Analysis in Econometric Modelling*. London: Prentice-Hall.
Harrison, M. (1985) *TV News: Whose Bias?* London: Macmillan.
Hartley, J. (1982) *Understanding News*. London: Methuen.
Hendry, D. and Doornik, J.A. (1994) 'Modelling Linear Dynamic Econometric Systems', *Scottish Journal of Political Economy*, 41(1): 1–33.
Herman, E.S. (1982) 'The Institutionalization of Bias in Economics', *Media, Culture and Society*, 4(3): 275–91.
Hetherington, M.J. (1996) 'The Media's Role in Forming Voters' National Economic Evaluations in 1992', *American Journal of Political Science*, 40(2): 372–95.
Höijer, B. (1989) 'Television-Evoked Thoughts and Their Relation to Comprehension', *Communication Research*, 16(2): 179–203.
Höijer, B. (1990) 'Reliability, Validity and Generalizability: Three Questions for Qualitative Reception Research', *Nordicom Review*, 1(1): 15–20.
Höijer, B. (1993) 'Reception Reconsidered from Comprehension Perspectives', paper presented at the 11th Norwegian Conference for Mass Communication, Trondheim, August.
Holbrook, T. and Garand, J.C. (1996) 'Homo Economus? Economic Information and Economic Voting', *Political Research Quarterly*, 49(2): 351–75.
Horn, R.V. (1993) *Statistical Indicators for the Economic and Social Sciences*. Cambridge: Cambridge University Press.
Hugemark, A. (1994) *Den fångslande marknaden: Ekonomiska experter om välfärdsstaten*. Stockholm: Arkiv.
Husbands, C.T. (1985) 'Government Popularity and the Unemployment Issue, 1966–1983', *Sociology*, 19(1): 1–18.
Hvitfelt, H. (1992) *Att berätta om räntor och människor*. Media Monitor: October 1992. Stockholm: Näringslivets Mediainstitut.
Hvitfelt, H. (1993) *Bankrutt: Ekonomi och banker i Aktuellt, Rapport och TV4-Nyheterna*. Media Monitor: June 1993. Stockholm: Näringslivets Mediainstitut.
Hvitfelt, H. and Malmström, T. (1990) *Ekonomi och arbetsmarknad: Journalistik i förändring*. Rapport nr 4/90. Stockholm: SIM.

Independent Television Commission (1996) 'Revealing Sources', *Spectrum*, 20: 23-4.

Jensen, K.B. (1986) *Making Sense of the News*. Aarhus: Aarhus University Press.

Jensen, K.B. (1987) 'News as Ideology: Economic Statistics and Political Ritual in Television Network News', *Journal of Communication*, 37(1): 8-27.

Jensen, K.B. (1990) 'The Politics of Polysemy: Television News, Everyday Consciousness, and Political Action', *Media, Culture and Society*, 12(1): 57-78.

Jensen, K.B. (1996) 'The Empire's Last Stand: Reply to Rosengren', *European Journal of Communication*, 11(2): 261-7.

Jordan, D.L. (1993) 'Newspaper Effects on Policy Preferences', *Public Opinion Quarterly*, 57(2): 191-204.

Jordan, D.L. and Page, B.I. (1992) 'Shaping Foreign Policy Opinions: The Role of TV News', *Journal of Conflict Resolution*, 36(2): 227-41.

Kask, P.J. (1997) *Vägen in i och ut ur krisen: Ekonomisk politik från Feldt till Persson*. Stockholm: Rabén Prisma.

Kinder, K.R. and Kiewiet, D.R. (1981) 'Sociotropic Politics: The American Case', *British Journal of Political Science*, 11(2): 129-61.

Lash, S. and Urry, J. (1994) *Economies of Signs and Space*. London: Sage.

Lewis, J. (1983) 'The Encoding/Decoding Model', *Media, Culture and Society*, 5(2): 179-97.

Lewis, J. (1985) 'Decoding Television News', in P. Drummond and R. Paterson (eds) *Television in Transition*. London: British Film Institute, pp. 205-34.

Lewis, J. (1991) *The Ideological Octopus: An Exploration of Television and its Audience*. New York: Routledge.

Lewis-Beck, M.S. (1986) 'Comparative Voting: Britain, France, Germany, Italy', *American Journal of Political Science*, 30(2): 315-46.

Lindhoff, H. and Mårtenson, B. (1995) 'Det värsta är över', Om ekonomin i budget-nyheter i TV i januari 1994, Seminarierapport. JMK, Stockholm University.

Lindhoff, H. and Mårtenson, B. (1996a) 'Dagens ekonomi: Går Persson stiger räntan' in K. Becker, J. Ekecrantz, E.L. Frid and T. Olsson (eds) *Medierummet*. Stockholm: Carlssons, pp. 164-94.

Lindhoff, H. and Mårtenson, B. (1996b) 'Structuring Economic News: A Study of Three Swedish Dailies in November 1995', paper presented at the Symposium on Media Space, JMK, Stockholm University, November 16-17.

Livingstone, S. and Lunt, P. (1994) *Talk on Television: Audience Participation and Public Debate*. London and New York: Routledge.

Lockerbie, B. (1991) 'The Influence of Levels of Information on the Use of Prospective Evaluations', *Political Behaviour*, 13(3): 223-35.

Lunt, P. and Livingstone, S. (1996) 'Rethinking the Focus Group in Media and Communication Research', *Journal of Communication*, 46(2): 79-98.

MacKuen, M.B., Erikson, R.S. and Stimson, J.A. (1992) 'Peasants or Bankers? The American Electorate and the US Economy', *American Political Science Review*, 86(3): 597-611.

Marsh, C. (1989) *Exploring Data: An Introduction to Data Analysis for Social Scientists*. London: Polity Press.

Mårtenson, B. and Lindhoff, H. (1995) 'Television Journalism and Economic Crisis in Sweden: Representations and Audience Interpretation', unpublished seminar paper, JMK, Stockholm University.

Merton, R.K. (1987) 'The Focused Interview and Focus Groups: Continuities and Discontinuities', *Public Opinion Quarterly*, 51(4): 550-66.

Miller, A.H. and Wattenberg, M.P. (1985) 'Throwing the Rascals Out: Policy and Performance Evaluations of Presidential Candidates, 1952-80', *American Political Science Review*, 79(2): 359-72.

Monardi, F.M. (1994) 'Primary Voters as Retrospective Voters', *American Politics Quarterly*, 22(1): 88-103.

Morley, D. (1980) *The 'Nationwide' Audience*. London: British Film Institute.

Morley, D. (1992) *Television Audiences and Cultural Studies*. London: Routledge.

Mosley, P. (1984) '"Popularity Function" and the Role of the Media: A Pilot Study of the Popular Press', *British Journal of Political Science*, 14(1): 117-33.

Mutz, D.C. (1992) 'Mass Media and the Depoliticization of Personal Experience', *American Journal of Political Science*, 36(2): 483-508.

Nadeau, R. and Niemi, R. (1995) 'Elite Economic Forecasts, Economic News, Mass Economic Expectations and Voting Intentions in Great Britain', paper presented at the conference on Elections, Parties and Public Opinion, London Guildhall University, 15-17 September.

Nannestad, P. and Paldam, M. (1994) 'The VP-Function: A Survey of the Literature on Vote and Popularity Function After 25 Years', *Public Choice*, 79(3): 213-45.

Neuman, W., Just, M. and Crigler, A. (1992) *Common Knowledge: News and the Construction of Political Meaning*. Chicago: Chicago University Press.

Newton, K. (1993) 'Economic Voting in the 1992 General Election', D. Denver, P. Norris, D. Broughton and C. Rallings (eds) *British Elections and Parties Yearbook, 1993*. London: Harvester Wheatsheaf, pp. 158-76.

Nichols, B. (1994) *Blurred Boundaries: Questions of Meaning in Contemporary Culture*. Bloomington Indiana: Indiana University Press.

Ormerod, P. (1994) *The Death of Economics*. London: Faber and Faber.

Page, B.I., Shapiro, R. and Dempsey, G. (1987) 'What Moves Public Opinion?', *American Political Science Review*, 81(1): 23-43.

Paldam, M. (1981) 'A Preliminary Survey of the Theories and Findings on Vote and Popularity Functions', *European Journal of Political Research*, 9(2): 181-99.

Parsons, W.D. (1987) *The Power of the Financial Press: Journalism and Economic Opinion in Britain and America*. Aldershot: Edward Elgar.

Philo, G. (1990) *Seeing and Believing*. London: Routledge.

Philo, G. (1993) 'Political Advertising, Popular Belief and the 1992 British General Election', *Media, Culture and Society*, 15(3): 407-18.

Public Communications Group, Liverpool University (1995) 'National Figures: Economic News as Public Knowledge', *Politics and Communications Studies Working Paper 2*, June.

Rae, J. and Drury, J. (1993) 'Reification and Evidence in Rhetoric on

Economic Recession: Some Methods used in the UK Press, Final Quarter 1990', *Discourse and Society*, 4(3): 329–56.

Reinius, U. (1996) *Stålbadet: Finanskrisen, Penserkraschen och Nordbankens rekonstruktion*. Stockholm: Ekerlids.

Richardson, K. (1997) 'Signs and Wonders: Interpreting the economy through television', in A. Bell and P. Garrett (eds) *New Approaches to Media Discourse*. London: Blackwells.

Robinson, J.P. and Levy, M.R. (1986) *The Main Source: Learning from Television News*. Beverly Hills, CA: Sage.

Rosengren, K.E. (1996) 'Review: Jensen, *The Semiotics of Mass Communication*', *European Journal of Communication*, 11(1): 129–41.

Sanders, D. (1991) 'Government Popularity and the Next General Election', *Political Quarterly*, 62(2): 235–61.

Sanders, D. (1995) 'Forecasting Political Preferences and Election Outcomes in the UK: Experiences, Problems and Prospects for the next General Election', *Electoral Studies*, 14(3): 251-72.

Sanders, D. (1996) 'Economic Performance, Management Competence and the Outcome of the Next General Election', *Political Studies*, 44(2): 203–31.

Sanders, D. and Price S. (1997) 'Disentangling the Relationship Between Party Support and Perceived Economic Competence: Some Evidence From the UK, 1991 to 1995', under review.

Sanders, D., Ward, H., Marsh, D. and Fletcher, T. (1987) 'Government Popularity and the Falklands War: A Reassessment', *British Journal of Political Science*, 17(3): 281–314.

Sanders, D., Marsh, D. and Ward, D. (1993) 'The Electoral Impact of Press Coverage of the Economy, 1979-87', *British Journal of Political Science*, 23(2): 175–210.

Schlesinger, P. (1987) *Putting 'Reality' Together: BBC News*. London: Methuen.

Schlesinger, P. and Tumber, H. (1994) *Reporting Crime: The Media Politics of Criminal Justice*. Oxford: Clarendon Press.

Schlesinger, P., Murdock, G. and Elliott, P. (1983) *Televising 'Terrorism': Political Violence in Popular Culture*. London: Comedia.

Schlesinger, P., Dobash, R.E., Dobash, R.P. and Weaver, C. (1992) *Women Viewing Violence*. London: British Film Institute.

Scott, M. (1996) *Wordsmith Tools*. London: Oxford University Press.

Severin, W.J. (1988) *Communication Theories*. London: Longman.

Silverstone, R. (1981) *The Message of Television: Myth and Narrative in Contemporary Culture*. London: Heinemann.

Silverstone, R. (1988) 'Television Myth and Culture', in J.W. Carey (ed) *Media, Myths, and Narratives: Television and the Press*. London: Sage, pp. 20–47.

Stubbs, M. (1996) *Text and Corpus Analysis: Computer-Assisted Studies of Language and Culture*. London: Blackwell.

Tunstall, J. (1996) *Newspaper Power: The New National Press in Britain*. Oxford: Oxford University Press.

van Dijk, T.A. (1988) *News as Discourse*. Hillsdale, New Jersey: Erlbaum.

Wernick, A. (1991) *Promotional Culture*. London: Sage.

Winston, B. (1993) 'The CBS Evening News, 7 April 1949: Creating an Ineffable Television Form', in J. Eldridge (ed.) *Getting the Message: News, Truth and Power*. London: Routledge, pp. 181–209.

Index